CW00408760

Advanced Praise

"In the wealth management industry, there are many charlatans: people who think they know the theory; but cannot actually manage wealth. Philip Marcovici not only knows the theory; he has been an eminent practitioner of it. One can only believe those who have experienced what they preach. All families should read his book."
—**David Chong**, President, Portcullis Group, Singapore

"Philip has lived through and helped shape an era unlike any other in the creation and management of private wealth over the past 50 years. This is a time of great global private wealth, of recognition that private wealth can help fund governments, that wealthy families can be global, multi-cultural, migratory and opportunistic.

Philip's book is a wise reflection on what he has seen and contains profound observations with respect to the distractions of family wealth and how they obscure the fundamental human needs for life's meaning. He lucidly explains technicalities and details all wealth holders need to know.

Philip reminds us that life is about living. This book should be read by wealth holder and wealth advisor alike; and it will be a lasting historical reflection of the challenges and failures of our era."
—**Charles A. Lowenhaupt**, Chairman, Lowenhaupt Global Advisors

"Philip is one of the few honest voices in the area of wealth planning. He highlights the importance of finding the right advisors and aligning their interests with yours, and always having checks and balances in place. The pitfalls of not doing so are well illustrated with many colourful stories; reading this book will ensure your family does not suffer a similar fate. A must read for anyone who has any amount of wealth (no matter the amount) and wants to ensure harmony within the family."
—**Leo Drago**, Co-Founder, AL Wealth Partners

"Congratulations to Philip Marcovici for a well-written and very easy-to-read book which has incorporated much of his personal experiences in dealing with a vast client base, especially Asian. Much of the material he has covered is consistent with my teaching syllabus. It will definitely be on my recommended reading list when it is released."
—**Professor Roger King** PhD, Director of the Thompson Center for Business Case Studies and the Tanoto Center for Asian Family Business and Entrepreneurship Studies, Hong Kong University of Science and Technology

"Philip is a long-time friend but more importantly a professional that I often seek guidance from for my ultra-high-net-worth clients. His expertise is not just his technical knowledge, but also the essential practical experience in how to manage or 'suffer' from wealth. This book illustrates many real life stories and should be read by all who have worked their entire lives to create wealth or a legacy for the family."
—**Anthonia Hui**, Co-Founder, AL Wealth Partners

"Other than wealthy families, this new book will also be useful to private wealth management practitioners and other professionals, such as tax advisors, accountants, lawyers, as well as law and business/finance students who are interested in learning about the basic tools of wealth and estate planning and issues related to cross-border taxation for high-net-worth individuals. In fact, I plan to use part of this book as reference material for my Private Banking and Wealth Management Course at the University of Hong Kong in the future. As Hong Kong continues to grow as an important wealth management hub in Asia, this book will be welcomed by wealth owners and people working in the financial services industry."

—**Professor S.F. Wong**, Professor of Practice in Finance,
The University of Hong Kong

"Very interesting! A must-read for everyone working in or anyone looking to enter into the world of Private Wealth."

—**Adrian Braimer-Jones**, Ensof Group

"This is a fantastic book and all families should read it. It is an education on wealth management entertainingly written. Well done! This book provides great guidance for any wealth owner and their advisors. Complexities are made understandable. Laughing is also included. Read this book and don't destroy your family."

—**Benedikt Kaiser**, Kaiser Partner

"Forget about complex family governance books, start with this read! *The Destructive Power of Family Wealth* contains a deep insight into the needs and psychology of the wealth owner and the challenges they face. It should be mandatory for every private banker and wealth adviser who wants to survive over the next 5 years and for every wealth owner who is concerned about what will happen if they are no longer around.

—**Jurgen Vanhoenacker**, Executive Director, Sales, Marketing & Wealth Structuring, Lombard International Assurance SA

"Who knew that philanthropy was not only about helping others? This book shows you how it can be a fantastic tool for family cohesion and to educate the next generation."

—**Maurice Machenbaum**, Co-Founder, Wise Philanthropy Advisors

"My initial reaction to Philip Marcovici's new book: I like it!"

—**Professor Joseph P.H. Fan**, Co-Director, Centre for Economics and Finance, The Chinese University of Hong Kong

"I thoroughly enjoyed reading this book as Philip Marcovici's style is very natural and 'colloquial' (in the best sense of the word) and conveys difficult technicalities across in a way that targeted families will understand as well; I can just picture him speaking on the subject of this book in public. The content is very relevant to any young wealth planner and anyone looking at a career in wealth management and planning will get absolutely nowhere without reading this book."

—**Britta Pfister**, Head, Rothschild Trust (Singapore) Limited

"This is fantastic stuff. Well done!"

—**Sharon Ser**, Regional Senior Partner Asia, Withers

A Few Extracts From *The Destructive Power of Family Wealth*

On the Needs of Wealth Owners

"Wealth owners have latent needs – they have needs, but don't know what they are. Knowing the right questions to ask is the key – no one has all the answers, but if a wealth owner does not understand their own succession plan, whether this involves the use of wills, trusts or otherwise, it can be very dangerous. Who has the power to make decisions if we are disabled or die? Who can replace the trustee? Who will monitor conflicts of interest, including how asset managers and others charge for their services? What can be done to manage the risks of divorce and other risks to wealth?"

On Succession Planning and Asset Protection

"The first step in succession planning is to understand that having no succession plan in place is a succession plan. If I die, something will happen to my assets, and this notwithstanding that I may not actually have thought about my succession or planned it at all."

"I have run into a number of cases over the years where trusts and foundations established by wealth owners were not disclosed to family members, something quite common in times when wealth owners in Europe and elsewhere were led to believe that good planning involved hiding their assets from the tax authorities and others. In too many situations, advisors ranging from lawyers to trustees to protectors and others ended up helping themselves to all or part of the assets involved. When families finally discovered the structures their deceased parent had created, it was often too late to recover the full value involved."

On Changing Demographics and Aging

"Do failing memories put assets at risk? It is wonderful that we are all living longer, but is it not the case that dementia and even simple forgetfulness that comes with aging put assets at risk if no one knows where they are? Early succession and asset protection planning is the key, and families increasingly need to consider the aging process and its effect on the safety of family assets and the maintenance of harmony within the family for the long term."

On "Gold-Diggers"

"I am often asked by families I work with about the risk of in-laws or others being gold-diggers, more interested in the wealth of the family than they should be. This is not a difficult evaluation to make, and my answer is always 'Of course your son-in-law or daughter-in-law is a gold-digger!' This is not because everyone is evil – but because money comes into every relationship – if not at the start of the relationship, at some point in future. I always advise families to hope for the best, but plan for the worst."

On Mistresses and Toy-Boys

"Mistresses are not an Asian concept. They are a global concept. Mistresses, toy-boys and other relationships all too often move into situations of blackmail, and there are approaches that wealth owners falling into common traps can employ to manage things effectively. One golden rule is to never give a mistress a lump sum of money – before long, she is back for more – why not use a trust or annuity that is designed to make payments over her lifetime, but conditioned on her keeping things quiet?"

On Divorce

"In the case of divorce, community property, co-habitation, and otherwise, it is easy to say that the rights of the spouse or other party are there because they need to be protected. And this is often the case, and why laws are in place to provide this protection. But for a wealth-owning family, and particularly where wealth is at the higher level, it is critical to understand how laws designed to protect a spouse can be abused to provide a spouse with rights to family businesses and wealth that by no stretch of the imagination should they have access to. And with lawyers charging on contingency, getting paid on the success of their efforts, is it fair that family wealth falls into the hands of those who fuel the flames of marital disputes?"

On Second (and Subsequent) Marriages

"Second and further marriages often cause more issues within families than the wealth owner establishing the new relationship thinks. The wealth owner often ends up in a difficult situation that jeopardizes not only the well-being of his children, but also the chances of success in his new relationship. As a believer that money comes into the picture in every relationship (because everyone is a gold-digger, at least to some extent), recognizing this is a first step toward finding approaches to help the process not be a destructive one."

On the Need for Women to Understand their Rights and Financial Position

"There is one very important reality about women and wealth. The chances are that they will end up with the money, one way or another – so they had better know where it is and how to deal with it. Women live longer than men, and in a marriage, it is likely that they will outlive their husband. And if the marriage fails, which many do, the wife will and should end up with something – so everyone needs to be prepared, and all too often, women are not."

On Who You can Trust

"Trust no one. This is not because no one can be trusted, but because the safest approach is to ensure that the right checks and balances are in place to deal with the reality that everybody has conflicts of interests. And for trustees, bankers and others, there is no client better than a dead client – dead clients do not complain about fees and do not fire you. Key is to ensure that those who succeed to your assets are able to properly keep an eye on trustees and others and remove and replace them when necessary."

On Family Business Succession

"Families that manage to keep their businesses intact over the generations tend to be families that are flexible in their understanding that it is inevitable that not everyone in the younger generation will see things the same way. Allowing for the likelihood that there will be family members who will not want to participate in and support the family business, and having clear procedures for how to buy out their interests and at what price has been a key way successful families have managed to keep businesses in family hands over the generations. Having the ability to 'prune' the family tree can be critical to the long term success of a family business."

On Tax Advantaged Investing

"There are many facets to tax advantaged investing, but in the simplest terms, to invest on a tax advantaged basis means focusing on the after tax and not the pre-tax return on an investment. It is very easy to get into an investment, but often not enough attention is paid to the question of how one will exit from the investment, and what the tax consequences of this might be."

On Taxation
"In a world where disparities of wealth are increasingly at the forefront of the political and social agenda, is 'hiding the money' either an option or the right thing to do? Advisors and wealth owning families have to change their ways, and in many cases, the ways of the past were not something to be proud of."

"[T]he only certainty in the tax world is that the laws will change, and constantly do. The wealth owning family does not need to become expert in the tax laws of every country that affects them and their investments. Rather, the wealth owning family needs to be able to understand the advice they receive and be able to challenge that advice, and ask the right questions. Being aware of how tax systems work can help families stay in control of the succession and asset protection planning put in place for their families."

On the Move to Tax Transparency and Automatic Information Exchange
"Is transparency in the tax world a rocky road that will create a new kind of refugee problem and a drain of capital and entrepreneurship from countries most in need? I worry that many developing countries are simply not ready for automatic information exchange. Politically motivated use of tax information, corruption, leakage of tax information to kidnappers and more will lead to entrepreneurs desperately needed by their economies realizing that they only have two choices – play by the rules or get out. And to play by the rules does not work if the tax system does not adequately protect taxpayer interests – so getting out will be the only choice. Who will replace the lost jobs and revenues of the developing countries involved?"

On Mobility
"Play by the rules or get out. These are the only choices wealth owners have – the third choice of staying connected to a country by residence, domicile, citizenship or otherwise and hoping that no one will find out is simply not an option in a world of growing transparency and where tax laws are increasingly and more aggressively enforced. Tax laws are laws, and there is no choice but for compliance with them."

"One simple guideline on mobility planning is that the best time to consider leaving a country is before that country begins to impose an exit tax. As the world moves to greater tax transparency and tax laws are enforced more vigorously, it is likely that more wealth owners will be using mobility as part of their planning, attracting more high tax countries to consider barriers to mobility, including exit taxes and tougher rules in relation to the question of who is and who is not a tax resident, particularly among those who were previously taxable residents of the country."

On Tax Planning, Tax Avoidance and Tax Evasion
"As a tax lawyer, my job has been to work with wealth owners and to help them legally plan their affairs such as to minimize tax exposures. But how far should one go to pay the least amount of tax possible? Is it an ethical obligation of wealth owners to pay headline rates of tax to help address wealth and income inequality and to not take steps to reduce tax exposures? Where is the line between legal tax planning and illegal tax evasion...and what of tax avoidance, something that used to be considered

legal and appropriate, but which is increasingly condemned by tax authorities and others?"

On Political Risk
"[T]here are many risks that a wealth owner is subject to that can fall under the heading of 'political' risk, including changes in the tax landscape, perhaps in part as a result of a new focus on income and wealth inequality... Addressing political risk will be an increasing need of wealth owning families worldwide. The current focus on income and wealth inequality, increasing populism in the political sphere and the difficult financial position of many countries is increasing risk, and not only in parts of the world one normally thinks of as unstable."

On the Wealth Management Industry
"Wealth management is a knowledge business, but sadly run by many who are more focused on their own interests than on the need to invest in and manage knowledge for the benefit of their clients. A wealth owner has little choice but to get a handle on what is relevant to their own situation, and be in a position to ask the right questions that will lead them to the right advisors. And for the wealth manager who gets it right, the opportunity to excel and attract clients is significant."

"Today, around the world, there are increasing regulations that require asset managers to provide transparency on charges to their clients, but there continue to be many circumstances of hidden charges that asset managers, such as private banks, impose on their clients. Is the client aware that the bank may have made arrangements to receive 'retrocessions' or kick-backs from investment funds in which they may invest the client money they have under discretionary management? Relatively recent court decisions in Switzerland require banks to refund retrocessions they historically received in a number of circumstances, but unsurprisingly the industry is pretty quiet about the rights their clients may have to obtain refunds of amounts their advisors secretly received."

On Independent Asset Managers and Family Offices
"Interesting to observe is that the independent asset manager and single and multi-family offices usually come into the picture when the wealth owning family gets fed up with the poor service they get from their traditional private bank. And while the private bank ends up being nothing more than a custodian, the independent asset manager or family office begin to focus on negotiating even these fees on behalf of the wealth owner, putting more pressure on the private banks."

On Compliance as a Client Need
"Compliance is a client need. Tax and related reporting requirements are only part of the picture, and too few banks realize that families need help to understand the choices they have on how to structure their affairs and ensure that they know who has what information on their family and assets and where that information is going to go. Delegating these things to the compliance department is not enough – helping clients deal with increasing compliance is part of the service an effective bank or trust company needs to provide."

The Destructive Power of Family Wealth

A GUIDE TO SUCCESSION PLANNING, ASSET PROTECTION, TAXATION AND WEALTH MANAGEMENT

Philip Marcovici

This edition first published 2016
© 2016 Philip Marcovici

Registered office
John Wiley & Sons Ltd, The Atrium, Southern Gate, Chichester, West Sussex, PO19 8SQ,
United Kingdom

For details of our global editorial offices, for customer services and for information about
how to apply for permission to reuse the copyright material in this book please visit our
website at www.wiley.com.

Wiley publishes in a variety of print and electronic formats and by print-on-demand. Some
material included with standard print versions of this book may not be included in e-books or
in print-on-demand. If this book refers to media such as a CD or DVD that is not included in
the version you purchased, you may download this material at http://booksupport.wiley.com.
For more information about Wiley products, visit www.wiley.com.

Designations used by companies to distinguish their products are often claimed as trademarks.
All brand names and product names used in this book are trade names, service marks,
trademarks or registered trademarks of their respective owners. The publisher is not
associated with any product or vendor mentioned in this book.

Limit of Liability/Disclaimer of Warranty: While the publisher and author have used their best
efforts in preparing this book, they make no representations or warranties with respect to the
accuracy or completeness of the contents of this book and specifically disclaim any implied
warranties of merchantability or fitness for a particular purpose. It is sold on the
understanding that the publisher is not engaged in rendering professional services and neither
the publisher nor the author shall be liable for damages arising herefrom. If professional
advice or other expert assistance is required, the services of a competent professional should
be sought.

A catalogue record for this book is available from the Library of Congress.

A catalogue record for this book is available from the British Library.

ISBN 978-1-119-32752-3 (hardback) ISBN 978-1-119-32753-0 (ebk)
ISBN 978-1-119-32754-7 (ebk) ISBN 978-1-119-32904-6 (ebk)

Cover design: Wiley
Cover image: © pking4th/Getty Images

10 9 8 7 6 5 4 3 2 1

Set in 11/13pt SabonLTStd by Aptara Inc., New Delhi, India
Printed in Great Britain by TJ International Ltd, Padstow, Cornwall, UK

To My Family
Peggy, Joshua, and Luca, With Love
and To All Families

Contents

Preface

Now retired from practicing law, I spent my career as an international tax and private-client lawyer, working with families, businesses, and the wealth-management industry, first in New York and Vancouver, then in Hong Kong and Zurich. I have also worked with governments seeking to address the global problem of undeclared funds, and have taught widely in Asia and Europe, learning while sharing my views on the potentially destructive nature of wealth and the failings of the wealth-management industry, and of advisors, to truly help the families they are meant to serve.

I began working with wealth-owning families on their succession and other needs early in the 1980s, in Hong Kong. Having studied law in both Canada and the USA, I had started out as a corporate tax lawyer in New York, and then moved to Hong Kong where I spent 12 years practicing law. The 1980s and early 1990s were interesting times in Hong Kong. Pretty much the most capitalist place in the world was soon to revert to pretty much the most communist place in the world. China, which was a very different country in the 1980s and early 1990s than it is today, was negotiating the return of Hong Kong by the UK. The UK had been governing Hong Kong under treaties that, in part, were coming to an end after a term of 99 years. The handover of Hong Kong to China was ultimately agreed between Margaret Thatcher and Deng Xiaoping and took place in 1997.

In the run up to 1997, many of Hong Kong's wealth-owning families began restructuring their businesses in view of perceived political risks and sought second (and third and fourth) citizenships and places of alternative residence. My work changed from being work for companies on their tax affairs to work for the owners of companies looking more comprehensively at their situation, mixing in issues of political risk and asset protection with tax exposures in the USA and elsewhere particularly those associated with cross-border investment and new residences and citizenships. Many of the wealth owners in Hong Kong came from families who had fled China on the arrival of the communists and who suffered the expropriation of their businesses and many other similar setbacks and challenges. They were not about to let themselves lose everything again.

My work with families in relation to their personal and business assets, and the protection of wealth, led to me working with the wealth-management industry – the providers of asset-management services, trusts, and other "tools" of wealth planning. Something I learned early on is that the industry all too often does not meet the comprehensive needs of the clients it serves. This led to me becoming active in training and education within the industry, and working on strategy for private banks and others interested in greater alignment with the needs of their clients. But overall, I was working in a major growth industry that was – to me – surprisingly chaotic (and often unethical) in its management and delivery of services.

In the mid-1990s, I moved to Switzerland, where I spent 15 years working with private banks, trust and insurance companies, and the global families that use their services. With young children, we were looking for a clean place to live in light of the growing pollution in Hong Kong. A partner of an international law firm, I had the opportunity to look at a map and broadly choose where I wanted to spend the next years of my career. We arrived in Zurich, and found the clean place we were looking for – air that was broadly unpolluted, a lake that could be swum in, and a population surprisingly obsessed with cleanliness. One of our many challenges in adapting to Switzerland related to the complexities of throwing out garbage, navigating a system that combined charges for unsorted waste and the encouragement of free recycling.

But while Zurich and Switzerland were certainly clean places, this was pretty much only from the point of view of the environment. While I was not naïve when arriving in Switzerland, I was still shocked at the unclean nature of the Swiss financial center and, in particular, its wealth-management industry. Now forced to change, the Swiss were, to me, clearly abusing their role as global champions of privacy, ignoring the real needs of their clients, which in my view include ensuring that families "play by the rules" of their home countries of residence and investment – including the tax rules of those countries. While tax evasion is a global problem, and the role of the wealth-management industry in facilitating tax evasion is and was by no means limited to Switzerland, I believe that Switzerland, as the dominant player in the wealth-management industry, had the opportunity to take leadership in addressing the issue. Instead, Switzerland and many other offshore banking centers misled their clients into believing that secrecy could be the solution to all problems.

Today, things are changing. Not only in Switzerland, where tax compliance and transparency are at the top of the agenda in the wealth-management industry, but around the world. Data leaks, most recently in Panama, have contributed to change, but the shift from an opaque world to one that is increasingly transparent will take time, and the road for many wealth owners will be a rocky one. Switzerland failed to take the global lead it could have on the issues of undeclared money, and today there remain, surprisingly, financial centers that continue to mislead families into thinking that hiding money is good financial planning. The USA is a particularly egregious offender, particularly given the way it has sought to protect its own tax revenues through aggressive attacks on Switzerland and others, while preserving the ability of its banks and corporate service providers to market secrecy over substance.

To compound these problems, in my experience, too many families have failed to understand their own planning needs and the conflicts of interest their advisors and banks have. Many of the families I have come across have neglected to focus on the critical issue of succession – in part due to an obsession with secrecy and an over-emphasis on tax exposures. Tax enforcement is a new reality, with many developments that are quickly changing the ways of the past. Notwithstanding these changes, I continue to have a real concern that families do not put enough emphasis on the key question or issue that they need to address – will wealth destroy their family?

In the 1980s a common line of thinking among my clients and friends was that things were different for Chinese families. I was told that I did not understand that the Chinese were close and loving families, where succession would never be something that would have a detrimental impact on family and relationships. This was in direct contrast to litigious Westerners lacking the respect for the older generation that the Chinese were innately meant to have. I later ran across Latin American families professing similar beliefs, this time on a theme of love and devotion (and music) that made them different. The sad reality, proven over and over by the many disastrous fights among Asian, Latin American, Middle Eastern, and other families of late, is that *all* families are the same – the children, holding hands, arrive at their parents' home for dinners and lunches, and after the passing of their parents all too often end up enriching the lawyers who are all too often happy to fuel the flames in disputes over murky succession arrangements left by the older generation.

There is no question that religious and cultural issues impact how families work as well as the succession process itself. But no family is immune to the dangers that wealth can generate, or the relatively new issues associated with all of us living longer and the succession changes that result because of changes in the demographic patterns. If Mom or Dad lives to 105, does that mean that I inherit when I am 80? And what of the growing incidence of dementia and all the problems that come with it?

Are these only problems of the "wealthy?" For me, the answer is no – all wealth owners, meaning anyone who owns anything of value that may pass to the next generation or to others, have the potential to destroy their families through a poorly planned or ambiguous succession process. In fact, families who have relatively little in the way of assets have a particular responsibility to ensure that what they have and hope to use to enhance the lives of the next generation does not end up in the wrong hands or result in the destruction of family relationships.

Who really is wealthy is, in any case, a very subjective thing – what is a fortune to one person may be a pittance to another. And there is a sad reality that human nature seems to make people think they always need more than they have to really be "rich." In the end, we do need money to survive, but how much is ever enough? Does wealth really create happiness? Or does it too often result in deep unhappiness and regret?

Perhaps the comedian Spike Milligan was right in saying *money can't buy you happiness… but it does bring you a more pleasant form of misery.* I actually think that he was too optimistic.

Acknowledgments

I have many to thank for help in writing this book, and have to acknowledge the outstanding support I received from a number of friends and colleagues. A surprising number of people took the time to read an advance review copy of the book, and I received many, many helpful comments.

The errors and judgements that I have made are, of course, my own responsibility, and I take particular ownership of the strong negative views I have of certain financial centers and of those who have led the wealth-management industry and its clients down a dark, dangerous path more about secrecy than understanding and meeting client needs. I believe that wealth-owning families have been let down by a business which has been too easily distracted by short-term, easy profits. These views are my own, and I take full responsibility for them.

I was fortunate in my career to have had the opportunity to work with families from around the world and, in my teaching, with students from around the world. I learned much from these experiences, and continue to do so. I was also fortunate to work with many advisors and regulators who not only share my vision of what wealth owners and the communities to which they are connected really need, but who are also leaders of change on many fronts. Sadly, the "stars" in the wealth-management industry and in the leadership of key financial centers are few and far between, but they do exist, and I have been fortunate to work with a number of them.

Pascal Saint-Amans, the Director of Tax Policy and Administration at the OECD, and his predecessor, Jeffrey Owens, were visionaries who generously supported my work in helping to address issues around undeclared funds, leading to the Liechtenstein Disclosure Facility and related arrangements between Liechtenstein and the UK. With the help of a very talented colleague, Lyubomir Georgiev, we, together with a number of others, were able to achieve what I believe was an example of what was needed at the time, but which received massive resistance from financial centers, law and accounting firms, and private banks and trust companies seeking to preserve the past. I think they regret this, as do many of the wealth-owning families connected to countries other than the UK, who would have benefitted from what was achieved – a confidential and sympathetic approach to moving from an opaque past to a transparent future. The arrangements would not have worked without the huge efforts of Andy Cole, former Director of Specialist Investigations for Her Majesty's Revenue and Customs. Now retired, Andy, a good friend, was appointed by the then Chairman of HMRC, Dave Hartnett, to negotiate the arrangements on behalf of the UK.

I received considerable input to my book, and I thank all those who took the time to share their thoughts. I have particularly to thank Stefan Liniger for his support and detailed comments. Stefan was a strong defender of Switzerland in his comments to me, and while only mildly successful in his efforts to have me tone down my criticism of Switzerland, Stefan shares with me a passion for excellence and a strong belief that Switzerland will rebuild its ability to be a long-term and respected safe haven for global families. Britta Pfister wore green eyeshades when reading my book, and not only provided important comments, but also line-by-line corrections that were much needed and appreciated. My good friend and colleague of decades, Paul Stibbard, provided not only detailed comments – correcting my English (and I very much trust his!) – but also important input on many aspects of my book and particularly my references to Islamic law, one of the many areas of his deep expertise.

Michael Morley was most helpful and supportive in his comments, and for years was one of the few leaders in the industry who I believe really understood what wealth management is about. Stephen Atkinson, Jurgen Vanhoenacker, Anthonia Hui, Leo Drago, Maurice Machenbaum, Amaury Jordan, Tom McCullough, and many others were also most helpful and generous in sharing their thoughts.

I also thank Annie Chen for her years of patient support and insight over martinis and otherwise, Lisbet Rausing for sharing her views over pancakes she made for me in London, and Michael Olesnicky, Jeff VanderWolk, and Richard Weisman for their input and friendship. Professors Joseph Fan of the Chinese University of Hong Kong, S.F. Wong of the University of Hong Kong, and Roger King of the Hong Kong University of Science and Technology were all of support and influence, along with many, many others.

I have been fortunate to work with John Wiley & Sons in relation to the publication of this book, and particularly want to thank Thomas Hyrkiel and Jeremy Chia for their professionalism and support.

Finally, my love and thanks go to my wife, Peggy, for her insights and consistent disagreement with almost everything I say.

About the Author

Philip Marcovici is retired from the practice of law and consults with governments, financial institutions, and global families in relation to tax, wealth management, and other matters. Philip is on the boards of several entities within the wealth-management industry, as well as of entities within family-succession and philanthropic structures. An adjunct faculty member at the Singapore Management University, Philip is actively involved in teaching in the areas of taxation, wealth management, and family governance.

Philip was the founder and CEO of LawInContext, the interactive knowledge venture of global law firm Baker & McKenzie. Philip retired from his CEO role with the company in 2010, and from his Chairmanship of the company in 2011.

Philip was a partner of Baker & McKenzie, a firm he joined in 1982, and practiced in the area of international taxation throughout his legal career. Philip was based in the Hong Kong office of Baker & McKenzie for 12 years, relocating to the Zurich office of Baker & McKenzie in 1996. Philip has also practiced law in both New York and Vancouver. Philip retired from Baker & McKenzie at the end of 2009.

Philip Marcovici is the former chair of the European tax practice of Baker & McKenzie and of the steering committee of the firm's international wealth-management practice, of which he was one of the founders. Philip was also one of the founders of the Baker & McKenzie Asia-Pacific tax practice and was involved in a number of firm and practice group management functions.

Among others, Philip Marcovici received the Citywealth Magic Circle Lifetime Achievement Award in 2009 and, jointly with Fritz Kaiser, the Wealth Management Innovator Award in 2011 for his work in instigating the Liechtenstein Disclosure Facility. In 2010 Philip received the Russell Baker Award from Baker & McKenzie in appreciation for his exceptional contributions to the firm's global tax practice. In 2013 Philip received a Lifetime Achievement Award from the Society of Estate and Trust Practitioners and in 2016 a Lifetime Achievement Award from Wealth Briefing.

Philip holds law degrees from Harvard Law School and the University of Ottawa.

Introduction

This book is designed to share my experience of working with families and their advisors around the world.

My hope is that this book will help wealth owners and their families understand their considerable opportunities to *avoid* wealth being destructive of their family and of the relationships that exist and will exist in future generations.

While my professional experience has been primarily oriented toward families at the upper end of the wealth spectrum, I am absolutely convinced that wealth can and does destroy *any* family, no matter what the level of wealth involved. A single asset, whether a piece of jewelry, a sum of money, or a small property, can carry with it enormous importance to the younger generation – either due to its value, or for sentimental and emotional reasons, or, as is more likely, both. How wealth transfers from one generation to the next, who gets what and when, carries messages that are remembered, rightly or wrongly, as being what the transferor "meant." Gifts of one asset to a son and another to a daughter may be well intended, but may also end up leaving one of the children with a false sense that they were less loved than their sibling.

I also hope that this book will be a guide to those beginning their careers in the wealth-management industry, and that it will help them to understand the real needs of their clients, leading them to become effective, trusted advisors. For the more experienced advisor, this book will, hopefully, help make them even more effective in their work with families. But I am sure that for some in the industry, there will be offence at some of my views. Here, I stand by my convictions – the wealth-management industry, sadly, is in chaos, and often does little to address the real needs of wealth-owning families. For those involved in management and strategy, this is a time of opportunity for those who can understand how an alignment of interests with those of client families can produce results.

The wealth-management industry is a substantial one, producing far more revenues for those involved than investment banking, and one that will grow significantly in the years to come. The Boston Consulting Group, in its 2014 Wealth Report, predicted that global private wealth will reach US$198.2 trillion by 2018, and states that in 2013 there were 16.3 million "millionaire" households around the world, a figure set to grow.

The business of serving wealth owners, from managing their money to offering advice and more, is massive. But there are too few stars who understand that success requires looking at things from a client's perspective. And my criticism of the industry also extends to many financial centers, including Switzerland, Hong Kong, the USA, and others, that have failed to take leadership in the interests of wealth-owning families and their communities.

Hopefully, some of my criticism may positively influence the way forward. For the wealth owner, understanding how the business of wealth management works is an important step toward taking ownership of the succession and asset-protection process, and helping to protect wealth and family relationships.

This book begins with some stories – stories about real families and the difficulties wealth has presented them with. Sadly entertaining, the challenges I outline are meant to show how easy it is for wealth to destroy families and relationships, and how advance planning can reduce the risk of the same patterns recurring. Throughout this book I continue to use both examples of real families whose situations have been in the news and examples from my experience of working with families over the years. In terms of my experience of working with families, I have made sure to reflect in my examples a mix of the issues I have seen occurring – this to ensure that no particular family will see any confidences breached. But I can say with certainty that I have seen far worse than some of my stories suggest.

I then move on to discuss some of the psychological issues associated with wealth that I have observed in my work with families and their advisors. There are many psychological issues that arise in and around wealth, and these impact the thinking of wealth owners as they get older and their life circumstances change. I also discuss the effect of gifts on the recipients of the gift – as well as the effect of not receiving the wealth that one may expect to receive. Gold-diggers, mistresses, toy-boys, illegitimate children, and many more interested players come into the mix. I am sometimes playful in relation to the messy relationships that come into the picture, but I do believe that there are some very practical lessons to be learned for all from reading this book. Not everyone is as evil as I might suggest, and there are many nuances to the complexity of human relationships. But protecting wealth, businesses, and families requires me to approach things in a frank and practical way. These psychological issues are often referred to as being part of the "soft" issues in wealth planning – but the reality is that they are not so soft and certainly are not unimportant, despite their neglect by many associated with guiding wealth owners through the asset-protection and succession process.

International taxation was the primary focus of my career, and clearly tax issues are relevant to most families considering the succession process and the protection of their wealth. Tax laws are ever-changing, and in too many countries unfair approaches to taxation are part of the political risk, making the navigation of the tax world a critical thing for any wealth owner. My view, however, is that all too often tax is a distraction in the succession-planning process. An over-focus on tax minimization leads to the neglect of what may be more important issues to the family. Where the wealth owner does not fully understand the tax planning being implemented, dangerous losses of control and other consequences result. All too often it is the tax advisor, obsessed with taxation and ill-equipped to address other areas, who handles succession planning for a family. The inevitable result is an insufficient focus on the many other needs of the family.

This book addresses the fast-changing global tax landscape, and my hope is to equip wealth-owning families with the information they need to understand the advice they receive, and to permit them to ask the right questions. But it is important to understand that tax is only *one* of the many needs families have, and this book also focuses on some of their other needs, ranging from protecting assets from political risk to dealing with second (and subsequent) marriages, divorce, and the many other challenges to wealth and family harmony that lurk around the corner. All wealth owners have needs, but many of these needs are latent – needs the wealth owner has but does not know he has. And if the need is latent, and the right questions are not asked, the succession and asset-protection plan may fail a family that neglected to address a need that only comes to the surface when it is too late.

Some of the needs of wealth owners are shared by all wealth owners, while others are needs particular to a family. Yet other needs are driven by the laws and circumstances of the countries to which the family is connected by residence, citizenship, or investment. Growing tax transparency, technology, and other developments are challenging the human right to privacy – and making the maintenance of privacy a key need of families globally. But is it politically correct to champion privacy in a world of growing wealth inequality? Or is privacy a real need in a world where dangers to those with wealth are increasing? The issue of inequality of wealth is a growing topic politically and otherwise around the world. What does this mean for the wealth owner, and are there risks of increasing taxes, overnight capital levies, and other means of wealth redistribution that may arise? Can a wealth owner protect their family against populist governments that may have other than the genuine best interests of society in mind? Has the abuse of secrecy laws in Panama, Switzerland, the British Virgin Islands, Singapore, and elsewhere created an environment where governments will over-react, against the interests of not only wealth owners but also their own economies?

How does the wealth owner address their needs? This is done using the help of advisors – lawyers, accountants, private bankers, trustees, and others. Advisors who, in turn, use the "tools" of wealth planning to address the needs of their clients. The "toolbox" is a big one, containing trusts, foundations, onshore, "midshore," and offshore companies, partnerships, insurance strategies, and many more structures and approaches that can be mixed and matched and adapted to meet changing circumstances. It is these too that the wealth owner and their family need to understand to be able to ask the right "what-ifs" and to make sure that the succession plan will do its job in addressing the holistic needs of the family. What is a trust, and how does it work? What are the right checks and balances to protect the interests of the family for the long term? Not every trust or foundation is the same – there are huge differences from one to the other, given how they are set up and maintained, and because of who is involved. This book discusses the various ways the tools of wealth planning can be used, and also how they are all too often misused.

Relevant to the use of wealth-planning tools and how they work is an understanding of the business of wealth management. Private banks, insurance companies, trust companies, lawyers, accountants, family governance advisors, asset managers, and many others participate in the process. Advice and help for many families is a real need, but it is key to understand the conflicts of interest that inevitably exist, and how those advising families should best be managed by the families consuming their services. Here, I try to shed light on an opaque industry, hopefully helping families to ask the right questions and make the right choices.

At the end of this book is a short glossary, designed to help readers in their understanding of some of the terms that are used in dealing with the succession and planning approaches taken – trusts and foundations, the role of the settlor or protector, retrocessions (a nice word for the kickbacks an asset manager may get for introducing an unwitting client to an investment), and so on. Hopefully the glossary will provide some help in allowing the owner of wealth to ask the right questions and to demystify the succession process.

Finally, a bit more on the soft issues. When should the older generation discuss succession with the younger generation? Should the details of assets be provided, and if so when? Should in-laws be involved in family retreats that are organized to allow the older generation to communicate matters relevant to succession to the family? Will wealth destroy the dreams of the younger generation, or are there ways to avoid this happening? Are there ways to avoid wealth coming in the way of family relationships, or is it normal for a parent to encourage their child to call their elderly aunt on her birthday *because if you don't, your cousin will get her money when she dies*? As wealth owners age, is there a risk of their becoming paranoid about staff and family members stealing, and are they afraid that if they give up their wealth their family will no longer visit? Do failing memories put assets at risk? Are the grandchildren only spending time with their grandmother for fear that if they don't, their cousins will, and that they will be disadvantaged in an inheritance? At what age should the younger generation come into wealth, and how do the decisions their parents and grandparents make affect their life? Is it fair for a grandparent to spoil a grandchild with money, destroying a parent's attempt to help their children lead a fulfilled life?

There are no right and wrong answers here, but what is clear is that the soft issues count. The families that get it wrong in dealing with the many issues that come up are the families that allow wealth to destroy relationships and enrich the lawyers who make a living from disputes among the younger generation.

Is it possible for a family to get it right?

1

Any Amount of Wealth is Enough to Destroy a Family

The Chadha Brothers – Could Thoughtful Succession Planning Have Avoided Their Deaths?

In November 2012, two brothers, Ponty and Hardeep Chadha, were shot and killed in a fierce gun battle at one of their family farmhouses in Chhatarpur, Delhi, in the Indian countryside. Kulwant Chadha, Ponty and Hardeep's father, had recently died without having left much clarity regarding how significant family business and personal assets were to pass to the next generation.

Accompanied by their bodyguards, Ponty and Hardeep were arguing over their inheritance and a settlement that had been brokered by their mother. The brothers were obsessed about a particular family farmhouse that their father had left to Hardeep. Ponty, the eldest son, had contributed hugely to the family business and believed he deserved the property. Hardeep felt that he had not only been bequeathed the farmhouse by his father, but that the overall deal on his father's estate brokered by his mother gave him too little.

For a family reported to have assets worth more than US$10 billion, it would be hard to imagine that Ponty and Hardeep's father had ever dreamed that his sons would die in a gun battle over an asset of relatively irrelevant value.

Jessica Schrader – Do We Need to Do Our Planning Much Earlier?

Jessica Schrader made a will in 1990 leaving her home, Southend Farm House in Essex, England, to her two sons. At her death at the age of 98, the house was worth just under US$500,000. Two years before Jessica died, at age 96, she made a new will leaving the house entirely to her older son, Nick.

A court dispute between the brothers resulted. With legal fees of close to US$170,000, Nick lost the battle, with the court reinstating Jessica Schrader's earlier will leaving the house to both of her sons in equal shares. The judge considered the bad feelings between the brothers, and Nick's perception that his parents had favored his brother Bill. Aggressive and violent, Nick had been jailed for assault, and was viewed as having exerted undue influence on his elderly mother, whom he had been caring for on a full-time basis, prior to her death.

One can imagine Jessica Schrader, in her 90s, being pressured into changing her will by her primary caregiver, her son Nick. Are only millionaires and billionaires at risk of having wealth destroy their lives and their families?

Nina Wang – Why it is Critical to Plan for the Worst, While Hoping for the Best

Nina Wang was a larger-than-life character and, at the time of her death in 2007, Asia's wealthiest woman, with assets of over US$4 billion. Her husband, Teddy Wang, from whom she derived her wealth, had been kidnapped twice, and was never found after his second kidnapping in 1990. Disputes over Teddy Wang's wills made front-page news. A first will divided the estate between Teddy Wang's father, who had started the family business, and Nina. A second will left everything to Teddy Wang's father, and was ostensibly put in place after Teddy found out about an affair Nina was having. A third will, hotly disputed as being a forgery orchestrated by Nina, stated that Teddy had "one life and one love" and purported to leave everything to Nina.

A lower court found Teddy Wang's third will to have been a forgery, and suggested that Nina had been responsible for its creation. On appeal to Hong Kong's highest court, the third will was found to be valid, and Nina escaped the charge of forgery and ended up with Teddy's entire estate.

Nina died in 2007 also leaving a messy estate. Her *Fung Shui* master, Tony Chan, who was having an affair with the much-older Nina, presented a will suggesting that Nina left everything to him, contrary to what was stated in an earlier will executed by Nina, which left her estate to a family charitable foundation. After a long period of litigation, the will Tony Chan presented was found to have been forged, and the charitable foundation was determined to be the proper beneficiary of Nina's estate.

Jonathan Griffin – An Extreme Example of How Succession Plans Can Affect Family Members

Jonathan Griffin, wearing combat gear, caused thousands of pounds of damage to his brother's farm in Dorset, England. Furious at having been excluded from benefit under his father's will, the family farm having been left only to Jonathan's brother and mother, Jonathan's relationship with his brother, David, was clearly destroyed. Jonathan had worked on his father's farm, and was shocked at his father having left him out of a share, ostensibly for tax reasons.

Tony Marshall – An Example of the Potentially Dangerous Consequences of the Fact that We All Live Longer and Need New Approaches to Our Succession Plans

Tony Marshall, aged 88, exhausted his last legal appeal against a jail sentence for having defrauded his mother, Brooke Astor, a well-known New York socialite and philanthropist, who died at the age of 105. Tony Marshall was convicted together with one of his mother's lawyers, Francis Morrissey, Jr., who was also disbarred.

Sentenced to prison terms of one to three years, Marshall and Morrissey were found to have schemed together to siphon funds from Brooke Astor and alter her will, after she was diagnosed as having dementia and suffering from diminished capacity.

Uncle Law – Lust? Use Caution

Uncle Law, a Hong Kong resident, was 79 when he met a young woman from mainland China in Hunan Province. They soon married and had a son. Six months after mother and son received residence permits to move to Hong Kong, the couple divorced and Uncle Law lost custody of his son and his tiny, 150-square-meter apartment. Left with nothing, Uncle Law had been humiliated and abused by his wife who complained of his impotence and lack of financial resources in front of friends and family.

The Hong Kong Agency Against Abuse, a welfare service for the elderly, reported that as many as 100 Hong Kong elderly men had sought their help in 2013 as a result of problems with much younger wives from the mainland who had apparently entrapped them into marriage to obtain residence permits and their modest homes.

Roy Lam Man-chiu of the Agency Against Abuse was quoted as saying "Lust? Use Caution."

Gore Vidal – The Importance of Considering Alternative Beneficiaries Early on in the Planning Process

The author Gore Vidal died in 2012 at the age of 86. In his original will, Vidal had left his entire estate (reportedly worth well over US$40 million when future royalties from his books were included) to his long-time partner, Howard Austen, who ended up pre-deceasing Vidal, dying in 2003. Vidal changed his will in 2011, leaving his entire estate to Harvard University, a school he was apparently accepted into but which he never attended. His surviving family members, some of whom challenged the will, received nothing. Vidal's long-time housekeeper and chef, Norberto Nierras, also received nothing. He was reported as having said: "I'm 60 years old and had planned to stay with Mr. Vidal until I retired. I will have to go back to the Philippines, I cannot afford to stay in America. I didn't expect he'd leave me anything – other people are surprised he didn't. If Mr. Vidal did leave me something, I would be very, very grateful as it would help with my retirement in the Philippines, as I have a small pension."

Vidal, in his later years, was in a seriously declined physical and mental state, and according to members of his family, was suffering from dementia and other maladies with symptoms that included confusion and hallucinations.

The Maharajah of Faridkot – Can You Trust Your Trustees?

The Maharajah of Faridkot was depressed after the death of his only son. When he died a short time after, his daughters, the princesses, were stunned to learn that a will their father had ostensibly signed left them virtually nothing. The princesses had expected that the Maharajah would leave them his lands, forts, palaces, jewelry, precious stones, classic cars, and other assets worth several billion US dollars.

All of the assets of the Maharajah were apparently left to a group of trustees, with the eldest daughter of the Maharajah, the child who would have been thought to receive the largest portion of his estate, receiving nothing under the trust. Similarly, each of the Maharajah's widow and surviving mother received nothing under the trust arrangements. The youngest princesses, under the trusts, received a monthly allowance of US$20 and US$18, respectively.

Finally, after lengthy litigation, and by then in their 80s, the Maharajah's daughters succeeded in showing that the will had been forged by their father's "trusted" aides, who named themselves, together with the Maharajah's lawyers, officials, and other servants, as "trustees" of the Maharajah's estate, taking control of his wealth. In the 20 years of litigation, one of the princesses had already died, and part of the Maharajah's estate had been squandered by his self-appointed trustees who threatened to continue the case, claiming that the will putting them in control of the Maharajah's wealth was valid.

These are a few true stories among, sadly, many reported in the press on a regular basis.

In the case of Jessica Schrader, pressured into changing her will at the age of 96, a house worth less than US$500,000 was what destroyed her family and her last years. Is it not a reality that those with less to pass on to the next generation have, in today's world, an even greater responsibility to ensure that what they do is not destructive? A small family business, a nest egg of savings, a piece of jewelry... all can have enormous importance to the younger generation and apart from value can carry with them perceived "messages" from the older generation that, if not sensitively handled, can leave generations of unhappiness. But did Jessica Schrader do anything wrong, leaving her home to her two sons in equal shares under her will? How could she have avoided coming under pressure to change things at a late stage in her life? Would an earlier transfer of the house to her sons, with Jessica keeping the right to live in it for her lifetime, have been safer?

The Chadhas had billions; the Schraders a few hundred thousand in the value of their mother's house. In both cases, families and relationships destroyed. For every family dispute we read about, many, many more take place outside the press. And how many situations have arisen where assets have been stolen, diverted, misplaced, or lost and no one in the family ever even found out?

If one child is a caregiver to an elderly parent and the other is not, is the caregiver entitled to a greater share of the inheritance? Are they able to abuse a position of trust and influence their parent into destroying family relationships, as occurred when Nick Schrader unlawfully influenced his mother to change her will?

The Nina Wang case fascinated Hong Kong and the world as it unfolded over the years. The press reported the kidnappings of Teddy Wang, the second of which was even rumored to have been engineered by Nina herself. Nina's alleged extra-marital affair, which had resulted in Teddy excluding her from benefitting under his will, also became a topic of gossip. But stripping away the dramatic elements of the story leaves a number of clear questions. What did Teddy Wang ultimately want in terms of where the family business he owned, which had been started by his father, would go in the event of his death? Were there steps Teddy, or perhaps better, his own father, could have taken to keep the business away from Nina if that was their intention?

Nina ended up being a good steward of the business after Teddy's death. Despite her eccentricity, the value of the business grew to over US$4 billion by the time she passed away. But could she have also considered succession plans that would have made it less of a risk that her *Fung Shui* master and companion would get it all by forging her signature on a will purporting to leave everything to him? As it turned out, even lavish gifts to her young lover were not enough to stop him taking illegal actions in an attempt to get it all.

Vincent Astor's father, John Jacob Astor, died in the sinking of the Titanic. Brooke Astor married Vincent, the heir of one of the wealthiest families in the world, in a time of reported financial distress after the death of her second husband. Vincent Astor was reported to be a difficult individual and husband and, perhaps fortunately for Brooke Astor, died only six years after their marriage, leaving her most of his wealth.

Anthony (Tony) Marshall, Brooke Astor's son from her first marriage, was reported to have had a troubled relationship with his mother, at least in part deriving from the abusive relationship of Brooke Astor with Tony Marshall's natural father. Marshall, who took the name of Brooke's second husband, also had a reportedly terrible relationship with Vincent Astor.

When Vincent Astor died in 1959, he left Brooke Astor US$120 million, half to her and half to a foundation she was to run. An enormous sum in 1959, Brooke Astor became one of New York's top socialites and philanthropists. As she aged, Brooke Astor was reported to be distant from her son, whom she referred to as "not an Astor," largely excluding him from participation in her philanthropic work and otherwise. While Tony was involved in managing a portion of his mother's money, Brooke planned to give most of her own money to charity rather than to him.

Over the years, and prior to her death at 105, Brooke Astor became more and more dependent on the care of her son and of others. Diagnosed with Alzheimer's, Brooke Astor's friends and several members of her family were concerned at what they viewed as "elder abuse" taking place at the hands of Tony. One of Tony's own children, Philip Marshall, initiated legal proceedings to have Tony Marshall removed as his grandmother's guardian. In the proceedings that followed, both of Tony Marshall's sons testified against him. The proceedings led not only to Tony's removal as guardian, but eventually to the filing of criminal charges against him and a lawyer involved, and their conviction and jailing.

Over her lifetime, Brooke Astor had executed more than 30 wills and amendments, and as the courts ultimately found, at least some of these were executed when Brooke Astor no longer had the mental capacity to understand her actions. Will amendments favoring Tony Marshall were made, according to Brooke Astor's own lawyer, at least in part on the instructions of Tony himself. Evidently, Tony Marshall was constantly working on his mother and her lawyer to make amendments in his favor.

Tony Marshall was ultimately convicted of having taken advantage of his mother who, suffering dementia, became more and more dependent on him. Among others, Tony Marshall was alleged to have encouraged Brooke Astor to change her will in his favor and, during her lifetime, to have helped himself to his mother's art, jewelry, and money.

Tony Marshall did manage to get himself released from prison for medical reasons after only two months of incarceration, but at the age of 89, it is hard not to conclude that wealth destroyed Tony Marshall and his relationships with his mother and his two natural children. But, in this saga, was Tony Marshall the only "bad guy?" Are there lessons here for all families, particularly in a time of changing demographics, and the reality that we are all living much longer than was the case in the past? What of the increasing frequency of cases of dementia and related problems facing the elderly?

I can envision conversations between Brooke Astor and her only son in the years leading up to her death being more about money and what Tony would ultimately get than about anything else. I believe that there are too many families where aging parents spend more time than they should worrying about succession issues that should have been concluded years before. Should someone who is in hospital be surrounded by lawyers and children positioning themselves for their inheritance rather than by family members who are there because they want to be? Should children and grandchildren feel they need to pay attention to their elders because they feel the need to protect their financial interests?

Would Brooke Astor have been able to reduce the risk of wealth destroying her family by letting her son know, early on in his life, that she would *not* be giving him much, her desire being to benefit charities with the bulk of her assets? Would Tony Marshall have been encouraged to build his own career rather than be so focused on his possible inheritance? Would the expectations of Tony's third wife, disliked by Brooke Astor and by most of the press covering the story, have been different had Astor been much clearer early on as to what Tony would get and when?

Brooke Astor remembered her daughter-in-law in her will, leaving her two used, size six mink coats, knowing very well that Charlene Marshall could never fit into them.

At what age should children of wealthy parents receive a good chunk of what they may ultimately get? With the death of Brooke Astor at the age of 105, Tony Marshall was 83 by the time he was able to inherit. Stealing from his mother was wrong, but under the unfortunate circumstances of the family, perhaps not that much of a surprise.

And were all of the lawyers and other advisors meant to be looking after Brooke Astor's interests really doing so, or were they listening to their future client, Tony Marshall, rather than focusing on the interests of his aging mother? Was Brooke Astor right to trust them? Perhaps Charlene, Tony's wife, was a gold-digger. How can we identify and deal with "gold-digging" sons or daughters-in-law?

I have some simple philosophies about trust, advisors, and gold-diggers. First, don't trust anyone. Second, don't trust advisors. And third, it is best to assume that *all* your in-laws are gold-diggers (and that your children likely are, as well). It is not that no one is trustworthy. I believe, however, that if the right oversight is put in place, the possibility of someone taking advantage can be much reduced. It is pretty rare for anyone to truly have no conflicts of interest. Key is to understand and manage the conflicts of interest that exist. In succession planning and dealing with how assets pass from one generation to the next, the need for checks and balances is significant.

For any lawyer, trustee, or other advisor, it is too often the case that there is no client better than a dead client. A dead client does not question fees or fire you; a dead client does not complain about poor investment performance. A dead client takes what they know with them, and if there is no one else in or out of the family who has the information, the advisor may have been accorded too much trust. And what if the advisor is trustworthy but they themselves pass away or become disabled? Are the right succession arrangements in place for advisors and can their successors be trusted? A wealth owner needs advisors, but needs to fully understand his own ownership and succession arrangements in order to be in a position to ask the right questions.

Uncle Law, apparently along with many other elderly men in Hong Kong, was taken advantage of by a young mainland Chinese woman who seemed to be more interested in getting a visa to live in Hong Kong and getting hold of his very modest assets than in Uncle Law's well-being and happiness. Clearly, Uncle Law married a gold-digger. But to me, the safest approach is to assume that *everyone* is a gold-digger. When marriages take place, those involved are, hopefully, attracted to each other. Even in less extreme cases than that of Uncle Law, it is, to me, the whole "package" that comes into the picture – how your potential spouse looks; how tall they are; how fit; their personality; whether they are from a good family; if they have good career prospects and some money.

The question is not whether your potential spouse or son or daughter-in-law is a gold-digger, but rather the *degree to which* they are a gold-digger. And someone who is not a gold-digger today may well develop into one over time or when circumstances change. So, wealth planning is about recognizing this reality, and planning for the worst. Wealth owners need to constantly challenge their succession plans to make sure that they can withstand not only gold-digging spouses, in-laws, and others, but many, many other challenges to wealth and, more importantly, family relationships.

The elderly are particularly at risk. Uncle Law was seduced by the interest he attracted from a young mainland Chinese woman who married him, had his child, and moved to Hong Kong. Sadly for Uncle Law, she soon sued for divorce, child custody, and support – and won, leaving Uncle Law with nowhere to live.

Gore Vidal, perhaps, intended to leave his family out of inheriting any of his wealth, and perhaps also planned to leave nothing at all to his long-term caregiver. But maybe, had he undertaken the work involved in succession planning earlier, before the onset of dementia, things would have been different. Certainly, the potential for dispute and unhappiness would have been reduced had he put his arrangements in place at a time when he was more clearly in command of his faculties. And thinking of a "plan B" is always critical – in Vidal's case, he had originally planned to leave his estate to his partner, who ended up pre-deceasing him. This led to wholesale changes in his planning at a time of life when he, perhaps, did not have the ability to really think things through.

Advisors are needed – but for the prudent wealth owner, understanding their own succession plan, and not allowing it to be kidnapped by advisors, is critical. In the case of the Maharajah of Faridkot, his substantial wealth fell into the hands of a group of "trusted" advisors who sought to exclude the family from any benefit at all.

Sometimes what happens is less dramatic, and less "black and white" – but perhaps the Maharajah of Faridkot's succession provides an example of the risks families face in a world of conflicts of interest. I have seen numerous cases of succession and asset-protection planning where an obsession with tax minimization has led the family to a complicated approach they do not really understand and in which the advisors all too easily "kidnap" the family structures. The advisors are not quite stealing the money, but the structures end up resulting in a never-ending flow of fees with little ability for the younger generation to step in and turn off the tap. For me, no advisor should be free of appropriate oversight and, most importantly, free of the family stakeholders having a clear view of their actions, with the ability to make changes if the need arises. Do you *really* trust your advisor more than you trust your children?

Today, virtually every family is international. Family members may live in different countries or hold different citizenships, and investments are increasingly likely to be maintained cross-border. Divorces, political risk, ever-changing tax laws, and an almost unlimited number of other threats to wealth add to the burden for those seeking to maximize what can pass from one generation to the next. Navigating a world of growing complexity and transparency is increasingly difficult, forcing wealth owners into the hands of private bankers, trustees, lawyers, and a variety of other specialists who make their living from the needs of the wealthy. But does the wealth owner and his or her family really understand the structures that are imposed on them by their advisors, and the many hidden charges and risks associated with typical wealth-planning devices? Is it safe to rely on outsiders whose interests may be starkly different from those of the family involved?

Earning appropriate returns, protecting wealth, and minimizing taxes are all well and good, but have you, as a wealth owner, considered that your wealth can destroy your family? Despite that, most of us think we would be happier if we had more wealth; a sad reality is that all too often wealth destroys relationships, families, and the dreams of the younger generation. This destruction *can* be avoided.

A wealth owner has responsibilities – and one of the most important of these is to really understand how one's own wealth is owned and how the structures implemented work – both in terms of their suitability to address the objectives for which they were created and in terms of their real costs and what security, if any, they provide against known and unknown risks. Even more critical is to understand what succession plan is actually in place, and its potential consequences for the younger generation.

For those who put off their succession planning, understanding that no plan *is* a plan is also vital. In the event of death or disability, something will happen to your assets regardless of whether appropriate planning has been done. Have you worked out what will happen if you pass away? Who actually knows about the assets you have and where they are?

News about the difficulties of well-known families and the failure of their asset-protection and succession plans seems to be growing in frequency and drama. The problems we hear about cross geographies and cultures. It is simply untrue that families from one part of the world or of a particular religion are truly different from others. The notion that *we all love each other and do not fight and involve lawyers the way westerners do* is just that – a notion that is sometimes a misleading dream of the older generation, thinking that everything will just work out. The children may well show up, holding hands at dinner at their parents' home every Friday evening, but sadly the children can also show up in the offices of their lawyers ready to do battle as soon as their parents are dead or incapacitated.

The stories we read about, while usually concerning the very wealthy and very famous, are sadly the same stories that plague every family, regardless of the level of wealth – because *any* amount of wealth is enough to destroy a family.

The Psychology of Wealth

It is human nature to think that if we had the wealth, we would be happy. But does being wealthy really bring happiness? Clearly, there is a need for a certain level of wealth to meet one's needs, but how much is ever enough? Research has shown that after a certain point, having more does not continually add to one's happiness, and from my experience, it is simply all too often that wealth is destructive of families and relationships.

I believe that it takes work to not only be happy with what you have, but to ensure that the next generation and others in any family are positively rather than negatively impacted by any wealth that might be shared. How succession plans are developed and implemented can have a dramatic effect.

Wealth is created in any number of ways. An entrepreneur can work hard to create a profitable business. Professionals can accumulate wealth through their work, and by investing their savings. Employees can come into wealth through bonuses and stock plans. Liquidity events on the sale or listing of businesses and otherwise can arise. Luck may play a role, as may family, political, and other connections. The creation of wealth can be fast and easy, or a long and slow road, or somewhere in between.

Wealth also comes through inheritance, gifts, divorce, and in many other ways.

How and when one arrives at wealth can have a big impact on the psychology of the wealth owner and on how the wealth involved will be grown, protected, and shared. Someone who inherits may never feel the wealth is really theirs, or that their input in the wealth-creation or preservation process was of any value. The successful entrepreneur who received help from a parent or in-law may not feel they did it themselves, and may thereby view wealth in a very different way than a wealth creator who started with nothing and did it all on their own. In families, it is often the case that while thought is given to creating wealth, not enough thought is given to how the wealth will be transferred and, importantly, the effect of a gift or inheritance on the individual receiving it.

How wealth is derived and the psychology involved also affects perspectives on how much is ever enough.

Is it possible to classify someone as "rich" when the term is so subjective? For the vast majority, having "enough" is something that never really happens, particularly given consumption and expectations – both of which are moving targets. Someone who is just starting out, and has virtually nothing, hopes for salary increases and opportunities. If your savings are in the thousands or less and your income just about covers your spending, it is easy to see someone who owns their own home and drives a nice car as being "rich"... but is that homeowner really feeling rich if their savings do not cover more than a few years of their current lifestyle? Are they looking out of the window of the home coveted by someone with less than them, gazing at a larger home that their neighbor owns, and thinking about how nice it would be to live there? Is the neighbor living in the larger home distracted from enjoying it by dreaming about owning a private plane or some other possession of one of their wealthier acquaintances that they think they would like to have?

I have worked with many, many families with wealth in the double digits of millions who definitely do not feel "rich" – yet for the vast majority, being a "millionaire" is something only for dreams. Families may own various homes, but this comes with the costs associated with running properties that are not producing any income. The cars, clothes, jewelry, schools, insurance, entertainment, travel, and other things enjoyed by those who can afford them come at a cost, and maintaining a lifestyle can get more and more expensive as wealth grows and consumption and expectations expand. As a result, there is little question that even the "rich" worry about money, and whether what they have will run out. The choices out there in relation to spending seem almost limitless... there is always a house, car, boat, or other thing that is a bit nicer or bigger than the one we have and which costs a bit more than we can afford. So is there ever really enough?

The question of how much we need is a difficult one, but it is highly relevant to the issues that come up in relation to transfers of wealth and how to best deal with the issue of succession. Even more important are the many psychological issues involved within and outside the family that come into the picture. The cast of characters can be a big one and, from a psychological perspective, the issues can be complex and ever-changing.

Looking at the typical players often involved is a good starting point to understanding the potential problems and, hopefully, avoiding them. We will come back to these characters in later chapters of this book, reflecting on how their differing psychological standpoints affect the planning process. Much of asset protection and succession planning is based on ensuring that all the relevant "what ifs" have been asked and addressed. Thinking about the possible actions and reactions of the different people in and out of a family interested in the family's wealth is a good starting point for some of the "what ifs" that are particular to the family involved.

The Wealth Creator

Family wealth almost always has at its origin an entrepreneur who created the wealth. This can be someone who started with nothing, and who built a business or career that changed the financial picture for the family. This can also be someone who started with substantial amounts from inheritance or otherwise, but who were themselves successful in wealth creation – perhaps through shrewd investments, excellent stewardship of a family business, or through the creation of new businesses for the family.

The origin of most family businesses is a hard-working entrepreneur who started with nothing. Grandfather may have emerged from poverty with the drive to build, and in his lifetime achieved amazing results, allowing the possibility of long-term financial security for his immediate family and descendants. But has grandfather so dedicated himself to his business that he lacks the other elements often needed for a balanced life, such as close friendships, family relationships, outside interests, and more? How does the move from poverty to comfort affect the wealth owner? Many never feel that they are really "safe" – and to protect their family and their wealth, grandfather may be surprisingly frugal, never able to accept that success has come to such an extent that there will be no return to the difficulties of the past. But how does this conflict with the expectations of a spouse or a child, or one of the in-laws marrying into what they perceive to be a "wealthy" family? And can these conflicts become destructive?

A wealth creator who started with nothing may also not be good at saying no to his children, spoiling them and their dreams with too much. And what happens – where the wealth creator has worked for years and years, living on little – when suddenly the business is sold and wealth comes fast and high? Is this change to the wealth creator's life positive?

It is easy to point out to the wealth creator the value of developing balance in their life, spending time on things other than their business and wealth, enjoying their family and developing outside interests that support a happy retirement. It is much harder to expect that the typical wealth creator will change. As a result, in working with wealth creators on the many issues that arise in asset protection and succession, it is important to try to understand things from their perspective, and to help them understand how their decisions (or lack of decisions) will affect their businesses and their families.

The super-successful wealth creator is often at the center of a complex set of family and business relationships, his or her success influencing a number of emotions among family, friends, colleagues, and others – emotions that the wealth creator himself may not understand or appreciate exist. Is the son or daughter of someone who is a larger-than-life financial success condemned to never being able to feel the sense of accomplishment that can be so important to the question of "happiness?" Can the wealth creator properly work on transition issues that will assure success of the family business as it moves to the next generation? Maybe there *are* steps the wealth creator can take to increase the chances that wealth and success will not be destructive of either their business or family relationships.

At one extreme, a wealth creator may get everything right. During their lifetime and career, the wealth creator might move from a singular focus on making money and building their business to spending more time with family, developing philanthropic and other interests, and thinking about how best to deal with asset protection and succession planning. Here, there is no one right answer for every family – but where the wealth owner involved puts enough time and thought into the ongoing process of putting in place what might work best in their circumstances, the chance of getting it right is certainly there.

Getting it right also means that the wealth creator understands that wealth is transitory and that it is not wealth that should be the glue that keeps a family together. If the wealth is gone, is the family also gone? Or does what family represents and the relationships involved survive and thrive whatever happens to family wealth?

The spending habits of the successful wealth creator are often interesting to observe. These can range from wealth owners who remain frugal and criticize spouses and children who "overspend," to wealth owners who themselves overspend, resulting in unrealistic expectations for those who may succeed them, lives destroyed at discovering that there is little left over, contrary to what they had expected and quietly planned for. To me, it is important for the wealth creator to understand how important it is to communicate clearly within a family, and also to understand how much of what our children learn comes from example. And for those whose achievements are enormous, how can they ensure that the achievements of their children, spouses, and other relatives are not diminished by the wealth creator's success?

Wealth creators are not always mothers and fathers affecting their spouses, children, and grandchildren with their succession and related decisions. Increasingly we see wealth creators who are young, and sometimes very young, and whose wealth has a tremendous impact on their relationships with siblings and fairly young parents who never achieved the success one of their children has achieved. Does a successful young person have an obligation to "share the wealth" with siblings or parents? How can family relationships best be preserved when there is outsized financial success by a family member?

Psychologically, the wealth creator is a difficult one to deal with, and the issues change as the wealth creator ages, and family dynamics change. The introduction of spouses, mistresses, toy-boys, second families, and more add to the complexity – and to the challenge of ensuring that wealth is not destructive of the family involved.

The Wealth Creator's Spouse

There is little in the world that is black and white, and this certainly applies to the spouses of wealth creators. Maybe the spouse is a second or third spouse, or a first love or arranged marriage that has lasted years. The spouse may have previously been a mistress or toy-boy, or may themselves have come from a family with meaningful wealth and/or position. Or the wealth creator's spouse may be a wealth creator themselves, either involved in their own business or career. Often, the spouse is an integral part of the wealth creator's business and success, working hand-in-hand with the wealth creator.

Family dynamics and the whole issue of asset protection and succession will be affected by the wealth creator's spouse, and where the spouse survives the wealth creator, his or her role can be ever more important in dealing with the question of whether wealth will destroy the family involved.

Relationships with the younger generation can vary... it is not every mother or father that is loved and respected by their children, and too often for good reason. And where the marriage is a second, third, or further marriage, relationships can be particularly strained, largely because money becomes a central issue.

Are things any different where spouses are of the same sex? In my experience, not at all – expectations and questions of fairness are the same, and often enough, children also come into the picture. But dynamics and the legal position can be very different, as can perceptions of siblings and others on what is their fair share when a succession event occurs.

I have worked with many wealth creators who, at some stage of their life, end up marrying a younger (and sometimes much younger) second, third, or further spouse. Almost inevitably, issues in and around the question of money arise. If, say, a father has three children in their 40s and 50s and remarries a younger woman, perhaps younger than his youngest child, financial issues invariably come into the mix. Is the new spouse a gold-digger? Of course! There is *never* a question of whether or not the young new spouse is a gold-digger. The new spouse *is* a gold-digger. The only open issue is the *extent* to which money came into the picture for the new spouse... and if she is not particularly attracted to the money, there is little assurance that she will not become a gold-digger at some point in the future.

This may sound like a very cynical view of relationships, love, and marriage. But the reality is that attraction involves a "full package"... looks, personality, fitness, intelligence, prospects, coming from a "good" family... wealth. So, in planning, my approach is always to expect the worst, and if things turn out for the best, all the better, but it is important to plan for what can and does all too often happen... a huge difference of views on money between the children and, in particular, a second or third (or further) spouse.

When Dad marries someone younger than his youngest child, it is rarely the case that this does not raise a question in the minds of the children regarding what this is going to end up costing them in terms of their interest in their father's assets. Where there are more children of the second or further marriage, the risks to the first set of children are even greater. From a legal perspective, marriage, co-habitation, divorce, having children, and adoption all have potential ramifications, and these are discussed later in this book. But there are also considerable psychological issues, often less easy to manage, that also arise.

The children may well not say anything to their father about their real concerns... how will the new wife their father has chosen affect their financial interests? This unspoken concern may end up poison-ing the relationship between the children and their step-mother, and also affect their relationship with their father, as the children evidence lukewarm (at best) support for the person their father has chosen to spend his life with.

Could all this bad feeling be addressed, at least in part, through some advance planning and greater communication within the fam-ily? What if the father, before marrying, makes irrevocable arrange-ments to make clear what his children will end up getting, either now or on his passing? And if, as part of the plan, Dad puts in place bind-ing agreements with his new wife, that she accepts, clarifying what she will end up getting if the marriage lasts and she survives her new husband, will this help ensure that the new relationship will work for all concerned? Could it be that once the question of money is off the table, the children will be more open to focusing on the potential happiness of their father and the reality that the new spouse may take away some of the burden they would otherwise be under to take care of their father in his old age?

Or will the father neglect the work necessary to minimize the risk of disputes, allowing even family photo albums carrying memories of his children's upbringing to pass to a new young wife who just throws them away when her elderly husband dies? Will a lack of foresight result in his relationship with his new wife moving into one where he increasingly depends on her care and she tightens the screws, focusing on the money she wants in exchange?

The broad range of spouses can include a spouse of a wealth creator who him or herself has meaningful assets, and perhaps their own family legacy that comes with those assets. I worked with a family where a woman in the older generation came from a wealthy and well-known family. Her father had employed the man who eventually became her husband, and provided him with what he needed to eventually start his own business. The wife used her own resources to support the growth of the business, and while she was not directly involved in the further wealth creation, spending her time raising a large number of children, it was pretty clear that her own family legacy and wealth was highly relevant to the success that her husband enjoyed. As the wealth of the family grew, so did the reputation and legacy of the husband. Increasingly, both within and outside the family, there was little recognition for the contribution of the spouse and her own family's legacy to the wealth created. This led to considerable differences of opinion in relation to the succession and asset-protection plan ultimately adopted by the family, and to the happiness of the aging spouse who was increasingly feeling left out of the process.

Understanding the dynamics of wealth and respecting the history of the family involved can be an important step in the succession process. And like all areas of asset protection and succession planning, the issues are not only of concern to those with millions or billions, but to all of us.

Aging Relatives – Alive… and Well?

The aging wealth owner is fast becoming a disaster area in wealth planning. This can be a grandparent or great-grandparent, a mother or mother-in-law, a father or father-in-law, or anyone else in the family. We are now living well into our 80s and 90s, with increasing numbers of people living well into their 100s. Accompanying this change in demographics are significant issues for families in relation to how wealth moves from one generation to the next, and when.

One simple question that aging populations give rise to is, when should the younger generation begin to benefit from assets that are intended to pass from one generation to the next? In the case of Brooke Astor, whose son ended up in prison for having, among others, helped himself to some of his mother's assets, her approach did not work. Brooke Astor lived to well over 100, delaying her son's inheritance until he was in his 80s. It is one thing to pass wealth to children on death when one lives until the early 70s, and the children are in their mid to late 40s, but if we add 30 years of life to the mix, is it really right to make children wait that long for their inheritance?

As we move into a time of aging populations, it is a responsibility of the older generation to make their plans clear, and to consider the possibility of finalizing their thinking on succession several decades before their death. If one's children are in their 40s or 50s, should this not be a time when at least some of the assets that are ultimately to pass to them are actually divided and transferred? Isn't this safer than holding onto assets until dementia sets in and household staff and others can interfere with the succession process, converting assets to their own benefit? I have been disturbed by reports of doctors and nurses caring for the aged becoming beneficiaries of their patients' estates, and have seen cases of trusted advisors, bankers, lawyers, and others worming their way into the succession process, taking advantage of their elderly clients. It is not only spouses and in-laws who are gold-diggers that need to be protected against.

As people age, there is a real risk of their becoming increasingly concerned that the "money" is what keeps their family interested in them. Members of the older generation are often afraid to let go of their wealth, thinking that their wealth is the main reason for their children and grandchildren to visit – a sad way for a successful wealth owner to feel, but a reality in how many do. I am a believer that a good succession plan is one that is adopted early in life, and which at the right time is discussed openly and sensitively within the family so that intentions are clear, reducing the risk of bad feelings and disputes when it is too late to adjust things. At the right time, the succession plan should be fixed, with changes only being possible if a majority of family stakeholders agree.

As people age, there is also the increase of varying forms of dementia. Memories fail, and as they do, paranoia creeps in. We forget where our glasses are, and this develops into thinking that someone stole our glasses. Sometimes this paranoia presents itself openly, with the older generation accusing household help or even family members of stealing. Often, the paranoia is internalized and translates itself into the aging wealth owner delaying any gifts of assets or openness on the estate-planning process. Hanging onto the assets and keeping secretive is a way of keeping control and power, and for someone challenged by the aging process, achieving control over something may seem critical.

There are many psychological issues that come into the mix when it comes to succession. Controlling your wealth until the very, very end may feel right, but all too often it means that there is no well-thought-out succession plan. Assets disappear for lack of anyone knowing where they are, possessions are stolen by those who know that they will not get caught, and individual siblings may press their own agendas with aging parents, resulting in long-term damaged relationships and potential for destructive family disputes. Anger with children may result in assets passing to grandchildren much earlier than they should, and with negative effects on the ability of the children to play their roles as parents.

The Second Spouse

Second marriages or other domestic relationships affect everyone in the family, both emotionally and financially. Sometimes the second marriage is encouraged by family members after the death of a spouse. In other cases the second marriage may have caused a messy break-up of a first marriage, and children and the former spouse will view the second spouse as an enemy from every perspective. Relationships can be very complex, including second and third domestic relationships that happen while the first marriage is still intact. In some religions and cultures this is accepted, in others it is not. But in all cases, issues arise, both emotional and financial.

The overall responsibility, in my view, is with the wealth owner. It is he or she, embarking on a second or subsequent marriage, who should consider the impact on their family and wealth and proactively address these issues to seek to protect the family from destroying itself and the wealth involved. Those "lucky" wealth owners who survive their second marriage with no legal or other challenges may well be leaving a legacy of problems, with the legal actions regarding their assets happening after they pass away.

In later chapters, the "tools" of wealth management will be a topic, and how these tools can be used to address family needs will also be described. But to really make these tools work, the wealth owner has to think about the "what ifs" in the context of what they know about their second spouse and of their first family. And if there are children and other stakeholders that the second marriage brings into the picture, the need for careful thought and planning also comes into the mix.

The reality is that the second or subsequent spouse will themselves benefit hugely from an open approach to financial issues. The more things are made clear at the outset of a relationship, the less room there is for uncertainty, and the more possible it is to anticipate that the relationship that develops will be less about money and more about what is important to really make the relationship work for all involved.

If the wealth owner fails to take early action in and around a second marriage, as sensitive as it may be, their own family should step in and encourage dialogue. Waiting for Mom or Dad to take action may leave things too late, and right or wrong, it is not uncommon to see virtually all the family wealth go to a second spouse where there is little upfront planning and discussion within the family. Timing can be everything, and from every perspective.

The First Mistress or Toy-boy

My eldest son was born at the Adventist Hospital in Hong Kong. I was standing in front of the glass window to the nursery looking for my son (I have to admit that all babies seem to look pretty much the same at that stage) when I noticed a client of mine also looking through the glass. He introduced me to the mother of his new child, who was sitting in a wheelchair, having just given birth. This was not his wife.

Living and working in Hong Kong, I developed a sense that mistresses are an Asian concept, having run across so many wealth owners with complex multiple relationships. I moved to Switzerland in the mid-1990s and began working with wealth owners from around the world, and increasingly realized that mistresses are not an Asian concept, but a *global* concept.

In some countries co-habitation can give rise to meaningful legal rights to assets and income. In all cases, out-of-marriage liaisons can disturb the succession process and, most importantly, family relationships.

And it is certainly not only about mistresses, but also the toy-boy, the male version of a mistress, with the terms "mistress" and "toy-boy" both being inappropriate in many cases. Out-of-marriage affairs can range from the most insignificant to meaningful, lifelong relationships and second families.

From the psychological perspective, all are affected – the mistress or toy-boy, the wealth owner involved with them, the wealth owner's spouse and family. Not everyone may know of each other, and this confidentiality may in and of itself be an objective of effective asset protection and succession planning. Approaches using the tools of wealth planning can help to prevent what so often happens – long-term out-of-marriage relationships coming to the surface after the death of the wealth owner.

For the mistress or toy-boy, there may well be plenty of non-financial reasons for the attraction. But can we really say that there are many cases where the money involved is not at least a factor? And maybe an important one? The wealth owner probably knows that his money is relevant, and may even think that the position is clear, with his paying the rent and providing gifts from time to time. But will the toy-boy stick to this price as he becomes less secure of his attraction as the years go by? Will a close relationship move from excitement and affection to blackmail?

There is one golden rule about mistresses and toy-boys. Never give them a lump sum of money. Within months, the mistress or toy-boy is back asking for more, having lost the money gambling or through some shady investment.

It is the wealth owner who is in control of decisions on how to financially deal with the situation of a mistress or toy-boy, or many of them. Not thinking about things is often a mistake. Like with families, openness with the toy-boy or mistress about the financial aspects of the relationship, and good use of the tools of wealth planning, can help. For example, a wealth owner can use a variety of structures to provide an annual allowance to the toy-boy, but only on the condition that he remains quiet about the relationship and does not make any other claims. If the toy-boy is cooperative, he receives the allowance. If he is not, he loses it all. Not a guarantee that there will be no trouble, but something that may help.

In my work, I was generally taking the side of the family – either looking at things from the perspective of the wealth owner or from the perspective of other family members. I often ran across situations of mistresses or toy-boys being egged on in relation to their financial expectations by outsiders – their own family and friends, and sometimes more sinister "handlers" with economic interests in the outcome.

The mistress or toy-boy will often have very different views on what is owed to them than the wealth owner has. But in many relationships, the mistress or toy-boy may have pretty valid reasons to think they deserve the share of the wealth they are seeking.

Within wealth-owning families, the issue of a mistress or toy-boy that a parent or spouse is involved with can be traumatic, and certainly not only from a financial perspective. A mistress or toy-boy will often come to realize that they had better get hold of some assets while wealth is still in the hands of the wealth owner – creating issues as the wealth owner ages, and as the relationship moves, as it too often does, from excitement to blackmail.

And like everything else having to do with families, it is not always black and white. It is sometimes the mistress or toy-boy who needs protection, and who is the one dedicating themselves to a relationship which might not provide them with the long-term financial security they deserve, particularly where they are the ones who are of real meaning to the wealth owner over the years. It again falls to the wealth owner to ensure that the right things are done at the right time.

The Second Mistress or Toy-boy… and the First is Not Thrilled

The reality is that the "value" of mistresses and toy-boys is at least sometimes their youth and the excitement of something new. The move to a new relationship will almost certainly raise many issues for both the new and the old playmate.

When the first mistress or toy-boy finds out about the new player, this is often a trigger for their wanting to assure their financial and family status. What was previously a private relationship that the broader family was not aware of may come out into the open, with financial and emotional consequences.

The second mistress may well be looking to establish herself by making herself known to the first – again creating havoc. For the wealth owner involved in these relationships, initial excitement may well turn into a nightmare. Making things clear on what the financial deal is and the consequences of causing trouble can help keep things under wraps, and is certainly worth the effort. It is easy to say that the best way to avoid difficulties is to stay away from toxic relationships – but this may be naïve given the realities in the lives of all too many wealth owners.

For both the new and old companion, financial issues are part of the relationship. It is the responsibility of the wealth owner to accept this reality, and to plan their affairs accordingly.

The Children in the Second Family

Each participant in a wealth-owning family has their own perspective on wealth and their entitlements in the succession process. But most important when thinking about children is how the succession process may affect their lives. There is no question whatsoever that growing up without wealth but with the right family support is much better than growing up in an environment of uncertainty as to how your mother or father feels about you, and confusion over whether financial "messages" are messages about the extent of how a parent feels about a child.

Having a mother or father who is the "second" spouse or playmate brings its own complications, given the emotions of the second spouse and his or her views about the first, and the children of the first, and the common financial preference of the children of the first relationship. Where family businesses are involved, the issues become even more difficult to manage, particularly where the wealth owner envisions his or her children, from whichever relationship, working together in harmony. This can work, but often doesn't, and the question that arises is whether there is anything the wealth owner can do early on to reduce the risk of disaster, both personal and financial.

But it is not only the wealth owner who impacts the well-being of the children of the second or third (or further family). The second parent, who may not be a wealth owner him or herself, will have a tremendous impact, as will step-siblings, grandparents, and others. Is bad feeling inevitable, or are there steps that can be taken to minimize the risks? And if you are the "victim" of a wealth-owning family, are there steps you can take yourself to protect yourself from a destructive family? Sometimes being destructive (or protective of your own interests, as might be your perspective) is the key, and understanding your rights and how they can be enforced (through persuasion or legal means) can be critical. This, of course, is something that all beneficiaries of wealth need to understand – wealth can destroy relationships, but early and clear action, based on understanding what is really going on, can be critical.

There are many practical and legal approaches that can help secure the financial position of members of a wealth-owning family. But at the end, the most important thing is to avoid wealth being destructive of one's life, and all too often the frustration of not getting what you think you deserve can become an obsession. The more each

individual can focus on themselves and building their own independence, both emotional and financial, the better off they will be.

The Sons

Much has been changing, but there is a reality that expectations and
arrangements involving male children *are* different. This sometimes
results from cultural differences, such as in traditional Chinese families where the older son, and sons generally, are favored in financial
support and inheritance. This also results from a broader reliance on
the older son as the one who has the responsibility to carry forward
the family legacy, including family wealth and businesses.

Religion can also come into it, and the *Shari'a* law, applying to
Muslims, generally hugely favors the male line, with sometimes dramatic consequences. As an example, the estate of a father who is a
Sunni Muslim in Lebanon leaving only daughters would go in large
part to the deceased's brother or his deceased brother's sons – this
regardless of whether the deceased was estranged from his brother
or nephews and regardless of the deceased father having wanted his
daughters to be the only beneficiaries of his estate. It is also the case
that in virtually all cases where the *Shari'a* law applies, sons will
receive twice the shares that daughters receive.

Even where cultural and religious elements do not come into it,
males are often, though clearly not always, the main breadwinners,
with women far more often being the ones to take a temporary or
permanent break from their careers to raise a family. Does this mean
that a son should inherit more than a daughter, the daughter being
less likely to need support from her parents given the ability to rely
on her husband? Should a son inherit less because of his earning capa-
bilities, with a daughter getting more because of the possibility that
she may not be able to earn throughout the period of parenting she
may undertake?

How do sons feel when they benefit more than their sisters,
for whatever reason, cultural, religious, or otherwise? I have seen
many relationships among siblings destroyed because of differences
in treatment by their parents, and the destruction is all the greater
where the recipients are of a different world than their parents. The
father or mother may come from a generation tied to religious and
cultural traditions and obligations, with the younger generation
much less so, if at all. If a son is then favored over his sister, does he

have an obligation to make things fair once the assets come to him? In the traditional Chinese family, the older son had the obligation to look after his sisters and younger male siblings. If the children are thoroughly westernized, will the older son, having received the bulk of his parents' assets, do the "right thing?" If he doesn't know how his sister feels about having received less, what will the effect of this be on their relationship? What if he does know how she feels, but likes the idea of having received more? If the son shares with his sister, is it enough, in her eyes, if the amount is not equal? And even if it is, does the son begin to affect their relationship by making his sister feel that she "owes" him for his generosity?

There are often reasons not to treat children equally in terms of gifts and inheritances, and certainly culture and religion are important elements in ensuring that wealth and the approach to its distribution within a family are not destructive. Where the religious or cultural elements are solidly believed in by all involved, problems are less likely to arise than in families without clear rules to guide them. But in my experience, distributing wealth unequally among children without adequate preparation and discussion within the family is one of the most destructive things a parent can do.

But is there value in an approach that puts the older son in charge of the family business and family affairs? Professor Joseph Fan of the Chinese University of Hong Kong has lectured and written on the failed performance of companies whose ownership passes to trusts rather than to a responsible family member, such as an older son, the favored approach in Chinese families. Meanwhile, Professor Roger King of the Business School at the Hong Kong University of Science and Technology has undertaken studies showing that the eldest son is the *least* able, psychologically, to ensure success. Professor King's research suggests that second and subsequent sons are more entrepreneurial than their careful older siblings.

For me, governance is the key, whatever approach is taken in succession, and whatever tool is used to achieve the future running of a family business or family wealth. Having a trust in place that is designed to protect the interests of the family does not mean that a business will fail if the trust contains the right governance checks and balances. Using structures that make it clear who owns assets among the younger generation, perhaps equally, but also putting the right incentives in place for those leading the business to feel that they are adequately rewarded for their efforts can be as effective (if not more so) as the traditional focus on the eldest son.

There is no one answer that fits all circumstances, but the issue of succession is one that requires considerable attention if assets, businesses, and relationships are to be preserved and enhanced.

The Daughters

The female line in a family can face a number of challenges, cultural, religious, or otherwise. I am a believer that since many daughters still have to take career breaks to care for their children, whether for a short period or otherwise, daughters have special financial needs. One which is of utmost importance is the need for lifetime financial independence, if the wealth of her family allows for this. If parents have wealth that might transit from one generation to the next, something to consider for both sons and daughters is to not have the value involved available to the next generation all at once.

A wealth-owning client of mine had a considerable estate he was planning the transition of. Planning for the next generation seemed straightforward to him, with his children all relatively successful in their early adulthood, well on the way to establishing their own young families. Perhaps a situation where the decision on how and when to distribute would be easy – just dividing the assets equally and having them shared among the younger generation. But one of his daughters had married into a mega-wealthy family... not millionaires, but multi-billionaires.

Did this mean that the one daughter, as opposed to her other siblings, should not receive anything, not being in need? Or would being fair and protecting the sibling relationships require an even distribution among the children? I asked about the daughter's spending habits, and how she was relating to the family she had married into. I asked whether she was spending within or above her means, and whether she was overspending, trying to keep up with her husband and in-laws, proving her status as herself coming from a wealthy family and not needing her husband's family's money. Not surprisingly, my client excitedly confirmed my suspicions. His daughter had been quickly going through the funds he had provided to all of his children as an interim distribution of his wealth.

While his other children were prudently investing what had been advanced to them, the daughter who had married into billions was using her own money to contribute to a lifestyle of private jets, couture clothing, and more. What I advised was that my client and his wife consider an estate plan that would *not* have his daughter receive her full inheritance on their deaths, but rather that, through the use of the "tools" of wealth and estate planning, she be provided with something more than just an inheritance – financial independence from her husband or anyone else for her entire life.

By holding back the full inheritance and having it made available in parts over her lifetime, whatever happened, the daughter of my client would avoid having to depend on her husband, and there would also be a level of control over her spending. She simply would not have the ability to "spend it all" in a few years, something not difficult to do notwithstanding that she was likely to inherit in the range of $15 to $20 million. Living amongst billionaires, and paying for her own clothes, jewelry, travel, and more to show her own wealth would have otherwise meant that she would have gone through her inheritance in only a few short years. Through some careful planning, this simply would not happen.

Divorces are all too common, and while we may lament this state of affairs, much, much worse are those who are confined to a dysfunctional and dangerous relationship for economic reasons. Providing any child (or anyone else) with financial independence is an important gift. The ability to walk out at any time can be critical.

But what of the other siblings in the case of my client? They were being prudent with what their parents had given them. Should we have arranged for different treatment of the daughter who had married into wealth from those who were doing it all on their own? I am not a believer in differences being made among children, except in the most extreme cases. As a result, I advocated a long-term approach being taken on the same basis for all of the children involved. This required some careful thinking and the design of an approach that would permit the next generation reasonable access to what they needed for the right reasons – education of the younger generation and the ability to deal with health care and other costs, and the ability to invest. But to me, the equal treatment of the younger generation is a key element toward helping to keep the younger generation together, and avoiding having wealth destroy the family.

Are these only issues for the super-wealthy? Or is it even more important to protect what may be left to the younger generation when the amounts involved are relatively small, but the needs of the younger generation and the effect of even modest financial help great?

The Sons-in-Law and Daughters-in-Law – A Broad Spectrum

What about spouses, and particularly those from modest backgrounds. Are they "gold-diggers" who need to be protected against? Did my new daughter-in-law marry my son for money? Is it safer for my son to marry a woman from a wealthy family?

In my years of working for wealth-owning families, I met many who engineered marriages among their children to families seen as their peers in terms of levels of wealth, thinking that this was a way to avoid the "gold-diggers." Is this a safer bet?

In my experience, the level of wealth of the spouse of a child from a wealthy family has little relationship to the threats to wealth that divorce gives rise to. And the reality is that the question of whether a son or daughter-in-law is a gold-digger is an irrelevant question to ask. Your son or daughter-in-law *is* a gold-digger. It is just a question of degree. And if they are not hugely a gold-digger today, they may well become one in future, as relationships and their own financial circumstances change.

All relationships involve money, at least to some extent. We are attracted to our partners because they have good personalities; they have a wide circle of friends; they are "buff," keeping themselves in shape and looking good; there is physical and emotional attraction; they have a good career and prospects for the future; they come from a wealthy family and can provide; they have the toys that make life more fun… The degree to which money comes into it may differ from relationship to relationship, but thinking that there is *no* element of money coming into it is all too often wrong. The wealthiest of potential spouses for your children will be thinking about what money your children might inherit or generate themselves. And if the issue is not at the forefront at the outset of the relationship, it can well move to the forefront later, when the financial position of the other party changes or when there is a rocky time in the relationship and a desire to "punish" comes into the picture.

The best option is to hope for the best, but plan for the worst, and to accept that every relationship involves money, at least to some extent.

Whether a spouse comes from wealth or not, having some understanding of how things work in the event of a breakdown in the relationship is very important for the younger generation. Pre- and post-nuptial agreements are only part of the picture. How one spends, and from where money is accessed, can have a big effect on who gets what in the event of a breakdown of the marriage. Whose money is used to pay for homes, education of children, and more is also an issue to be considered early on. Money can run out, and if the safety net is represented by the savings or inheritance of one of the spouses, what happens to that if the marriage breaks down?

It is often much easier to sort things out upfront when the intended spouse of one of your children does *not* come from wealth. This may sound mean, but it is much easier to come to clear financial arrangements with someone from a modest background than with someone who sees themselves as financially ahead of the family they are marrying into. Which means even more care is needed if your child is marrying into a family of wealth, to avoid your child, and your wealth, becoming victim to what could happen.

Should spouses be excluded from family discussions in or out of "family retreats" in the case of a wealthy family? How much should they know about family wealth? More on this later in relation to pre- and post-nuptial agreements, and the destruction of wealth that divorce can give rise to, but it is important to remember that the wife or husband of your child will be raising your grandchildren, and will be involved in protecting their interests. Total exclusion from the family is not the answer, but neither is unlimited trust. In fact, trust no one.

Where the in-law is from a wealthy family, this is not an answer to the many questions that have to be asked as part of the "what-ifs" an effective asset-protection and succession plan needs to address. In fact, the wealth of your son or daughter's partner may be the basis on which your child overspends… trying to prove their own independence. Reliance on the wealth of their partner can result in your child losing the important financial independence that your wealth should be able to offer.

And wealthy families often get there for a reason – they are not stupid, and have money as their focus. Upfront, the man or woman your child may be planning a future with may themselves be carefully planning their own financial protection, allowing your child to be the spender, while they are the saver. When a divorce is looming, wealth can be the basis of investments in the best lawyers, experienced in ensuring the destruction of the wealth and well-being of the victims of attack. Your child marrying into wealth means more prudence, not less, in a world of danger and destruction of wealth and relationships.

There are also plenty of psychological issues that come into the mix. How sad for a successful mother and father to have worked hard to provide a solid start for their children, to have one of their children feel "poor" given the wealth they have married into. How sad to have a son or daughter, successful in their own profession or business, be undervalued given the success of their father-in-law or mother-in-law. We need to find ways to ensure that our children do not measure their success by how much money they have in the bank, or what they are able to consume or earn. It is too easy to fall into the trap of measuring your success by the wrong things, and it is here that parents can do much to help their children avoid money being destructive of their lives and relationships.

From white to black, there are many shades of gray. And sons-in-law, and daughters-in-law, will fall on every point of this broad spectrum. But it is safest to take the view that they are all gold-diggers, and none are to be trusted... not because they are or will be gold-diggers, or are not trustworthy, but given that without the right protections in place, wealth and relationships will be at risk. The right planning means hoping for the best, and planning for the worst. Checks and balances, and ensuring that wealth goes to who you really want it to go to, is key.

I have seen many situations of families where sons-in-law and daughters-in-law have played a critical role in not only protecting family wealth, but also hugely growing family wealth. I have also seen families where, for cultural and other reasons, hugely talented in-laws (and their children) have been excluded from family businesses.

I was approached by a Chinese family divided between Hong Kong and Singapore not too long ago, and was asked whether I could contribute to the family's thinking on the next steps of their estate plan. A well-known family, the plan, at its early stage, was to document the historical ways of the family: only sons bearing the family name could enter the family business – daughters would be given some liquidity, a small fraction of what would have been an equal share of the family business, and their children, not bearing the family name in most cases, would be permanently excluded from the possibility of entering the family business. Does this make sense? I indicated that I would certainly not be the one to decide for the family, but given my involvement I would at least want to put on the table the possibility of the family moving to a more "modern" approach to succession, allowing for the possibility of talented daughters, sons-in-law, and the children of daughters, whether bearing the family name in whole or in part, being able to participate in the family business. I was not invited back for a second meeting.

I have also seen situations where family wealth, due to the premature death of an only child, fell into the hands of a son-in-law who then used his in-laws' assets to establish himself in his second marriage and family, favoring his new family over the grandchildren of the wealth creators. The wealth-owning parents had left their assets to their daughter, leaving it to her to decide how to plan for the future. The daughter, sadly, died young, without any planning, resulting in most of the wealth passing to the control of her young husband. Perhaps safer would have been for the older generation to have made clearer provision for their grandchildren, protecting against what ended up happening.

Checks and balances; trusting no one; assuming the worst. In-laws step up to the plate more often when things are kept in check, as with anyone else. Making things clear and fair, and, most importantly, understanding the succession plan and the "what-ifs," is key to protecting wealth and relationships.

The Grandchildren

Should we just leave our wealth to our children, and leave it to them to work out what is best for their own children? It is compelling to do this, and there is sense in accepting that only your children will be in a position to monitor how your grandchildren develop and what their real needs are. But the tax laws and other challenges that can threaten wealth dictate that one should plan for not only grandchildren, but also further generations.

Inheritance taxes apply in many countries, and with the focus on wealth and income inequality, their application may increase rather than decrease in the future. In many cases, skipping a generation in the estate plan allows for inheritance taxes to also skip a generation, resulting in enormous wealth preservation. If I leave $1 million to my son, and he does not spend the capital during his lifetime, he will leave the $1 million to my grandchildren. If there is a 40% inheritance tax that my son is subject to, the grandchildren get $600,000. If I had left the capital to my grandchildren directly, and perhaps only the income to my son, my grandchildren would get the full $1 million. Different countries treat these things in different ways, but the principle of considering longer-term transfers to younger generations can be important.

From the perspective of asset protection, including protection against divorce and other claims, skipping a generation may also be valuable. For example, in the case of divorce, courts increasingly look to the assets and income available to a spouse – regardless of whether these are in a trust or other structure. If I leave my assets to my son in a trust, but my son benefits from that trust while married, it may well be that what is in the trust can be considered to be subject to division in a divorce. This could mean that an important family business falls at least in part unfairly into the hands of an undeserving spouse. Could more protection be achieved by leaving the business to future generations, with only income interests, or other assets, being available to those marrying and potentially divorcing?

It is often also a good idea to consider reserving a portion of wealth for grandchildren and further generations, as a way of ensuring that at least some portion of family wealth is protected against many risks, including bad investment decisions by our children, legal claims, and more. But should a grandparent determine the age at which a grandchild comes into significant wealth? There may be circumstances where this is appropriate, but to me, it is better to carve out wealth for future generations, but leave decisions on when grandchildren should receive this wealth (other than money for their education and healthcare) to their parents, who may want to ensure that their own children do not get too much too soon. Is it right for a grandparent to generously provide for grandchildren, but for this money to then go to the grandchild when he is 22, perhaps at a time when his parents believe he would benefit from focusing on completing his education and building a career? Could coming into money too soon compromise the parenting that is ongoing? Grandparents can be generous – but to me it is often a better bet to leave most of the decisions on when grandchildren should best benefit to their parents.

The Siblings

Not easy, but worthwhile to try for, is having a set of siblings who together support the succession process and encourage dialogue with their parents on the subject. In a world where it is difficult to trust, a set of siblings who can really rely on each other is a tremendous gift.

Sadly, it is often the case that siblings do not get along, and that they have their own psychological issues associated with the wealth that may eventually come to them. When siblings marry, their spouses come into the mix, and almost inevitably change the balance among siblings. One in-law may be a success on their own; another may be dependent on the wealth of the family they have married into. One in-law may contribute to the family business; another may be taking advantage of the good nature of his mother-in-law and father-in-law. And are the in-laws involved in encouraging their spouses to "grab" assets from their parents, fueling bad feeling among siblings?

There is work that families can do early on to help encourage siblings to communicate better and openly discuss issues that, when covered up, can simmer into disputes. But it is also critical to realize that trying to keep the children "together" is not always the best way to go. Using the tools of wealth planning, planning for the worst, and hoping for the best, is often the best way to go. This means thinking carefully about whether trusts, companies, or other structures require the younger generation to stay together, and if they do, whether there are solid approaches on means to resolve the disputes that are pretty inevitable to arise. How can a disgruntled sibling be bought out, and their children, wanting again to be part of the family business, buy in? How can assets be protected from those in and out of the family who may be destructive of not only family wealth but also family relationships?

The Friends

Having wealth affects not only relationships within families, but also friendships, business relationships, and otherwise. Here too, the amount of wealth doesn't matter – having more than others (or being perceived to have more than others) affects all relationships, and care and preparation is often needed.

In the work I do with families, I try to emphasize to the younger generation the need to keep a low profile, and the advantages of being discreet about wealth. How to deal with friends and business contacts seeking financial help, whether through loans or investments, is also a topic worth spending time on when families meet to discuss their wealth and to consider what they can do to preserve both relationships and money. With friends, it is sometimes best to simply have the philosophy of never lending them money – if they really need help, just make a gift, as getting paid back is so often a rarity. Lending money is a good way to lose friends. And in business and business ventures, everyone needs to be vigilant – scams abound, and the best way to deal with friends and contacts promoting investment and business ventures is with a high degree of professionalism. All members of wealth-owning families can learn from the need to ensure that any investment is well considered, well documented, and based on the reality that it is very easy to invest, but not always easy to get your money back.

Even the wealthiest and canniest of families get dragged into scams, some of remarkable complexity and which in hindsight carried all the warning signals that should have been heeded. An investment approach promoted by someone with little understanding themselves of the investment involved; hoped for returns that simply do not reflect the realities of the investment world; complexities that even professional advisors do not understand. I have seen so many scams over the years that I believe every wealth-owning family needs to discuss with all generations how these work, and the reality that many are implemented through the unwitting involvement of friends and business contacts of wealth owners who themselves may not realize that a scam is underway.

So, as is the case with everyone else, when it comes to friends and business contacts, trust no one. Not because your friends and colleagues cannot be trusted, but because with the right skepticism, wealth, friendships, and relationships can be preserved.

CHAPTER

3

The Move to Transparency

The tax landscape for wealth-owning families has been fast changing. Transparency and tax compliance are becoming the norm. This is a positive development given the financial challenges faced by governments seeking to address the needs of their populations and the growing inequality of wealth. But the road to transparency is not a smooth one.

Wealth-owning families need to understand how the world is moving to transparency and the critical importance of tax compliance, but also how tax laws work and develop, and how wealth owners can legally and properly take advantage of approaches that will help protect wealth and avoid unnecessary tax exposures. But there is one bottom line: a wealth owner only has two choices. Play by the rules of your country, or get out of your country. There is no choice, despite the ways of the past, that allows for sitting in your country and hoping no one will find out about hidden assets and income. And the ability of tax authorities to find out about hidden assets and income is getting better and better.

For many years, the wealth-management industry directly or indirectly supported the misuse of bank secrecy to the detriment of both interested governments and wealth-owning families. Today, families are increasingly realizing that apart from being the right thing, tax compliance can be far cheaper and safer than tax evasion. There have, of course, been a number of voices pushing for transparency and compliance over the years, but the approach of too many in the industry had been to resist change and to perpetuate the ways of the past – which are inappropriate in today's world. Transparency in relation to taxation is now fast developing, and families and their advisors have much to do to be prepared for the changes that have and will be taking place.

There are Only Two Choices: Play by the Rules, or Get Out

Wealth-owning families need to hear the truth, and to be guided by their advisors on how best to navigate a fast-changing and increasingly transparent landscape. And for the wealth owner, it is critical to understand how tax systems work and change, and how to be in a position to understand the advice they receive and make their own decisions on the right approaches to take. For wealth owners still following the advice of those encouraging them to hide, it is urgent to become very skeptical, and to seek better guidance.

In the case of the private banking and trust world, secrecy was all too often the historical basis for planning, with aggressive or outright evasive approaches being adopted on the logic that "no one would ever find out." Indeed, private banks and trust companies in a number of jurisdictions marketed bank secrecy and, in effect, tax evasion, as a luxury product, available to those with the wealth and contacts needed to attract them offshore. In this regard, it is easy to think of Switzerland as the dominant player, but it would be incorrect to fail to recognize that the issues of abuse of bank secrecy and tax evasion are not Swiss issues – they are and will continue to be global issues.

Switzerland and bank secrecy provided important protection to many families in and around the turmoil of wars, expropriations, corruption, and more. But bank secrecy has been abused – and not only in Switzerland. Data leaks in Panama and elsewhere make it easy for the press and others to bash offshore "tax havens" and those involved in promoting the use of opaque structures designed to hide assets. Not enough is being done, however, to have an open dialogue about the reality that the USA is one of the best places for money to be hidden, given its lack of regard for the needs of countries other than the USA to get information on companies, trusts, and assets connected to the USA.

There is also not enough dialogue about the reality that not all countries are ready for transparency. Countries with tax systems that cannot be trusted, in a world of transparency, will face a reality that the wealth-owning entrepreneurs they need for their economies to survive will be forced to relocate, creating a tax refugee crisis that negatively impacts those countries most in need – countries that are still developing and where tax revenues are critical to address poverty and starvation.

With the tax landscape changing quickly, many banks and trust companies are looking to protect themselves ahead of looking to address the needs of their clients – wealth owners need to be aware of this. For advisors to families, understanding that compliance is a client need, and that there is huge value in helping families navigate a changing world, may help to provide an edge to not only retaining clients but also building new relationships as clients realize that they need something different from what they received in the way of help and advice in the past.

The wealth-management industry has not done a good job of proactively leading on issues in and around growing transparency. To a large extent, the industry has been reactive, defending the past rather than working out how best to cooperatively address the needs of all stakeholders. This lack of strategy has resulted in the future of the wealth-management industry being dictated not by the industry itself, but by others, including onshore governments, which themselves are not necessarily achieving what it is they set out to achieve. The leaders of private banks have been among the worst offenders, looking more to short-term profits than to the long-term best interests of their clients and society. Governments interested in perpetuating the ways of the past, such as Switzerland and other successful wealth-management centers, have done far too little to show the way forward.

Forced to change, financial centers are adapting to new rules on exchange of information and otherwise. But they have failed, for the most part, to play a role in helping to address the real needs of all stakeholders, to the detriment of all involved, including their own economies.

Similarly, the wealth-owning community has not taken leadership in showing responsibility and being proactive in shaping how tax laws should work to fairly address the needs of governments for revenue and the need to address poverty and inequality. But are governments to be trusted when led by populists thinking of their own short-term interests? Are wealth owners safe in a world where corruption, political misuse of tax systems, and unfairness in tax systems abound? How much tax is a fair amount of tax, and at what stage does a tax actually become confiscation of assets?

For many years, arguments on behalf of offshore centers seeking to preserve the past have focused on the notion of a "level playing field," pointing to bank secrecy and the use of opaque structures in countries such as the USA as a rationale for continuing past practices. It is true that the USA is probably the best place in the world to hide money given its own bank-secrecy rules and limited ability to exchange information with other countries. The reality, however, is that onshore countries have every right to tax their residents (and sometimes citizens) as well as those who invest in their countries. The industry failing to recognize this reality and its clear abuse of bank secrecy has led to a *tsunami* of overreaction, to the detriment of the wealth-management industry and the families it serves.

Over-reaction by governments has ranged from punitive and intrusive reporting and taxpaying requirements associated with the use of trusts to aggressive attacks on private banks and others for past practices. Compliance requirements are out of control, and getting more and more complex, dangerous, and difficult to deal with. Wealth-owning families are increasingly destroyed as the practices of the past are coming under attack, with significant penalties, jail sentences, and sometimes worse being the consequences of the sudden move from hidden money to transparency.

There is a need for wealth owners to understand the impact of global change in relation to tax enforcement and transparency, and also to participate with the wealth-management industry in helping to educate onshore and offshore governments and helping to smooth out the rough road to transparency ahead. To date, not enough has been done.

It is time to be far more proactive, to the benefit of all stakeholders. It is also critical for wealth-owning families and their advisors to understand what is really going on.

Tax Evasion and the Misuse of Bank Secrecy is a Global Problem

Many things have been happening to help move the world into transparency, and the secrecy landscape has been changing fast and in a very public way. These changes are happening on a global basis, but with somewhat less effect in some places than others. The reality, however, is that the issue of misuse of bank secrecy and tax evasion is a global one.

Interestingly, but not surprisingly, respect for tax laws seems to have carried greater sway when the laws involved were those of the jurisdiction or advisor involved rather than those of another country. For example, it is not unusual to see American private banks having evidenced a history of being far more careful about US tax evasion than the evasion of other countries' taxes by their clients. Similarly, UK, Dutch, French, and other banks seem to have evidenced greater sensitivity to what they do with clients from their own countries as opposed to others. This said, recent data leaks show that the Swiss private banking industry has paid particularly little regard to global tax laws in their short-term focus on easy profits, something that has led to many wealth-owning families having too late realized that they were misled and mis-sold advice in relation to their tax positions.

What is particularly worrying is that the over-reaction of onshore governments is quite likely to lead to a very problematic picture for wealth owners, and will force many out of their countries, to the long-term detriment of the economies properly seeking to increase their revenues.

The adoption of varying standards of ethics on the issue of tax compliance has also extended to the community of advisors and others involved in the industry. In my experience, even top tax lawyers in Miami and New York tend to pay far more attention to the question of US tax compliance than the tax compliance of global families in their home countries. Today's advisor (and, frankly, yesterday's) must look at tax compliance as a *global* issue, meaning that when a Chinese, Venezuelan, or Mexican invests in the USA and is guided by a US tax lawyer, that lawyer should properly liaise with Chinese, Venezuelan, or Mexican advisors to ensure that the overall approach adopted is tax compliant – not only in the USA but also in all relevant jurisdictions of residence and investment. The foreign investor has often been misled by advisors who fail to take the global picture into account, and in today's world, anyone failing to anticipate the fast pace of change relating to transparency is making a big, big mistake.

Undeclared funds are a global problem, and measurement of the amounts involved is very difficult. The Tax Justice Network has reported the figures involved to be as high as over US$30 trillion. Oxfam has estimated that if taxes were properly paid by those earning the income involved, global poverty would be eliminated twice over.

These issues affect wealth owners, advisors to wealth owners, and interested governments, both onshore and offshore. For the wealth-owning family, the explosion of transparency underway as a reaction to historical tax evasion on an industrial scale is going to have more than just tax consequences in the future.

How Do Tax Authorities Find Out About Undeclared Money?

There are many ways that tax authorities get the information they need to enforce their tax laws, and this ability is fast increasing. Automatic exchange of information is changing the global landscape, and will bring an unprecedented level of transparency, for both better and, sadly, for worse. Wealth owners need to be ready.

Information has traditionally come to tax authorities through many means, including the old-fashioned tip from jealous neighbors, friends, disgruntled employees, and spurned spouses. Sometimes blackmail is involved, a trusted secretary or other employee is fired, and then threatens to report the tax evasion they were aware of to the authorities if not paid off. In divorces, the threat of being turned in has too often led to settlements beyond those that would otherwise have occurred.

In some countries, such as the USA, the tax authorities actually reward those who turn others in to the authorities. Bradley Birkenfeld, an American private banker working for UBS in Switzerland, received a reward of US$104 million – an astounding amount, but actually lower than he might have been eligible for given the US$780 million fine paid by UBS for its activities in and around US tax evasion by a number of its American clients and the many, many millions of dollars recovered by the American tax authorities from wealth owners whose information came to light in the process.

Tips to the authorities can be about individual taxpayers on a one-on-one basis, but increasingly have come through stolen bank information, something that has affected banks ranging from Julius Baer, to LGT, HSBC, and others. In some cases governments actually buy the stolen information – in others it is just given to them, sometimes by other governments who have received the information. Recent data leaks in Panama show only a small part of the extent of assets that have been hidden.

What of credit cards, and the role of technology in helping tax authorities to find things out? Many countries now get and use credit-card information to check on the expenditures of their taxpayers, reviewing whether reported income is sufficient to substantiate what people are spending. And information from credit-card companies that a government gets may be shared with other countries through, among other methods, "spontaneous information exchange" under tax treaties, meaning that a taxpayer in, say, Indonesia using a credit card on an undeclared account while traveling in the USA may well find that information on their spending activities and account relationship finds its way back to their home country. The lesson is not to avoid using credit cards and online payment services but, in a world of technology, that it is very hard to think what one spends or has cannot be discovered.

Many banks have come under attack by tax authorities for their role in the tax evasion of their clients, and to a great extent the "business" of extracting money from banks by governments has only just begun. UBS, in addition to its US$780 million fine recently found itself again under investigation by the USA for other possible misdeeds, and faces potential fines to France of over US$6 billion. Credit Suisse settled with the USA by paying a fine of US$2.6 billion. Almost the entire Swiss banking community is still in the process of working out their obligations to the USA, and governments worldwide are only beginning to make moves to collect their fair share. But what does all this mean for the wealth owner?

First, it is important to understand that not every bank can afford the fines that are being doled out, meaning that some will close their doors. This has already begun, and is likely to continue, particularly for banks whose economics were based on the low-cost business of misusing bank secrecy and just hiding the money. In the mainstream banking world, more and more banks will be pulling out of private banking services, and where they are in the business, they will focus even more on what too many have always focused on: their own interests well before those of their clients. Institutional risk associated with working with wealth owners holding undeclared assets and income means that banks will increasingly refuse to be involved, and in a number of cases will be the source of information provided to governments.

For those who advise wealth owners, whether from within the financial services industry or outside of it, understanding the real needs of families is what it is about. A time of change is also a time of great opportunity, as wealth owners are more clearly able to articulate what they are looking to their asset managers and advisors to help them with.

For those who spend time in countries but pretend they don't, it is important to understand that governments are improving their ability to track the time people spend in a country, through both technology and greater alignment between border entry controls and the tax authorities. Most are not there yet, but it is only a question of time – and not too much time – before it will become totally clear that there really are only two choices: play by the rules, or get out.

Automatic Exchange of Information Backed Up by Anti-Money-Laundering Rules – But Will it Always Work?

There is now rapid progress toward the adoption of global approaches to automatic information exchange, a dramatic departure from the methods of information exchange of the past, such as information exchange upon request. What does "automatic" exchange of information actually mean?

The global community is moving toward a system that has financial intermediaries, such as banks, obtain information on the residence (and sometimes citizenship) of their clients, which information then results in details on earnings and assets being reported directly to the client's country of residence – automatically, and without any request for such information having been made. The rules and procedures are well developed, and implementation is in progress, with a large number of countries having already committed to adopting the approach. Under rules that are already agreed, it is not information about the companies or trusts that hold accounts that will be exchanged, but rather information about "beneficial owners" – the individuals behind structures that have, in the past, sometimes been misused to obfuscate ownership. The approach to reporting that is being developed involves the "common reporting standard" or CRS, which is part of the move to automatic exchange of information coordinated by the Organization of Economic Co-operation and Development, the OECD.

For a wealth-owning family, it is absolutely critical to understand who has what information on their family and wealth, and to whom that information will go. With banks and other financial intermediaries seeking to ensure that they do not expose themselves to fines and other sanctions, some have compliance approaches that may go beyond what they are actually required to do; some wealth owners may find that the information their financial intermediaries hold is inaccurate or out of date. Just leaving things to chance is a dangerous approach, given that information on income and assets may simply find its way into the wrong hands. Tax compliance is a given, but the road to transparency is a rough one.

The USA has made great progress in implementing the Foreign Account Tax Compliance Act (FATCA), legislation oriented to ensuring tax compliance by US citizens and residents maintaining financial arrangements outside of the USA. Participation by the global community in FATCA has made it easier for the OECD, with the support of the UK and others, to develop a global standard for automatic information exchange. The European Union (EU) has been successful in closing loopholes on exchange of information that had already been in place in Europe, and has now moved to fully automatic exchange of information in a very comprehensive way.

So, tax transparency and automatic information exchange is no longer just something affecting Americans – we are fast moving to global tax transparency, and to information exchange that takes place without the taxpayer necessarily being aware of it.

The ability of automatic information exchange to address the global issue of undeclared funds is substantial. An important, but sometimes overlooked, element of tax enforcement relates to the move to have anti-money-laundering rules include tax crimes as "predicate" offences, something that has already been introduced in many countries, including the UK, Singapore, and Hong Kong. Through initiatives of the Financial Action Task Force, among others, we are a short time away from comprehensive anti-money-laundering rules in key financial centers that include tax offences as anti-money-laundering offences.

What do anti-money-laundering rules that include tax offences as predicate offences do? If a wealth owner approaches an advisor, be it a real-estate broker, an accountant, or a banker, that advisor, on learning that monies being handled are tax undeclared, may have a legal obligation to turn the wealth owner in – filing a "suspicious activity report" to the authorities, and with an obligation to *not* tip off the wealth owner that the report is being made.

Combining the impact of anti-money-laundering rules that are effectively enforced (today, they are not) with automatic-information-exchange arrangements, undeclared money will clearly be significantly reduced. A bank, for example, in a traditional bank-secrecy country will, where the anti-money-laundering rules so provide, have to be comfortable that monies on deposit are tax declared in the home country, failing which anti-money-laundering reports will need to be made. Parallel to this will be automatic-information-exchange agreements, whether or not part of comprehensive tax treaties, requiring information to be automatically exchanged regarding the earnings and assets of taxpayers connected to countries that have entered into automatic-exchange agreements. It is important to note that anti-money-laundering rules will apply even where there is *no* automatic exchange of information yet agreed with the relevant home country.

Developments toward global transparency include initiatives to require the creation of public registers on beneficial ownership. While the debate continues, there are moves toward this for companies, trusts, and other investment and asset-holding vehicles. This links closely to automatic exchange of information, and data leaks in Panama, which led to massive global press coverage and new calls for transparency, are helping to ensure that transparency initiatives accelerate. New and sometimes duplicative approaches to information exchange and disclosure are being discussed, and some of the proposals are certainly over-reactions and may carry with them many problems over and above the challenge to the human right to privacy. But where things are going is clear, and wealth owners need to be ready for the substantial changes that are coming.

Something many are not aware of is that automatic exchange of information will include information that goes far beyond the information governments actually need to enforce their tax laws. For example, among the information that will be exchanged is information on the total value of assets held in a bank account – not only the income from investments, and this even where the country receiving the information does not need information on the assets involved or their value to enforce their tax laws. And countries whose tax laws do not include reference to overseas income, such as Hong Kong and Singapore, will be receiving information that they do not necessarily need. Are wealth owners aware and prepared for this? Are there wealth owners living in Hong Kong who may have had historical connections to mainland China and who may be concerned that information on their foreign holdings will be sent to the Hong Kong tax authorities? Are there possibilities that the information the Hong Kong tax authorities get may find its way to mainland China through spontaneous information exchange or otherwise?

Where countries have the economic and other power to be early on the list for automatic exchange of information, these countries will benefit their tax systems early on. This is already happening in relation to the USA, with its rollout of FATCA, and will be the case for many European financial centers, and others, as part of OECD and EU initiatives.

Two realities, however, among many.

First, countries will only have the capacity to negotiate and enter into a limited number of automatic-information-exchange agreements in the short and medium term, and the priority will clearly be to do so with countries, like the USA and certain western European countries, that are pushing this on their agenda, and who have the negotiating power to force counterparts into such arrangements, such as where a comprehensive tax treaty can be threatened if automatic exchange is not agreed to. While there are multilateral agreements relating to automatic information exchange, and a push by the OECD and others toward multilateral implementation, the reality for the moment is that much of automatic information exchange will be implemented on a bilateral basis. Singapore and Switzerland are good examples of countries that have made it clear that they *only* intend to exchange information with countries that will have the laws necessary to protect the information provided and under certain other conditions. However, the extent to which countries such as Singapore and Switzerland can, over even the short and medium term, avoid being forced into very wide automatic information exchange remains to be seen.

Second, a number of financial centers are adopting strategies designed to "go slow," in the sense of allowing loopholes in anti-money-laundering rules (this through the requirement of "double criminality," among others, which means that if something is not a tax offence in both countries involved, no reporting arises) and through a selective approach to entering into bilateral exchange-of-information agreements. For example, if a taxpayer from one country is subject to a tax on their wealth, and has assets in a second country that only taxes income, if the wealth tax in the home country has not been paid, will an anti-money-laundering suspicious activity report be filed in the second country? If a requirement of double criminality applies, the answer would be no, as while evading the wealth tax is illegal in the home country, there is no wealth tax in the second country, and hence no crime there. For wealth owners, this is of very short-term protection, as pressure from the international community and otherwise is pushing all countries to not require dual criminality for anti-money-laundering rules to apply.

Broadly, the financial services industry and financial centers are focusing on the USA and certain western European countries as the first countries in respect of which tax evasion is being targeted... low on the priority scale are countries most in need of tax revenues, those that are developing and which may have other problems with their tax systems. These countries, which are most in need, may be the least likely to gain in the short or medium term.

Are All Countries Ready for Automatic Exchange of Information?

While, for the moment, anti-money-laundering rules are generally not being overly enforced when it comes to taxpayers from many developing countries, as such rules become better known and focused on, the risks to wealth owners from fragile countries will increase. Automatic information exchange is in the process of being implemented on virtually a global scale. However, the reality is that not all countries are actually ready for the full tax transparency that the world is working toward.

What happens where a taxpayer is a resident of a developing country, the tax system of which does not respect privacy, meaning that information the tax authorities have is improperly made available to journalists and others, perhaps including kidnappers interested in knowing who has what? What if there is corruption in the tax system, and tax proceeds are, maybe in part, diverted improperly? What if information on an individual's assets and income lead to a corrupt approach to a bribe to avoid a full tax audit? And what of countries that use tax information to attack the political enemies of those in power?

Taxpayers connected to countries whose tax systems are not ready for full transparency will be forced into finding ways to avoid new reporting and compliance systems, in part relying on the insufficiency of the home country tax system to fairly tax income. In some cases, taxpayers will be encouraged to abandon their residence to avoid being taxpayers, something that contributes little to the local economy. In other cases, untaxed assets might well be converted into investments that do not yet attract the tax compliance that passive investment portfolios with banks now attract.

For example, instead of holding a bank account that earns interest and which holds equities producing capital gains and dividends, the wealth owner might be tempted to hold a safe deposit box with diamonds and gold. Unlike the bank account, the safe deposit box, at least under present rules, does not attract automatic information exchange.

Again, not something that encourages investment into the home country which needs it most. It is the entrepreneurs, who can hugely benefit a home economy with their knowledge and experience of the country, who are encouraged to invest abroad and find ways to distance themselves economically and otherwise from the place they know best. Meeting the tax laws of many developing countries is simply not an option given the practicalities of how the tax system operates.

Wealth owners and the wealth-management industry have a key role to play in helping the world address the issue of undeclared money. A continuation of a reactive approach to change badly serves both the industry and wealth-owning families. There is a need for leadership and dialogue, with a focus on outcomes that can benefit all stakeholders.

Most important, though, is for the wealth-owning family to understand enough about the changing tax world and how tax laws work if they are to avoid the many challenges to preserving and enhancing wealth, and most importantly, the financial and non-financial best interests of their families.

For Countries That are Not Ready for Transparency, What Kind of Alternative Tax System Could Work?

The simple reality is that wealth owners need to be ready for transparency. For many, the risks are enormous, particularly where they are connected, by residence, investment, or otherwise, to countries that are not ready for transparency given the political and legal framework of the country involved.

I believe that there are approaches that the global community could take to improve the situation, but am not overly optimistic that much will actually be done. Like with so much else associated with asset protection and succession planning, the best approach for a wealth owner is to hope for positive change, but to plan for the more likely reality that good sense will *not* prevail.

I advocate more openness and discussion on the reality that not every country is ready for full transparency. I also believe that one approach that could address the needs of both the home country and the individual taxpayer would involve having a suitable non-governmental organization, perhaps Transparency International, evaluate the tax and legal systems of countries, measuring levels of corruption, misuse of taxpayer information, and other characteristics relevant to the determination of which countries are actually ready for full tax transparency.

Where countries are not ready for full transparency, financial centers and their banks and trust companies could agree to ensure tax compliance by identifying the relevant owners of assets and income, and agreeing to withhold tax on initial capital and annual income, say, at a figure of 10%. The proceeds of the withholding tax would be maintained in a fund that would be made available to the home country involved under certain conditions. Because the taxpayer would be considered tax compliant in the financial center involved, no anti-money-laundering or other reports would need to be filed. This would be very different from Switzerland's failed "Rubik" strategy – a weirdly complex system of withholding requiring the input of mathematicians, and oriented to precisely the wrong countries – the UK, Germany, and others clearly *ready* for automatic exchange of information. You may or may not like the UK or German tax systems, but the reality is that both countries have tax and legal systems that protect taxpayer rights and are generally free from corruption and political misuse.

The approach I advocate would involve a simple and transparent approach to anonymous withholding that is attractive to taxpayers and reflects the reality of tax collections rather than "headline" tax rates. Should there be withholding at 40% if the effective tax collections in the relevant country are at 10%? Most importantly, unlike Switzerland, which focused its now abandoned withholding thinking on the UK and Germany, two examples of First-World tax systems fully ready for automatic exchange of information, the withholding approach would be used for countries that are *not ready* for automatic exchange of information – countries that do not properly protect taxpayer information, countries where tax proceeds are corruptly converted to incorrect use and where information on financial affairs is used for political or other wrongful purposes.

On agreeing to accept the funds held for it as settlement of tax due in relation to assets subject to withholding, the withheld amounts would be paid over to the home country. It would also be possible to have withheld amounts be the subject of disbursement with international oversight, something that may be particularly appropriate for countries where tax revenues are improperly applied. In some cases, the tax withholdings might have a role in repayments of outstanding international loans or otherwise.

The idea here would be to allow a wealth owner resident in a country not ready for transparency to be tax compliant without putting their assets and families at risk. If I live in a country that uses tax information to achieve political objectives, or where such information leaks out to kidnappers, I will not remain a resident given the risks this will give rise to. If there is corruption in my tax system, information my government gets may simply result in my being subject to additional blackmail by low-level or other tax officials. Rather than being forced to leave my country, what if there were an alternative system, designed to operate until such time as my country cleans up its act? The alternative system might actually accelerate the ability of countries to root out corruption and put in place proper legal and practical approaches to protecting taxpayer information and rights.

Short term – immediate revenues that can be applied as they need to be given the circumstances of the country involved. Medium and long term – an influence on what the country needs to do to establish an effective and fair tax system that can operate in the interests of the country and its taxpayers.

But will issues relevant to countries not ready for automatic information exchange be smoothly addressed in the years to come? Or will the industry and relevant financial centers again fail to take leadership? Are international organizations like the International Monetary Fund (IMF), the OECD, and others more focused on the longer-term need to establish effective tax-administration systems in developing countries rather than on the shorter-term need to ensure that there are tax revenues which are applied appropriately to those in need? I have met with the authorities of several financial centers to discuss my ideas, and am not optimistic that any are ready to proactively address the real need of wealth owners connected to countries that have corrupt tax systems.

So for the wealth owner, there is no choice but to be ready for the chaos to come.

Tax Competition, Mobility, and Countries Not Ready for Full Information Exchange

Like all competition, tax competition is healthy and necessary to ensure that countries are imposing tax fairly and efficiently. If something is not done to address the reality that not all countries are ready for full information exchange, however, wealth owners faced with a corrupt or otherwise defective home country tax system will be encouraged to relocate, taking advantage of the tax savings and privacy protection afforded by this. One element of the reality of tax competition is that countries with attractive and reliable tax systems will be safer for wealth owners to be connected to than countries lacking the basic legal and political protections a proper tax system should provide.

For example, a wealth owner who has international business activities, and who is based in a country that is unstable and developing, may fear having the local authorities be aware of global wealth. With growing transparency, and anti-money-laundering rules that include tax as a predicate offence, a wealth owner may be forced to relocate to avoid putting their family at risk by complying with home country disclosure requirements. Relocation may be to a country that "competes" with its tax system – for example, the UK, at least for a set period of time, does not generally tax the unremitted foreign earnings of those who are "resident" but not "domiciled" in the UK. Similar benefits can be achieved by relocating to a number of other places, including Hong Kong and Singapore, given their territorial tax systems.

This competition is healthy as it encourages home countries to review their tax systems and to ensure that they are fair... but this process can be a long one, particularly in the case of fragile, developing economies – another attraction of an interim withholding-based taxation regime or other approach designed to retain wealth owners in the countries that need them.

Should Tax be the Driver in Asset Protection and Estate Planning?

Historically, there has been an over-emphasis on taxation in asset and succession planning, something fueled by advisors focused more on bank secrecy than understanding the real needs of their clients. These real needs are varied, and include needs that are particular to the family involved, such as where there is a child needing special protection. Other needs of wealth owners are driven by the laws and structure of the home country and the countries of investment. For the latter, issues such as forced heirship, political risk, and many others come into the mix. Yet other needs apply to all families, such as how best to deal with the succession of assets and the many other issues all wealth owners face.

The over-emphasis on taxation notwithstanding, it is critical that wealth owners and their families understand their tax position, learning from advisors and being guided by them, but not allowing them to "kidnap" the family's wealth, keeping the family in the dark about how their own structures really work. If the wealth owner understands the tax systems of his countries of residence, citizenship, and investment, he is in a better position to guide his advisors and make the right decisions in the succession process.

For advisors to wealth-owning families, it is important to understand that it is of huge assistance to your clients to just be able to help raise the right questions, and to help wealth owners identify the right advisors to address their concerns. In an increasingly complex world, no one has all the answers. Being able to ask the right questions is the first step to really being of help and value. Even a top tax specialist will be unable to address all the tax issues typical wealth owners face given the international nature of families, the structures they use, and where they invest.

An important overlay to how tax systems and planning work is to also understand the changing world of tax enforcement, and the reality that the luxury product offered by the private banking industry in the past – secrecy without much more – is fast falling away. This has real importance not only for families connected to countries at the forefront of tax enforcement, such as the USA. In some ways the issue is of even greater importance for families connected to countries whose tax systems are just developing, and where corruption and misuse of tax information is rife. The combination of anti-money-laundering rules and heightened institutional risk is driving advisors and intermediaries, such as banks, insurance companies, accountants, and others, to turn their clients in to the authorities. A wealth owner needs to understand these developing risks. And in a world where disparities of wealth are increasingly at the forefront of the political and social agenda, is "hiding the money" either an option or the right thing to do?

I have worked with many wealth owners who are in the younger generation, and who on inheriting assets from their parents have negotiated "voluntary disclosure" arrangements with tax authorities, essentially coming clean on the past tax evasion undertaken by earlier generations. The costs for this are often higher than the costs would have been to the older generation had they paid their taxes, and undertaken legitimate and legal ways to reduce exposures. Was the older generation right in believing that they were doing the younger generation a favor by salting the money away in secret accounts and opaque structures?

And for those who do not take advantage of tax amnesties or voluntary disclosure, what is the consequence of getting caught? In many cases, tax authorities and those involved in prosecuting tax cases are looking to make examples through severe penalties and jail sentences. It is not always only about punishing tax evasion, but also about making an example to scare others into compliance. Is it worth the risk for a wealth owner who has spent their life building their business and their wealth? Is this the legacy to be left to the younger generation?

The move to tax transparency also brings with it the question of privacy, and whether privacy of one's financial affairs can be legally achieved. I am a believer that privacy is a human right, and that privacy and tax compliance can go hand-in-hand. But it is not always straightforward, and the approaches open to wealth owners very much depend on their countries of citizenship, domicile, and residence. We are in times of enormous change, and in times where headline tax rates are probably much higher than they should or need to be – in a world of full tax compliance, governments would be collecting enough revenue to permit tax rates to decline substantially, but we are likely several decades away from this being able to happen.

Many countries have misleadingly high "headline" tax rates, allowing politicians to claim that they are adequately taxing the wealthy. But actual tax rates reflect deductions and other tax reliefs, and faulty collection systems further influence the huge gap between the headline or published top tax rate and what countries actually collect.

We are also decades away from all governments having tax systems that can be trusted; tax systems free of corruption and political misuse of tax information; tax systems where information the tax authorities hold is truly kept confidential. We are also, fortunately, nowhere near a global tax system – despite the efforts of some countries – meaning that tax competition is, for the most part, alive and well.

Countries compete for investment and business on the basis of their tax systems, and as the world moves to greater tax transparency, the role of mobility in tax and privacy planning becomes increasingly important. Interestingly, the world is also getting smaller, with wealth-owning families becoming more and more international. Mobility therefore becomes an important element of planning – carefully choosing where to be resident and how to manage the time spent between different countries. Citizenship can also be an issue here, and one that in the years to come may be more and more important.

While tax is important, and in succession and asset-protection planning is a key issue to be managed and minimized, it is critical to keep tax in its place – and to *not* allow tax planning to drive the succession plan and to distract the family into allowing tax advisors and tax objectives to kidnap the family's asset-holding and succession structures, something that in my experience is too often the case. I have come across a remarkable number of situations where the older generation has worked hard to achieve secrecy, managing to leave their assets in a messy labyrinth of secret structures, facilitating theft and abuse and leaving a legacy of mistrust and unresolved tax liabilities to their family to sort out.

Tax laws are difficult for anyone to understand. Even the most sophisticated tax advisor will not have all the answers. Today's wealth-owning families are international families. Family members may live in different countries, the family is likely to invest in a number of places, and citizenship can sometimes play a critical role in the tax picture. Where grandchildren are born, and the citizenships of sons and daughters-in-law can all have an impact. And the only certainty in the tax world is one: the laws will change, and constantly do.

The wealth-owning family does not need to become expert in the tax laws of every country that affects them and their investments. Rather, the wealth-owning family needs to be able to understand the advice they receive from experts, and needs to be able to challenge that advice, and ask the right questions. Being aware of how tax systems work can help families stay in control of the succession and asset-protection planning put in place for their families.

There also remains much that wealth owners, the wealth-management industry, and the financial centers involved can and need to do to address the sometimes conflicting needs of wealth owners with the needs of governments to enforce tax and other laws.

More on this is contained in the Addendum.

Understanding the World of Taxation

Wealth owners have plenty to worry about in dealing with their businesses and investments, and the many issues that affect the question of whether wealth will be destructive of their family. It is, however, the case that a wealth owner, and every member of their family, needs to have some understanding of the tax world to properly understand and guide the advisors they may be using to ensure that they are being tax efficient while being fully compliant with the tax laws relevant to them.

Why are taxes important? Depending on the countries involved, taxes may eliminate a high percentage of income and assets. With all the work put into building and maintaining wealth, navigating the tax world is critical. And with the notion of hiding money being a thing of the past, understanding how tax systems work, and the legitimate planning approaches that families can adopt, is increasing in importance.

Tax is also a form of political risk. As the world moves toward tax transparency, governments will be getting hold of much more information than they actually need to enforce their existing tax systems. What will they do with this information? Will populist governments impose new "taxes" as a means of expropriating the assets of wealth owners, as a way to address perceived inequality? Will corruption in tax systems be helped by the massive amount of information that will now be available to governments that are in many ways not ready for automatic information exchange?

Wealth owners need to understand these risks, and also the opportunities to legally address risks by choosing which countries to live and invest in. Sad to say, but transparency, in many cases, will not result in developing countries receiving more in the way of tax revenues. I fear that wealth owners who create jobs and economic activity will be forced to exit countries that others are not keen to invest in.

This chapter of the book is not designed to turn the wealth owner or their advisor into tax experts, but is meant to help them raise the right questions, and be in a better position to understand and evaluate the advice they receive.

Tax Evasion, Tax Avoidance, and Tax Planning – the Years to Come

Attitudes and approaches in relation to tax evasion and aggressive avoidance are fast changing.

Tax evasion, the illegal non-payment of taxes due, is something that is usually pretty clear. A rule applies, and one actively fails to comply with that rule, breaking the law and committing the offence of tax evasion. Bank secrecy, opaque ownership structures, and noncompliance with reporting made tax evasion a pretty easy thing for wealth owners to commit, sometimes with clear intent, but sometimes unwittingly, perhaps encouraged by those "selling" bank secrecy and opaque structures, and sometimes by accident or neglect.

Mobile wealth owners connected to multiple countries may wittingly or unwittingly become taxable residents of the countries they spend time in, but may not tell anyone, particularly the tax authorities of that country, that they have been present in the country for a sufficient number of days to be considered tax resident. This, one of many forms of tax evasion, is becoming increasingly dangerous as authorities are becoming much more able to track where people actually are. And tax authorities are always motivated to severely punish the tax evaders they catch as a means of scaring others into compliance.

Tax avoidance, once largely considered to be legal, is different from tax evasion. Avoiding tax by skirting a rule in place is increasingly under attack with a range of "anti-avoidance" rules that countries put in place to address arrangements that lack commercial substance and take advantage of unintended loopholes.

There are many gray areas in and around tax avoidance, and what works and does not, and what is right and what isn't. A wealth owner needs good advisors, and the ability to make their own judgement about what advice is safe to follow. Denis Healey, a former Chancellor of the Exchequer in the UK, was quoted as saying that the difference between tax avoidance and tax evasion is the *thickness of a prison wall.*

Today, perceptions of inequality and abuse of tax rules by corporations as well as individuals are leading to new tax rules, new transparency through reporting and other requirements, and an environment where wealth owners and businesses face negative perceptions and publicity when found to have taken aggressive advantage of (albeit legal) "loopholes" to reduce or otherwise avoid taxation. In other words, it is no longer enough to just ask whether a tax strategy is legal. One must also ask whether it would be considered acceptable in the current environment and what the consequences might be if the approach, as it is likely to, comes to light.

Tax planning, which refers to understanding the tax rules that have application and navigating them so as to legitimately pay the minimum of tax that is actually required, is perfectly legal, and what a well-informed wealth owner seeks to do. The tax laws of countries may be designed to encourage investment in certain areas, providing tax advantages as an incentive; wealth owners can choose where in the world to live and to invest; giving away an asset to children before it increases in value may result in lower tax on the gift of the asset than the inheritance tax that might arise if the asset is given away years later – these are all simple examples of legitimate tax planning. In a world of transparency, good tax planning is particularly important.

However, the tax world is fast changing, and in the next years, more and more difficulties will be faced by the world's wealth owners as the rough road to transparency leads governments to be better able to enforce their tax laws. I have a vision of a world in which tax laws can be simple and predictable, with modest tax rates, and where full compliance results in a significantly higher level of tax revenues for countries that can efficiently and transparently administer a tax system that addresses income and wealth inequality and the needs of a fair society.

But moving from a world where the wealthiest often pay much less in the way of tax than they should, to one where there is real fairness, will be a long and rocky road, and one where the human right to privacy is compromised, and where populist and sometimes corrupt governments will destroy wealth and lives. And complexity leads to the wrong people getting the revenue – accountants, lawyers, and other advisors rather than governments seeking to cover social and other costs.

A wealth owner needs to be well equipped with the knowledge necessary to know how best to proceed.

Different Kinds of Tax Systems

Different countries have different tax systems, and these vary significantly, both in terms of complexity and in terms of the tax rates that apply. Understanding how a tax system that one is subject to works is a first step to understanding the input tax advisors provide in relation to asset protection and succession planning. Also key is to understand which tax system actually applies – for many wealth owners, there is never only one tax system that is relevant. A wealth owner may live in one country and invest in another, and this in and of itself may attract the application of the tax laws of two countries. Usually, however, it is even more complex – a wealth owner may spend time in several countries, and the question may arise as to whether he is resident, for tax purposes, in more than one. And investments are increasingly global, and the structures used to hold assets may themselves be located in yet other countries, the tax laws of which come into play.

Will There be One Global Tax That Applies, or Will Tax Competition Survive?

I do not believe that we will see one global tax system for many, many decades and this despite the rush toward increased tax information and enforcement cooperation between countries. Like all competition, tax competition is important and beneficial, keeping governments in check in relation to their policies, and allowing taxpayers to choose where to live and to invest, reflecting not only the services and protections different countries provide, but also the cost, benefit, and risk of living or investing there.

There are moves, however, to address what governments sometimes see as unfair tax competition, and this can be seen in the EU in particular, as the practices of Luxembourg and other countries that have used their tax systems to attract business come to light. It will be interesting to see how the UK navigates its exit from the EU, and whether it will seek to increase its attractiveness as a location for business and residence by taking advantage of additional freedom in relation to its tax policies. Europe is certain to object, and the issue of tax competition is very likely to be a key element of Brexit negotiations.

But my belief that tax competition is a good thing does not necessarily mean that all governments agree. Evidence of the abuses of bank secrecy, tax havens, and opaque structures by companies and individuals is encouraging governments to do things that are not in the best interests of wealth owners, and often not in the best economic interests of the countries involved.

Short-term politics often wins out over long-term good planning, and this will increasingly have a negative effect on the tax laws wealth owners need to navigate.

Countries That Do Not Impose an Income Tax

The simplest tax system of all is where a country does not impose tax. Such jurisdictions do exist, and among these are Dubai, where there is no personal income tax. Other kinds of tax do apply, but for an individual who resides in Dubai, there is, simply, no income tax at all.

There are many other countries that also impose no tax, and these include a number of offshore Caribbean and other centers, such as the Bahamas.

Countries that impose no personal income tax often do have other taxes designed to raise revenues for the government. These can include taxes on particular industries (as is the case in Dubai), taxes designed to force pension savings for individuals, sales taxes, and others. Later on, some of the kinds of tax that can apply will be discussed, but where a country does not impose an income tax, it generally leaves a wealth owner free of the main taxes that affect wealth, including taxes on capital gains, salaries, dividends, and other revenues, as well as transfer taxes, such as gift or donation taxes and estate or inheritance taxes.

Living in a tax-free country sounds attractive, but this does not mean that the taxes of other countries do not apply. If a wealth owner invests in other countries, tax exposures may arise, and depending on residential and citizenship connections, other exposures to tax can arise, based on these connections.

Territorial Tax Systems

Next to countries with no tax on income at all, jurisdictions that impose tax on a territorial basis are the next simplest to understand. The definition of what constitutes a "territorial" tax system can vary dramatically, but for my use, I refer primarily to jurisdictions that tax only income that is locally sourced – meaning that income from outside the country involved is generally tax free. Good examples of territorial tax systems are Hong Kong and Singapore, though there are many others that also impose tax on this basis, in full or in part.

Where a jurisdiction imposes tax on a territorial basis, the focus is not on where the taxpayer lives, is domiciled, or has citizenship, but rather on the source of income. In the case of Hong Kong and Singapore, whether or not someone actually lives in Hong Kong or Singapore is not generally relevant to determining tax exposures – the tax question is simply whether the income involved is of a Hong Kong or Singapore "source." In the case of Singapore, residence can affect the tax rate, but the main issue remains the question of where the income is sourced.

Many rules and interpretations apply in relation to what constitutes Hong Kong or Singapore "source" income, but in simple terms, earning a salary from working in Hong Kong or Singapore would clearly produce locally sourced and taxable earnings. Similarly, if a business is conducted in either place, and the revenues are all earned from activities that take place only in the jurisdiction involved, tax will arise.

Most important in relation to territorial tax systems is that there is no tax on income that is foreign sourced, meaning that earnings properly earned through activities conducted outside of, for example, Hong Kong or Singapore are entirely free of taxation. In the case of Hong Kong and Singapore, tax rates on even locally sourced income are relatively low, generally around or under 20%. In Hong Kong, there is no relevance to whether tax-free foreign-sourced income is "remitted" or brought into Hong Kong. In the case of Singapore, this also has no relevance for individuals, but is an issue in the case of corporate taxation, where remitted income can become taxable – but keeping that income out of Singapore, even in the corporate context, can retain tax-free status in Singapore for foreign-sourced income.

As outlined below, there are varieties of tax that countries can impose... and in the case of Singapore and Hong Kong, many of these do not apply, even if the income involved is locally sourced. Hong Kong and Singapore do not impose tax on capital gains or dividends, and also do not impose tax in relation to gifts or transfers made on death.

Linked to the benefits of living in a jurisdiction with no taxes or with a territorial system of taxation is the privacy regarding foreign income that this gives rise to – privacy that is now compromised by the approach of automatic information exchange and how it will apply. Under domestic tax laws, the general principle is that where there is no tax on foreign earnings, there are also generally limited reporting requirements on foreign earnings. A resident of Hong Kong or Singapore who has a bank account in, say, Switzerland, has not had to report the capital in the account or the earnings from the account given that there is no tax on foreign-sourced income.

But what is the effect of automatic exchange of information on the privacy benefit of residing in a place that imposes tax on a territorial basis? Something that few are presently aware of is that automatic exchange of information will result in the sharing of information that goes well beyond what information a tax authority actually needs to enforce its tax laws. For example, when Hong Kong enters into automatic-information-exchange agreements with Switzerland or the UK, will this result in the Hong Kong government receiving information on the assets, income, and gains associated with a Swiss or UK bank account of a Hong Kong resident? Under Hong Kong tax law, this information is not strictly needed by the Hong Kong authorities to enforce the territorial tax system in place in Hong Kong, but may well be information that Hong Kong will get in future. And what of moves to ensure the disclosure of beneficial owners in high-value real estate in London, New York, and elsewhere and how this fits into the picture, along with new beneficial-ownership registers and other transparency initiatives? What if the taxpayer in issue has connections to mainland China and would prefer that information on their foreign assets did not find its way to China's tax authorities? Will there be an ability for this information to be shared by the Hong Kong government with the authorities in mainland China?

Worldwide Taxation on the Basis of Residence

The most common system of taxation is that based on residence, and where the tax that arises is then imposed on a worldwide basis. This means that if the wealth owner lives in a particular country, that country will tax all of the wealth owner's income, wherever in the world that income may arise.

This form of tax system applies in countries throughout the world. But there are significant differences in how these tax systems work.

A first question in relation to a tax system that imposes tax based on residence is whether or not the individual taxpayer is a resident for tax purposes. If I own a house in the USA, for example, but spend little time there, am I a resident of the USA? The USA has separate tax rules that apply to citizens and "green card" holders, discussed later; but if I am neither a citizen nor a green card holder, does having a house in the USA or just spending time there each year cause me to be a resident, subject to American tax on my worldwide income?

In the case of the USA, the question of whether an individual who is neither a citizen nor a green card holder is resident there for tax purposes is based on a purely objective test, meaning that tax residence has little to do with intention, and much to do with how much time one physically spends in the USA. Like many things to do with American tax laws, the rules are not simple, but the bottom line is that if an individual never spends more than four months a year physically in the USA, they will *not* be resident for tax purposes, meaning that exposure to tax on a worldwide basis will not arise.

More technically, the residence rules in the USA count days of presence on a rolling three-year basis. To know whether I am resident in, say, 2016, I count my days of presence in 2016, add to those my days of presence in 2015, divided by three, and my days of presence in 2014, divided by six. If I spent at least 31 days in the USA in 2016, I will be a resident for tax purposes if the total under this formula comes to 183 days or more. Many exceptions can also apply, including exceptions for qualifying students and others. It is also possible to overcome being considered a resident under what is known as the "substantial presence" test by showing closer connections to another country, and spending less than 183 days in the USA in any year. This requires, however, the filing of a tax form, among others.

It is not the detail of how the US residence rules work that a wealth owner needs to focus on. With the help of advisors, a wealth owner can be guided on the residence rules of any country. What is important to realize is that when one spends time in different countries, it is critical to understand how those countries' tax laws work in terms of determining whether taxable residence arises. While the American approach is objective in looking at the number of days of presence in the country, other countries include subjective elements in their residence tests, making it tricky to determine whether residence does or does not arise.

In Canada, for example, spending 183 days or more a year in the country gives rise to resident status, an objective test. But Canada also considers as resident those who "in the settled routine of their lives regularly, normally or customarily live in Canada." This rather subjective test makes it tricky to know for sure whether one is resident in Canada for tax purposes given that many factors come into the picture, including residential, personal, and other ties. And the question of residence is critical from a tax perspective – someone who is resident in Canada is taxable in that country on their worldwide income, and at tax rates that can reach 45% or more.

Other countries have very sensitive residence rules in the sense that even minimal presence, under some circumstances, can give rise to taxable residence and tax exposures on a worldwide basis. In Germany, for example, just having a home available there can result in an individual being considered to be domiciled in Germany, and thereby subject to worldwide taxation.

Tax Treaties and the "Tie-Breaker" Rules

A very important exception to the residence rules of countries and their application comes up where there is a tax treaty that applies. Tax treaties, which are generally bilateral agreements on taxation between countries, can provide critical tax benefits to wealth owners, and one important one relates to how they apply in the area of determining tax residence. Most comprehensive tax treaties contain what are known as "tie-breaker" rules, which avoid the possibility of the countries that have entered into the treaty both treating the same individual as resident in their country.

In the absence of a tax treaty, there is nothing to stop two or more countries treating the same person as a tax resident. Double or triple or more taxation could arise on the same income. Application of a tax treaty in the case of multiple residence can therefore be critical.

Here is an example of how a tax treaty can work to help deal with the possibility of being treated as a tax resident of more than one jurisdiction. If the wealth owner is a Hong Kong native and has lived and worked in Hong Kong his whole working life, he will have been "ordinarily resident" in Hong Kong under Hong Kong's determination of who is and who is not resident. This test of "ordinary residence," which also applies in Hong Kong's tax treaties to determine whether someone is a resident of Hong Kong, does not look at the days of physical presence in Hong Kong, but rather at many factors, including where one has chosen to establish a residence for settled purposes. The wealth owner in the example has always lived in Hong Kong, has close personal and economic connections to Hong Kong, perhaps has planned to be buried in Hong Kong, and maintains club and other social memberships in Hong Kong.

If, after retirement, the wealth owner establishes a second home in Canada, perhaps close to where his children and grandchildren live, and spends a substantial amount of time in Canada (maybe even more than 183 days a year), there can definitely be exposure to Canadian tax on the basis of Canada treating the wealth owner as a resident under Canada's domestic tax rules. This would result in worldwide tax at significant tax rates. If the wealth owner, however, continues to maintain a home and strong residential and other connections to Hong Kong, as would often be the case, taxation in Canada as a resident may be avoided, something that would provide a substantial tax benefit given that Hong Kong does not tax on a worldwide basis, and taxes even Hong Kong-sourced income at moderate rates.

Given the way the treaty works, only *one* of Canada or Hong Kong can treat the wealth owner as a resident. If, under their rules, both do so, "tie-breaker" rules apply to work out the answer. First, the question is where the individual maintains a permanent home – if in both locations, as is the case in this example, then the question becomes where the individual's personal and economic relations, or center of vital interests, is closer. As is often the case for wealth owners, this would, in the example, be in both countries. The next test is the location of the individual's "habitual abode" – and again, this may exist in both Canada and Hong Kong. Finally, if this is the case, if the individual is not a citizen of Canada, but has the right of abode in Hong Kong (a formal designation in Hong Kong), then the individual is *not* tax resident in Canada.

Most tax treaties, for the final tie-breaker rule, focus on citizenship, but in the case of Hong Kong, the formal right of abode is used in place of the citizenship test. Only if the individual is a citizen of both countries, or if, in the case of Hong Kong, they have the right of abode in Hong Kong *and* citizenship in Canada, is the question referred to the authorities to determine between them which of the two jurisdictions has the ability to tax on the basis of residence.

The impact of a tax-treaty "tie-breaker" rule can be substantial, as can be seen from the Hong Kong/Canada example. If the taxpayer is considered resident in Hong Kong, but not in Canada, the tax benefit is meaningful, particularly given that Hong Kong does not tax a wide range of income, including foreign-sourced income, capital gains, dividends, and more. While not all tax treaties involving jurisdictions that do not tax certain income provide full protection where a tie-breaker rule applies, understanding the role of tax treaties is critical. In the case of the treaty between Canada and Hong Kong, specific protection is given for income that is not of a Canadian source, and which is earned by someone determined to be resident in Hong Kong and not Canada – only the country of residence has the right to taxation.

This is all very complex, and enough to give the wealth owner a headache. But the headache is more pleasant than being taxed on worldwide income at substantial tax rates. Understanding how residence rules and treaties work can help the wealth owner establish a way of living that legally and effectively minimizes their global tax exposure.

It is also critical to remember that in an increasingly transparent world, it is not a question of whether a country will know how much time you spend there. You need to assume that they will. The only planning that a wealth owner can adopt is to *play by the rules, or get out.*

There are Many Differences between Worldwide Tax Systems Based on Residence

Each country has its own tax system, and the fact that many countries have in common the approach of taxing residents on a worldwide basis does not mean that there are not important differences between tax systems. Tax rates, of course, vary widely, and many other factors can be relevant in determining just how much tax a worldwide taxpayer actually has to pay. Very relevant is also the question of how the problem of possible double taxation is dealt with. Where a country taxes its residents on a worldwide basis, what happens if the taxpayer is also subject to tax in another country on the same income?

Whether or not one is a resident of another country, tax exposure in that country can arise if income sourced in that country arises. Virtually all countries that have an income tax will tax at least some forms of income that arise in their country, regardless of whether the person earning the income is or is not resident there. In very general terms, if an individual lives in one country, but earns income in another, say by working in that other country or investing there, that income may be taxed in the country in which it was earned. If the individual is resident in a country that taxes on a worldwide basis, both countries will be seeking to tax the same income. This potential for double taxation is dealt with in a number of ways, and avoiding double taxation, needless to say, can be a very important (and legitimate) objective in tax planning.

Back to tax treaties. Where a tax treaty applies, one of the areas commonly covered is assurance that double taxation will not arise. This is achieved in any number of ways, including through assurance of the availability of foreign tax credits or exemptions. In simple terms, tax treaties will usually make it clear which of the two countries involved have the right to tax any particular item of income and, in the case of the source country, often to what extent.

An example would relate to income from real-estate investment. Treaties generally protect the source country in the sense of allowing the country in which the real estate is located to tax income relating to the real estate under its own rules, and then requiring that the country of residence of the taxpayer (if it is going to tax the income under its worldwide taxing approach) provides a "credit" for the tax paid, thereby avoiding double taxation. If the country of residence taxes at 45%, and would charge a tax of $45 on $100 of net income from real estate, a credit would be provided for the tax imposed by the source country – say a tax of $35 on the same income. The final tax payable would be $35 to the country where the real estate is located, and $10 to the country of residence ($45 less the credit for the $35), thereby resulting in the final collective tax rate being the higher of the tax rate in the two countries involved.

Even in the absence of tax treaties, most countries that impose tax on a worldwide basis provide tax credits for taxes paid on income earned in other countries. How these credits work can be very different, and important steps may need to be taken to ensure that the credit can be obtained. In some countries, rather than a credit for foreign taxes, a deduction is provided. This can work out to be less valuable than a credit, resulting in an overall tax rate higher than the highest rate of the two countries involved. In other countries, Switzerland being an example, certain foreign income that is allocable to a foreign permanent establishment (as would be the case where a Swiss resident owns foreign real estate) is entirely exempt from Swiss taxation. This is highly attractive, as the exemption does not require that the income from the investment in the foreign country actually be taxed in that foreign country. As with tax credits, making sure that the availability of the exemption is maintained can be a critical element of legitimate tax-minimization planning.

A mistake that many wealth owners make, sometimes based on the legacy and incorrect approach of not properly disclosing foreign income and assets, is to own an income-producing investment through a company or other intermediate entity without having made sure that this does not result in double taxation. For example, a wealth owner may live in a country that taxes on worldwide income at the rate of 40%, but only provides tax credits on foreign taxes that are directly imposed on the wealth owner. If the wealth owner earns $100 of income in a foreign country, and pays $25 of tax in that country, that tax would be credited against the $40 of tax on the income in the home country, resulting in a total tax of $40 − $25 paid to the foreign country, and $15 to the home country. If, however, the wealth owner owns the shares of a company that makes the investment in the foreign country, it is the company that may then pay the $25 in tax in that foreign country. When the remaining $75 is paid to the wealth owner as a dividend, it may then be that the full $75 is taxed at 40% in the home country, resulting in a tax payment to the home country of $30. The total tax paid in the home country and the foreign country comes to $55, meaning that the total tax is higher than it would have been had the wealth owner held the investment in the foreign country directly, and obtained a foreign tax credit.

This example is one of many that begin to point toward a topic dealt with in the next chapter, tax-advantaged investing. This means thinking carefully about the tax effect of how investments are made, and focusing on not only the potential of return and risks taken, but the reality that returns are very much affected by tax. Key is to focus on the after-tax return, and not the pre-tax return, and to do so by looking at tax not only in the country of investment, but also in the country in which the wealth owner lives (and/or maintains citizenship, which may also be relevant).

Offshore Companies and Worldwide Tax Systems

Individuals living in countries imposing tax on a worldwide basis have long looked for ways to "defer" or delay their tax exposures, allowing them to accumulate income and reinvest it on a pre-tax basis, enhancing returns, before exposing the earnings to tax in their home countries. Suppose, for example, that an individual is living in a country that imposes tax on a worldwide basis at a rate of 40%, and invests $1000 in another country that does not impose tax on the type of investment being made. If the individual earns $100 of income from that investment, there would be $60 left to invest after the 40% tax is paid. But what if the activity or investment is not conducted by the resident individual, but rather by a company that the individual has set up? The individual could contribute the $1000 to a company in a country that imposes no tax, say the British Virgin Islands, and that company could then invest the $1000 in the country where the income is to be earned. If the income of $100 stays in the company and is not distributed to the individual shareholder by way of a dividend, is the full $100 then available to reinvest, as opposed to only $60, which would have been all that was left after the home country tax of 40% was paid?

The answer is that it depends. Some countries that impose tax on a worldwide basis allow for the deferral, or delay, of tax that the example suggests. Switzerland, which subject to limited exceptions for some foreigners, taxes its residents on a worldwide basis, is an example of a country where tax can, if certain steps are taken, be deferred in this way.

Other countries have a number of "anti-deferral" rules that can apply, including what are sometimes referred to as "Controlled Foreign Corporation" or "CFC" rules. These rules focus on the use of foreign corporations, and limit the ability of a taxpayer to "defer" or delay tax exposure. If an individual resident in a country that has these rules owns a bank account in another country, tax cannot be delayed by having the bank account transferred to a corporate vehicle. The individual, if taxed on a worldwide basis, would pay tax in his home country on the income earned from the account despite the fact that the account is not located in his home country. If the individual transfers the account to an offshore company owned by him, while the offshore company itself may not be taxed in the individual taxpayer's country of residence, the individual shareholder can be treated as taxable on the earnings of the company, even if the company does not distribute a dividend and holds onto its earnings.

Generally, controlled foreign corporation rules look at the nature of the activity of the offshore company. Where it is involved in passive investments as opposed to independent active business, the controlled foreign corporation rules can apply to tax the income on a current basis. Even where active business is conducted, some countries have complex rules to evaluate circumstances where tax can be deferred, making a review of the issue complex.

Controlled foreign corporation rules tend to focus on companies that are "controlled" by taxpayers from the country whose tax laws are in issue. However, even where such control does not exist, anti-deferral rules can have application where a country focuses not only on "controlled" foreign corporations, but also on "passive" foreign investment companies, where the anti-deferral effect arises even when the taxpayer owns only a small part of a foreign passive investment company.

In simple terms, an individual living in a country that taxes on a worldwide basis needs to understand how their tax system generally works, as only then can the wealth owner begin to be in a position to understand their own succession and asset-protection plans, asking advisors the right questions and guiding them in the planning process.

Also relevant to wealth owners living in countries that impose worldwide tax based on residence is the question of where the foreign company they have established is itself resident. While where a company is incorporated is a very important element in determining tax residence, many countries also treat companies as resident where the company is "managed and controlled." A Swiss-resident wealth owner who owns shares of a British Virgin Islands company that, in turn, owns assets outside of Switzerland will not be taxable on the earnings of the British Virgin Islands company, as Switzerland does not have controlled foreign corporation rules. But if the British Virgin Islands company is viewed as being "managed and controlled" in Switzerland, as would be the case if the wealth owner, from Switzerland, "calls all the shots," then the company itself would become taxable in Switzerland, losing the ability to help in achieving tax deferral. Careful planning, and ensuring that management and control takes place outside the home country, will be critical to avoid current tax exposure.

"How will anyone find out?" has been the basis of defective and historical tax "planning" – advisors and taxpayers asking themselves how, in a world of bank secrecy and opaque ownership possibilities, anyone will know about offshore companies used by taxpayers, or of other cross-border structures that might be taken advantage of.

The move to transparency is an unstoppable one, and in the next few years, the amount of information that tax authorities (and others) receive will be unprecedented. For wealth owners seeking to manage their tax exposures through legitimate tax planning, it is key to navigate the ever-changing tax laws and to ensure that the structures they use have the substance they need to withstand full scrutiny.

Moves to transparency are not limited to a focus on the taxation of individuals, and automatic information exchange implemented through a focus on the banks and other financial intermediaries they work with. In parallel, there is a focus on ensuring transparency in relation to the corporate tax world and, in particular, the use (and possible abuse) of "offshore" companies and inappropriate transfer pricing. In broad terms, governments are moving toward requiring information, from taxpayers, from tax authorities abroad, and from other sources, relevant to understanding the full global tax picture for corporate groups, whether or not they are owned by individuals.

Simply allocating a portion of income to a company in a tax haven is not tax planning – it never really was. But if no one ever found out, and there were positions that could be taken, was the planning legitimate? The "offshore" world of tax-haven companies developed in the shadows of an opaque world where the main countries of residence of individuals and corporations would not have a full picture of what was going on globally. In a world of transparency and focus on transfer pricing – the allocation of earnings and profits between related entities – this is fast falling away. The possibility of allocating earnings and profits to an offshore company with little substance or activity, and not paying any tax on this in the home country, is becoming part of history. While the use of tax havens and offshore companies will continue, the shift is to substance – and to the need for the use of jurisdictions that can offer real infrastructure to support that substance, as well as favorable tax rates, a wide network of tax treaties, and more. Such locations are not often found in the offshore world of the Caribbean, but rather in the "midshore" world of locations like Singapore and others offering infrastructure, treaties, and moderate taxation.

The starting point in any tax analysis is always to understand how the home country taxes the wealth owner. If a wealth owner is investing abroad, a mistake often made is to start the analysis in the country in which the investment is made. The right first step is to first understand how the home country, through its tax laws, affects the wealth owner and to then marry the tax planning that might be possible in the country of investment with the rules applicable in the home country. Relevant here will be, among others, whether the home country taxes overseas income; whether dividends from foreign companies are taxed; whether there are controlled foreign corporation rules; and whether there are issues that can arise in relation to "management and control." Effective tax planning means putting together the rules applicable in all relevant countries.

The USA and Worldwide Taxation of Citizens and Green Card Holders

The USA, in addition to taxing those who are resident in the USA on a worldwide basis, taxes its citizens and permanent residents (known as "green card" holders) on a worldwide basis regardless of physical presence in the USA. A number of countries in the world look at citizenship as a factor in some taxes that are imposed, but the USA is the only country in the world that imposes its taxes comprehensively on those who hold citizenship or "green card" status virtually regardless of their physical presence in the USA.

In the case of a permanent resident of the USA, full taxation on a worldwide basis can sometimes be avoided if the green card holder is also resident in a country that has a tax treaty with the USA and the relevant treaty "tie-breaker" rules apply. Treaties, however, do not generally protect US citizens from worldwide taxation.

Citizenship of the USA has long been viewed as a great benefit by wealth owners, particularly those linked to countries with political risk and uncertainty, and where home-country passports do not make travel easy. Many wealth owners in India, Pakistan, Indonesia, China, and other places have sought to obtain US citizenship to provide them with a passport that allows travel to many countries without a visa, and to afford their families the possibility of "escape" to the USA in the event of political or other problems in their home countries. Some families have gone to great lengths to obtain American citizenship for themselves or their children, but many of them have not been clear about the tax effect of having US citizenship. Under US tax laws, exposure to tax (and numerous reporting requirements) arises where a wealth owner is a citizen, and this regardless of where the wealth owner actually lives and whether they spend any time in the USA. This is also regardless of whether the wealth owner has a valid US passport or multiple citizenships.

Becoming a US citizen is remarkably easy, and automatically includes those born in the USA, as well as many circumstances of those born outside the USA to a US parent. There are certainly many situations where one may be a US citizen and not even be aware of it!

Boris Johnson, the Mayor of London at the time, found out about the difficulties faced by American citizens living abroad the hard way. A British national born to British parents, Boris Johnson was also a US citizen as his mother gave birth to him in New York. As a result, on selling a house in the UK, he discovered that he did not only have to navigate the UK principal-residence exceptions having application, but also US taxation on his gain. As a US citizen, he was subject to hefty capital gains taxes in the USA on his sale of a home in England, and this reportedly outraged the outspoken mayor, resulting in his stating that he simply would not pay. It didn't take long for Boris Johnson to learn that you really only have two choices – play by the rules, or get out. And in his case he was reported to have had to do both. First, to pay the taxes due in the USA (playing by the rules) and second, to give up his US citizenship in a formal way, getting out of the US worldwide tax system going forward.

Historically, it has been difficult for the USA to ensure that its citizens, particularly those living outside the USA, meet all of their tax and reporting obligations. This, however, has been fast changing as banks in particular have been brought into the picture through reporting requirements backed by tough tax and penalty rules designed to ensure compliance.

For US citizens, whether living in the USA or not, getting out of the tax system means not only not spending more time in America than the US residence rules allow, but also giving up citizenship. And before giving up citizenship, it is key to sort out the tax issues of the past, meaning that if tax and reporting requirements have not been complied with, voluntary disclosure is the only way to go.

When a tax authority catches a wealth owner who has not been compliant with tax and reporting requirements, it is often not just about punishing the taxpayer, but also about making an example of them to scare others into compliance. Voluntary disclosure, which means going forward to the tax authorities to sort out historical non-compliance, can often avoid many of the penalties associated with illegal tax evasion, and in the case of the USA, like other countries, there are from time to time procedures in place in relation to voluntary disclosure that can provide very favorable results to wealth owners seeking to "come clean."

For those who do not come clean with the American tax authorities in relation to undeclared income, even if they do not get caught in their lifetimes, there is generally no time limit that applies to tax claims in and around undeclared situations. "Transferee liability" may also apply, meaning that if my mother was an American citizen, and regardless of whether I am one or not, I may be responsible for her unpaid US taxes if I inherit from her. Wealth owners need, in my view, to leave a clean slate to the younger generation, and it is not only in the context of untaxed monies owned by American citizens at death that this is of relevance.

There are Many Kinds of Tax

Countries impose a wide array of taxes, and for the wealth owner, it is critical to understand which do and which do not apply.

Indirect taxes, being taxes that are applied on goods and services rather than on income and gains, are increasingly relied on by governments as an easier way of collecting taxes. The most common of these are "value added" and other sales taxes imposed on consumption. For wealth owners, indirect taxes can be important, and this particularly in relation to real estate, with a number of countries increasingly focusing on stamp duties as a means of raising income.

Of even greater focus for wealth owners are direct taxes on income and gains.

Income taxes generally include taxes on salaries and other income, but with considerable differences in how countries tax different items and at what level. For example, in some countries, dividends may be subject to income tax, while in others, some or all of a dividend may be exempt from tax. Investment income in the way of interest income is usually taxed, but some countries provide exemptions for certain interest income earned by non-residents as a means of encouraging investment into the country.

Capital gains are different from normal income and in the case of some countries, capital gains may be tax free. In other countries, capital gains may be taxed at lower rates than ordinary income. What constitutes a capital gain can, therefore, be a very important thing to determine. An occasional sale of a real-estate investment may give rise to a capital gain; a trader in real estate selling a piece of real estate may be considered to not be earning a capital gain, but rather fully taxable trading income, given that they are in the business of buying and selling real estate.

Transfer taxes – taxes on gifts and on death – can be very important to wealth-owning families. While some countries do not tax transfers made during life or at death, many do, and at sometimes very high tax rates that are not based, like an income tax, on profits, but rather on the value of assets that are transferred. The current global focus on income and wealth inequality is suggesting that we may see more in the way of transfer taxes being imposed in the future, albeit that rules vary country by country.

For example, in some countries the tax is imposed on the giver of the gift or the estate of the person whose assets pass on death; in other countries it is the recipient that is taxed. A common mistake made by wealth owners and their advisors is to not enquire about the tax residence of the recipient of a gift or bequest. A resident of the Bahamas, for example, may assume that a gift made to a child is tax free given the absence of gift taxes in the Bahamas, but in certain jurisdictions, such as France, Ireland, and Spain, a recipient resident there may become taxable on receipt of a gift.

In cross-border gifts and inheritances, avoidance of double taxation also becomes an issue, and here too tax treaties can have an impact, with a number of countries having in place bilateral estate and gift tax or similar agreements designed to help avoid double taxation.

Wealth taxes are imposed by some countries, and these taxes are particularly of concern to wealth owners given that taxes can exceed income. If, for example, the wealth owner owns a particular asset, and the asset does not produce any income, then the value of the asset will still be part of the tax base for determining exposure to the wealth tax. Tax will be payable, regardless of the fact that the asset does not produce any income. Wealth taxes are also of concern given the disclosure that providing information on one's net worth results in. In a world of populist governments and changing regimes, it is not always a safe option for wealth owners to provide this kind of information to the government of the country they may live in.

There are many other taxes that can also be critically important to wealth owners, and which will affect how assets are owned for succession and asset-protection purposes.

Increasingly, countries are focusing on the taxation of real estate, both through indirect taxes, such as stamp duties, and direct taxes, such as income and inheritance taxes. There are ever-changing rules on how high-value property is taxed and on how different ownership structures used by wealth owners affect the tax position. Real estate is not a very mobile asset, and for countries seeking to raise revenues, taxing owners of real estate is an increasingly attractive taxing option. Real estate is also coming under scrutiny as an investment class that permits an opaque approach to ownership, with the frequent use of offshore companies and other vehicles as owners, masking beneficial ownership. This scrutiny is resulting in new reporting requirements both inside and outside the world of automatic exchange of information, and is likely to intensify.

Mobility and Citizenship Planning, and Fixing Historical Tax Non-disclosure

Play by the rules, or get out. These are the only choices wealth owners have – the third choice of staying connected to a country by residence, domicile, citizenship, or otherwise and hoping that no one will find out is simply not an option in a world of growing transparency, and where tax laws are increasingly and more aggressively enforced. Tax laws are laws, and there is no choice but to comply with them.

Getting out means sorting out any historical tax liabilities, and then moving on to exiting a tax system and finding a new one, and ideally a more favorable one, to become subject to.

In addressing historical tax liabilities, a first and important step is to work out what they are. This may not be easy given the difficulty of finding historical records on the income involved, and the forensic work necessary can sometimes be difficult. Where one inherits undeclared funds, working out the past can be even more complex.

Sadly, where assets and income have been hidden, steps may have been taken that make tax exposures higher than they would otherwise have been, and more difficult to calculate. This is particularly the case where offshore companies, trusts, foundations, and other structures come into the picture. In other words, had the older generation played by the rules, less in the way of tax would have been payable than what the younger generation has to pay to come clean when they come into the money. This highlights the need for the older generation to take charge and not leave a legacy of problems to those who may inherit from them.

A next step in figuring out tax exposures associated with undeclared money is to determine whether there is an applicable limitations period that may apply. In some countries, statutes of limitations may prevent a tax authority from having the ability to look back more than a few years in relation to undeclared and untaxed income. In other countries, no limitations on time may apply. The effect of death and the existence of "transferee liability" will also be relevant. If my father died and left me assets that he did not declare to the tax authorities, am I responsible for the taxes he did not pay? There are few things my father may have done wrong that I am legally responsible for, but tax may be one of them. Again, the answer to this question will vary country by country, and will have a major impact on my determination of how much tax, if any, I owe in relation to undeclared income and assets.

Different countries, at different times, offer programs designed to encourage taxpayers with historical non-disclosure issues to come forward voluntarily. These can be forms of amnesties or voluntary disclosure procedures, all designed to encourage compliance. Related to growing transparency, and moves to automatic information exchange, is that more in the way of voluntary disclosure procedures is on offer. In most cases, these facilities provide much more efficient, safe, and inexpensive ways for taxpayers to "come clean." Failing to take advantage of these opportunities is often a mistake, particularly given that, when countries catch a tax evader (as opposed to when one voluntarily seeks to come clean), it is not just a question of punishing the taxpayer and imposing taxes, interest, and penalties, but also making an example that will scare other taxpayers into compliance.

The more wealth is involved, and the better known the taxpayer is, can sometimes make things particularly risky for taxpayers given the good "example" their being punished may provide. Increasingly, governments seek to "name and shame" those who break the tax laws with a view to making it clear to other taxpayers that tax compliance is their only choice. Rather than becoming an example for tax authorities, voluntary disclosure can be an important way to put the past behind you in a safe, predictable, and confidential way.

Given the upcoming automatic exchange of information between countries, many countries are moving to ensure that there are reasonable means for taxpayers to regularize their historical tax affairs, recognizing that this will increase revenues and help ensure longer-term tax compliance.

The Golden Rules of Undeclared Money

Despite huge increases in global transparency and tax enforcement, undeclared money remains a major issue around the world. For years, I have put forward a set of three "golden rules" in and around undeclared money.

Don't Make Someone Else's Problem Your Problem

Whether you are a banker or other advisor, or simply being asked by a family member, friend, or business associate to help, it is important to understand how easy it is for someone else's problem to become your problem in the area of undeclared money. Tax evasion is a crime, and helping someone to commit a crime is itself a crime. In the tax area this can come up in any number of ways, including through a conspiracy to commit tax evasion, aiding and abetting, or otherwise. If a banker or other advisor assists a client to disguise the real source or ownership of income or assets, this can easily turn into a crime. A wealth owner living in one country may be asked by a friend from another country to hold assets in their name with a view to a future gift to the children of the real owner or otherwise – lots of variations on a theme, and all examples of easy ways that someone else's problem can become your problem. In today's transparent world, the only option for the real owner of the assets or income is to play by the rules, and where there is historical non-reporting, to regularize this through voluntary disclosure or similar procedures.

In Today's World, No New Undeclared Money

Looking back in time, it is understandable, in many circumstances, why wealth-owning families may have undeclared money. This may have arisen through inheritance or otherwise, or because of historical issues faced by the family given their background or countries to which they are connected. During the Second World War, many families lost everything through expropriations, and, not trusting governments, took advantage of bank secrecy to protect a portion of their family wealth; in many countries in the world corruption, political risk, and other factors forced wealth owners to keep a portion of their income and wealth undisclosed. But in today's increasingly transparent world, the wealth owner risks more by keeping things undeclared, and other, legitimate approaches to wealth protection need to be undertaken. So, while there may have been a historical rationale for keeping money hidden, there is no room for this today, and in respect of new flows of income, legal approaches to achieving confidentiality and tax minimization need to be adopted.

No New Bad Guys – Keep the Younger Generation Innocent

Today, the best approach for a wealth owner to take where there are historical non-disclosure or other issues is to undertake voluntary disclosure – going forward to the relevant tax authorities and seeking to address issues of the past. Where a taxpayer makes such an approach, in the case of most countries the position is hugely different from where a taxpayer gets caught with undeclared money. And in many, many cases, the more innocent of wrongdoing the person coming clean is, the less in the way of penalties and other negatives arise. Where the older generation has an ownership interest in undeclared funds, likely the older generation has signing authority and other incidents of ownership over the relevant funds. They may have a history of using the funds and may even have been involved in steps taken to disguise the ownership of the funds – all steps that turn them into "bad guys" in the sense of their having broken the laws of the country whose taxes are in issue. Keeping the younger generation of the family out of any wrongdoing can be critical if it is the younger generation, on inheriting the assets involved, who will come clean with the relevant authorities. Do not add your children as signatories to the account; do not have your children access the funds or be involved in structures that may wrongly be used to disguise actual ownership. If those in the younger generation are innocent of wrongdoing, on inheriting the assets they may be in a much better position to undertake voluntary disclosure in a way that will result in a minimum of penalties.

Getting Out

Once historical tax issues are addressed, and the wealth owner is clearly "playing by the rules," a wealth owner can consider the important question of whether "getting out" is a good option.

Mobility, and taking advantage of the ease with which a wealth owner can move from one country to another, is an important element of not only tax planning, but also the achievement of a number of other objectives the wealth owner may have. The reality is that different countries have different tax rules, and where someone lives (and in some cases, where one holds citizenship or is domiciled) may drastically affect tax exposures. Apart from tax, residence choices will affect the question of what information which government will hold about a wealth owner's income and assets, an important issue in a world where challenges to wealth are only increasing, and where it is not always safe for information about wealth to be in the hands of governments, where such information can fall into the hands of kidnappers or be misused politically or otherwise.

Achieving the objectives of mobility does not necessarily require that the whole family relocates. Sometimes just having one or two members of the family take up residence in an appropriate country may facilitate a solid tax-minimization and asset-protection plan for the family. For example, a family living in a particular country may have a business there, and a number of family members involved in various aspects of the business, both in the home country and abroad. If one or two members of the younger generation relocate to a more tax-advantaged country, and become the owners of new family businesses established there, they may be able to own the new businesses, and even transfer them to tax-beneficial structures that benefit the entire family. Ownership of the new assets may not be part of the reporting requirements of the country that has been exited, and a number of tax and non-tax objectives of the family may thereby be met.

The first step in mobility is the question of how to exit the country you are currently connected to. Those looking at mobility almost always begin by asking the wrong question – how long do I need to spend in Monaco or the Bahamas or wherever to be a resident there? The reason that this is the wrong question is because the key first step is to work out how to exit the country you are currently connected to, whether by residence, domicile, citizenship, or a combination of them.

As discussed earlier in this book, many countries impose tax on a worldwide basis on those who are resident in that country. A first step in mobility planning is to understand the residence rules and to work out how they apply to those giving up residence, and how much time going forward you will be able to spend in the country you are leaving without continuing to be a resident, or resuming residence once residence has been given up. Usually, this involves carefully monitoring the number of days of physical presence in the country one seeks to exit, though in some cases also relevant will be whether accommodation is retained in the relevant country and what personal and economic ties continue to exist after departure.

Very relevant to exiting a country may well be the presence of a favorable tax treaty between the country one is departing from and the country one is moving to.

Touched on earlier, tax treaties, which are generally bilateral agreements between countries, contain residence "tie-breaker" rules that prevent an individual being considered to be resident in both countries at the same time. If the conditions of the treaty are met, domestic tax rules, which might otherwise cause the individual to remain taxable in their original country of residence, may be supplanted by the application of the treaty, which provides protection against the individual still being considered to be a resident of the country involved. A good example would arise in relation to Germany, where a long-term resident seeking to leave Germany and give up residence may find that the maintenance of accommodation in Germany, even if accompanied by a minimal physical presence, will result in a taxable domicile in Germany, and continued tax exposure on a worldwide basis. This domestic rule, however, could be overcome if the individual involved establishes sufficient connections to their new country of residence and that new country of residence has a suitable tax treaty with Germany. Exposures to gift and inheritance taxes similarly apply in many cases, and inheritance and gift tax treaties can also be of importance.

A growing issue relevant to leaving the taxing jurisdiction of a country is the question of whether exit taxes apply. An increasing number of countries impose an exit tax on those who give up taxable residence (and in the case of the USA, citizenship or long-term "green card" status, elaborated on below), often through a deemed sale of assets at fair market value on the date of departure. Canada, for example, has long had an exit tax that operates in this way. A resident who leaves the country is taxed on their departure on the basis of their being considered to have sold their assets when they leave. If the individual owns appreciated assets, exposure to capital gains taxes thereby arises.

Basically, exit taxes of this kind seek to tax the appreciation in assets that occurred during the period of residence, ensuring that a departure from the country does not permit this "pregnant" gain to avoid taxation.

A number of European countries also impose exit taxes, though in recent years how these taxes apply has had to be adapted to ensure that the taxes remain valid in light of the freedom of movement assured under agreements that form the EU. Even with such freedom of movement, a number of European countries, such as France, do have exit taxes that are now compliant with EU rules, and which require careful planning and navigation where mobility planning is underway.

One simple guideline on mobility planning, however, is that the best time to consider leaving a country is before that country begins to impose an exit tax. As the world moves to greater tax transparency and tax laws are enforced more vigorously, it is likely that more wealth owners will be using mobility as part of their planning, attracting more high-tax countries to consider barriers to mobility, including exit taxes and tougher rules in relation to the question of who is and who is not a tax resident, particularly among those who were previously taxable residents of the country.

Where exit taxes apply and there are rules that deem the sale of assets on departure, it is useful to consider an exit when asset values are low, such as during an economic downturn. In a wealth-owning family, it is also relevant to consider having those in the younger generation of the family undertake mobility planning before and not after they come into wealth.

In relation to the USA, it is not only the giving up of taxable residence that is important in mobility planning, but also the giving up of citizenship or green card status. The reason for this is that the USA is virtually the only country that currently taxes citizens and permanent residents on their worldwide income, regardless of how much time they spend in the USA. In the case of citizens and long-term green card holders, giving up citizenship or green cards can result in an exit tax applying, depending on, among others, the individual's net worth and income and certain other factors. Giving up citizenship before a family member in the younger generation comes into wealth can often be an important thing to take into account.

When one considers giving up citizenship, the question comes up of what replacement citizenship can be obtained. Citizenship planning is also relevant to wealth owners seeking second, third, and further nationalities, something of interest to those whose existing citizenship gives rise to political risk or inconvenience. There are many wealth owners from countries that are politically unstable, and the passports of which do not afford easy travel. Here, too, interest in obtaining second or further citizenships arises.

Once planning in relation to getting out of a country has been undertaken, the question arises as to where the wealth owner can go. A sometimes related question is where a wealth owner can obtain a second or further citizenship.

Where mobility planning is undertaken, there are often many choices regarding where a wealth owner can move to. Obvious tax-advantaged choices include jurisdictions that impose no tax at all, such as the Bahamas or Dubai. Other choices can include countries that impose tax on a territorial basis, such as Hong Kong or Singapore, where a resident (or non-resident) only pays tax on their locally sourced income, not on worldwide income. There are also a number of countries that offer special "deals" on taxation for specific groups of taxpayers. In Switzerland, in some cantons, it is possible to negotiate a "lump-sum" taxing arrangement where taxes are imposed on the basis of a fictitious income figure that is calculated on the basis of expenditures in Switzerland for housing rather than on the basis of actual worldwide income. In Thailand, retirees can avoid being taxed on their non-Thai-sourced income. And in the UK, many wealth owners can find themselves in the attractive position of being resident in the UK, through physical presence, but not domiciled in the UK, either because their father was domiciled outside of the UK, or because they have established a domicile of choice outside of the UK. A resident, non-domiciliary of the UK, rather than being taxed on a worldwide basis, can choose, at a cost after a set number of years, to be taxed in the UK only on their UK-sourced income and only that portion of their foreign income that they "remit" or bring into the UK. This attractive taxing regime was recently the subject of focus and review, resulting in limits on, among others, the number of years for which beneficial non-domiciled status can be retained. Non-domiciled status is now limited to 15 out of 20 years.

In all these cases, care needs to be taken in planning one's affairs to reflect the way in which one's new country imposes tax, and it is critical to consider planning that is done on a "pre-immigration" basis – taking steps before one becomes a resident of the new country.

While many countries offer tax advantages to wealth owners establishing residence, it is important to pay attention to the reality that where a tax system discriminates against "locals" as opposed to "foreigners," political and other pressures can result in many changes to the rules, and increasing costs to the new resident. Good examples here would include Switzerland and the UK, where those on "lump-sum" tax arrangements in Switzerland and who qualify as "resident, non-domiciliaries" in the UK have found their status to be under constant review and change, with costs increasing and uncertainties regarding long-term reliance on the special taxation system arising.

Pressures from neighboring countries, and in the case of the UK, from the EU, are inevitable as more and more wealth owners choose to "get out" as a means of managing their tax exposures. While the UK's exit from Europe may suggest that it will have more freedom to "compete" with its tax system, Europe is likely to put even more pressure on the UK to not do so and may well use this issue as a negotiation point in the UK's quest for trade and other benefits from the EU. On this front, jurisdictions that impose no tax on both local and foreign individuals, or which, like Hong Kong and Singapore, do not tax the foreign income of both local and foreign taxpayers, may have a longer-term future as interesting locations for wealth owners to consider moving to.

Demand in relation to mobility is increasing, and this results in not only more in the way of exit taxes, but also more difficulty in obtaining resident permits in places like Hong Kong and Singapore, and higher costs for those seeking to take advantage of tax-advantaged locations.

Interestingly, there is much in the way of planning that an individual can undertake before a move to even what may be perceived as a high-tax country. Here, pre-immigration planning again comes into the picture, and a variety of approaches, sometimes involving the use of trusts and other wealth-planning "tools," become relevant. In very simple terms, for a retiring couple, for example, some simple steps can reduce the tax dramatically before a move to a new country. Gifting assets to children, directly or through structures, if properly done, may well result in the assets no longer being owned, meaning that tax in relation to income earned on those assets will be avoided in the new country of residence.

Citizenship is available in a number of circumstances, and a good starting point is often to consider what citizenships may be available as a result of family history or religion. A number of countries have laws that consider the children and further descendants of a citizen to be a citizen. So if your mother or grandfather was born in a particular country, you may find that you are eligible to become a citizen of that country. In fact, you may already be a citizen, and it is only a case of proving your right to obtain a passport as proof of that citizenship.

In the case of Israel, a right of "return" open to all who are Jewish makes it possible for Israeli citizenship to be available to those who can prove they are Jewish and who establish residence in Israel.

There are also countries that, in effect, sell citizenship. This is often achieved through investment and other programs, and in some cases the countries involved are even members of the EU, affording their citizens freedom of movement within Europe and wide access to visa-free travel to many countries. Other countries require a considerable period of physical residence before citizenship can be obtained, and this includes countries like Australia, Canada, and the UK. But, unlike the USA, these are countries where once citizenship is obtained, if one is not resident in the countries, there is no exposure to worldwide taxation – like any non-resident, whether a citizen or not, tax only arises on locally sourced income if one is not resident there.

In the longer term, it is likely to become more and more difficult to obtain and keep second, third, and further citizenships. Like in the area of mobility, where there are an increasing number of countries that impose exit taxes and whose residence and related rules are getting tougher and tougher, it is likely that more countries will seek to limit the circumstances in which second, third, and further citizenships are permitted. For now, however, multiple citizenships can be an important safety net for wealth-owning families, and not only from a tax perspective.

The world of taxation is not a simple one, but tax is an important area for wealth owners to navigate. The only certainty in the tax world is one of change – tax laws rarely stay the same, and the complexity of cross-border investment and global families all too often results in wealth owners losing the ability to really understand their overall tax position and the structures that their advisors put in place for them. Most important, however, is for the wealth owner to have enough of an understanding of their tax position to be able to ask the right questions, and also to realize that while tax is important, it is only one of many needs wealth owners have and need to address in their succession and asset-protection planning.

5

The Needs of Wealth-Owning Families

Wealth-owning families have many needs.

Some needs affect all families, and relate to issues like succession and asset transfers, something that everyone has to face at some point.

Other needs may be specific to a particular family, such as a need relating to a disabled family member requiring special care or some other issue specific to the family, such as a second marriage, or concerns about particular assets in which the family has an interest.

A third category of need is driven by the tax and other laws that apply to the family – either by virtue of where the family maintains residential or citizenship connections, or by virtue of where they invest. Religion can also come into the picture in this third category, with the *Shari'a* law being an example. For Muslims, religious law governs many aspects of inheritance, as well as other areas of economic life, and these rules are part of the laws of most, if not all, Muslim countries.

Set out below are some examples of the different kinds of need that wealth owners have, and some first indications of how they can be addressed. Very important to keep in mind is that a family never has only one need, albeit that a particular issue, relating to taxation or a special dynamic within the family, may drive the planning process. Successful succession and asset-protection planning requires that a holistic view of needs be undertaken, and that these needs are all addressed as part of the approach to be adopted by the family. And as needs change, whether due to changes within the family or in the external world, the approaches taken need to adapt.

Knowing Where the Assets Are – And Not Having a Plan *is* a Plan

A fundamental and seemingly straightforward need of every wealth owner is to understand the basics of succession in relation to their assets and their hopes for how their assets will pass to others in the event of their death or disability.

The first step in succession planning is to understand that having no succession plan *is* a succession plan. If I die, something will happen to my assets, and this notwithstanding that I may not actually have thought about my succession or planned it at all. The laws that apply where I live and where my assets are located will come into the picture, and in most countries, the succession of those who die without having made a will or taken other steps in planning will set out who will be entitled to the assets of the deceased. In most countries, the assets of one dying without a will go in set shares to a surviving spouse, children, and depending on the circumstances, to more distant family members. So a very first step for any wealth owner is to understand what happens if there is no planning, and to make sure that the default plan is one that the wealth owner is comfortable with and understands.

But there are many issues with not thinking the succession plan through. One fundamental need of any wealth owner is simply to ensure that the assets they have will really go where they want them to go, and here a first step is to ask the question whether the right people know about the assets and where they are.

If I ask most wealth owners what they have, the answer is not always as straightforward as one might expect. A typical wealth owner, if they tell me the truth, will describe a number of bank accounts, not all of which their families may know about; safe-deposit boxes in different banks, and sometimes countries, with jewelry and other valuables – in some cases, *jewelry from my mother that she didn't want my wife to have... she wanted the jewelry to go to my daughters, so my wife doesn't know about the safety deposit box.* The list goes on to include shares of companies that the wealth owner has invested in; amounts owed by friends and business colleagues the wealth owner may have loaned money to; maybe interests in companies in countries with foreign-ownership restrictions, such as Indonesia, where the shares are in the name of an Indonesian friend or business associate *who knows that if I die the shares should go to my children...* and more assets that only come to mind later in the process of trying to get a grip on what the wealth owner has.

A number of years ago I was working with a wealth owner who was a particularly well-organized person. He had good records and lists of assets, and a solid recollection of the many small and larger businesses and investments he had interests in. When I suggested to him that part of the succession-planning process would require identifying what he actually owned, and how such ownership was documented, what he thought would be an easy process ended up taking more than two years to complete. The wealth owner kept remembering investments he had made and assets he had, and then had to search for documentation on them. Ownership records on offshore companies, real-estate investments, and many other items had to be reconstructed, as not everything turned out to be as well documented as he thought. Keys to safe boxes had to be found, and arrangements made for ensuring that the right people would have access to the safe boxes at the right time. Some of the companies he had set up over the years had their records maintained by lawyers who had retired, and quite a bit of work had to be done to track things down.

If it is so difficult for a well-organized wealth owner to quickly identify their own assets and ownership structures, what happens when a wealth owner dies, and his spouse, children, or others have to work out what they had, where those assets are, and what they are worth? If the safe box containing valuable jewelry is in a country like Canada, the UK, or the USA, even if the wealth owner is not a resident or citizen of the relevant country, tax exposures can arise given that valuable assets are actually physically located in Canada, the UK, or the USA, countries the wealth owner may have believed would be safer locations in which to keep valuables than the wealth owner's country of residence in Latin America or Asia. Taxation based on the location of physical assets arises in some countries but not others. Yes for art collections in the UK, no for the same art collections located in Switzerland when owned by a foreigner. This information is highly relevant to the decision on where to keep valuable items.

And what of personal possessions, such as art, jewelry, and other valuable collectibles? Is death a time when doctors, nurses, household staff, and others have an opportunity to help themselves to items that those meant to succeed to the estate may not have knowledge about or an ability to track down? Will the friend in Indonesia in whose name the shares are registered given foreign-ownership restrictions do the right thing and acknowledge that they own interests for the benefit of the family, or will they "forget" to say anything about it and even if asked claim that they owned the assets themselves?

When people die or become disabled, their assets all too often just disappear, and there are many circumstances where what one has worked hard to keep for the next generation or for others simply falls into the wrong hands.

It saddens me to watch the many different versions of *Storage Wars*, a television reality series that focuses on storage units that have been forgotten or abandoned, with the contents auctioned off when rental payments have not been kept up. I cannot help thinking about the owner of the goods that someone has bought at auction and is sifting through, who may have died or become disabled before having been able to arrange for what they owned to pass to the next generation. The "big win" in the reality program is when one of the storage units includes something of real value... but who is the winner? Is it the person the real owner of the assets wanted to benefit, or some stranger who bid on a storage unit's contents without even knowing what was inside?

At every level of wealth, I am a great believer that it is very important for the wealth owner to ensure that those who are meant to benefit from the assets know about the assets and where they are. A good succession plan is well thought out, and ideally those who will be inheriting assets are part of the succession process and are in a position to make sure they actually get what they were supposed to get.

I have run into a number of cases over the years where trusts and foundations established by wealth owners were not disclosed to family members, something quite common in times when wealth owners in Europe and elsewhere were led to believe that good planning involved hiding their assets from tax authorities and others. In too many situations, advisors ranging from lawyers to trustees to protectors and others ended up helping themselves to all or part of the assets involved. Where families finally discovered the structures their deceased parent had created, it was often too late to recover the full value involved.

While the wealth owner is alive, things often go pretty much according to plan, with advisors seeming to do the right thing. But after death, the question arises as to who will actually make sure that the trusted intermediary does what they are supposed to do. And where individuals are involved, what if they become disabled or pass away? Is a successor in place and, if so, is the successor trustworthy?

In one case I was involved with, an American lawyer had made use of the entire trust fund after the death of his client, and by the time the family found evidence of the existence of the trust and took action, the lawyer involved was in his late 80s and claimed he had Alzheimer's, with no recollection of anything to do with the trust.

What rights children have in relation to being the beneficiaries of trusts, and the responsibilities of trustees, and other such things are discussed in the next chapter. But the example brings out some important lessons for any wealth owner. Where secrecy is the overriding objective, there is a much higher degree of risk that the right oversight will be missing from the structure.

Fortunately today, fewer wealth owners are falling into the trap of tax-undeclared money, given global transparency and increased tax enforcement, but for those who – for any reason – opt for approaches that focus on secrecy, it is important to not lose sight of the many other needs a wealth-owning family has. An overriding need is for a succession structure that ensures the right people, such as the wealth owner's children, come into the assets, and that advisors and intermediaries have someone, or more than one person, keeping an eye on them. If those meant to benefit do not know anything about the asset-holding structures that are in place, they will simply be unable to enforce their rights.

I am a great believer that a safe succession structure requires that those who are to benefit have at least some idea of who to call and where to get the information they need about what may be coming to them. It may not always be appropriate, given ages or otherwise, for the younger generation to know the specifics on amounts or other details regarding what they may come into, but knowing what they should be looking for and what to do on the passing of their parents is critical. This is something the wealth owner has to anticipate, failing which there needs to be more than just one person who has the obligation to follow up and do the necessary.

For a wealth owner, not having a plan *is* a plan, and if there is no clarity on who gets what, there is much in the way of confusion and unhappiness that can result. Mother and father may have retired, and now spend time with their son and daughter, each of whom have their own families and homes in different places. Mother leaves some of her jewelry in a safe in her daughter's home for use when she visits; father leaves one of his important antique wristwatches in a safe in the home of the son. When mother passes away, to whom does the jewelry belong? What of the watch when father passes away? If in their wills (or maybe there are no wills) the specific items are not mentioned, who will get the assets? What if the son argues *Dad gave me the watch, that is why it is in my safe*. Does the watch then fall outside of the estate on death, not being an asset divided between the son and daughter (if that is what the will provides in relation to assets), as it was gifted to the son earlier? Will the lack of clarity create a division between the son and daughter, giving rise to wealth being destructive of family relationships?

Wealth owners need to make things clear, and also need to understand that the risk of the wrong people coming into their assets is much greater the less clarity there is about what they have and the steps that need to be taken on their passing.

A colleague of mine had been advising a Latin American family where the very significant family business involved was ultimately owned by a Panamanian holding company. Now out of favor in most jurisdictions given moves to transparency, the company had issued "bearer" shares, shares which are not registered in the name of any particular shareholder, but rather where the share certificates themselves represent the ownership of the company. Like currency, whoever has the shares owns the company and, indirectly, all its assets. The owner of the business had a mistress, and maintained an apartment he shared with her. His children worked with him in the business, and when he died, they assumed that the business would become theirs, together with the other assets that passed to them on the death of their father.

The children were in the process of restructuring the business when they were asked by their bankers, as a formality, to prove their ownership of the company. The children hunted through their father's papers, searching for evidence of their ownership. Learning that the holding company had issued bearer shares, they conducted a search for them. After some time, their father's mistress was contacted as the search extended to the apartment the father had shared with her. It was only then that the mistress revealed that she had the bearer shares, claiming that they had been given to her well before the death of the father – meaning that the shares had not passed to the children together with the other assets of the father that went to them on his death. The children ultimately prevailed, in lengthy litigation that proved the father's intent to have the shares pass to his children, but the lawyers involved did very well financially out of the dispute, and not every similar case ends as happily for the younger generation of the wealth-owning family.

It is useful and important for wealth owners to keep an inventory of their assets, and regularly review and update both the inventory and the approaches in place in relation to what is to happen in the event of death or disability.

Regular stress tests should be conducted to ensure that everyone knows what will happen if there is an unexpected event that gives rise to death or disability. Advisors should be in place in a way that provides for effective oversight, perhaps with one unrelated advisor keeping an eye on another, and with clear instructions in place to family members and others about who should do what in the event of death or disability. And most important is the need for good communication within the family, in age-appropriate ways, about the succession process. This can ensure that those who may come into assets are aware of what is planned, something important not just for tracking down the assets, but to avoid misunderstandings and allow the succession process to be a collaborative one that has the chance of preventing wealth becoming destructive of family assets and relationships.

Succession, Wills (Including "Living Wills"), and Probate

The reality is that we will all die one day. Death and preparing for the possibility of disability represent more needs that apply to all wealth owners.

Succession, wills, and what happens on death are subject to the laws that apply to the estate of someone who passes away. Similarly, in the event of disability, what happens to assets and their management is subject to the laws that may have application. For a typical wealth owner, what law applies is not always clear, particularly where the wealth owner may be a citizen of one or more countries, resident in another, and have assets in a number of other countries. Conflicts of law may arise, and the law governing how assets are to be dealt with may be far from clear.

There are some general principles that wealth owners should be aware of regarding the succession process. A first general principle is that where there is no will that governs the estate, something will still happen to the assets on death, but this will be determined not by what the wealth owner intended, but by the applicable law. The applicable law will likely be the law of the jurisdiction where the wealth owner was domiciled, resident, or a national of at death, but this may be affected by other factors, including the location and nature of the assets on death and the law applying there. The law that governs in the place the assets are located may well provide for a different approach to succession than the law of the domicile of the wealth owner.

In most countries, where one dies without a will, the assets, on death, go to specified family members – perhaps a surviving spouse and parents, and if there are children, often in shares to the surviving spouse and children. If there are no close family members, then the assets go to more distant relatives in specific shares, and sometimes simply to the relevant government once there are no relatives surviving.

For an estate governed by Islamic law, at least four different issues become relevant. First, not only the spouse and children will be forced heirs, but also any surviving parents. Second, if the spouse is not a Muslim, such spouse will not receive a forced heirship entitlement. Third, if a child is adopted or illegitimate, that child will receive no share of their father's estate. And fourth, Islamic law does not provide for a *per stirpes* approach to succession, with each branch of a family receiving a share. Instead, the Islamic rule of degree applies, meaning that if the deceased had two sons, one of which pre-deceased leaving a grandson, the whole of the estate will pass to the surviving son, and nothing at all to the orphaned grandson.

A change of religion from, to, or within Islam can result in the inadvertent disinheritance of family members who do not themselves convert. Further, conversion away from Islam can result in the individual undergoing conversion themselves losing inheritance rights. In jurisdictions with split systems, such as Bahrain and Lebanon, a change from the Sunni to the Shia school of Islam, or vice versa, may affect what forced heirs get in, for example, the case of a testator who has only daughters surviving him.

The most important thing is to understand who is going to get what given your circumstances and planning (or lack thereof). And then it is key to ask yourself the critical question: who is going to make sure that all goes as it should, preventing assets being stolen by employees or others who have access to them?

If there is one, the will usually determines where the assets go, but for wealth owners having assets in multiple jurisdictions, having more than one will may be something to consider. If I have a will drawn up in my country of domicile and die with assets in another country, it is important to understand the procedures in that other country that will be necessary to cause the assets to pass from having been in my name into the name of those I want to benefit from the assets. In some cases, easier and quicker than "proving" a will from another country might be to have a separate will for assets in a particular country. If there are multiple wills, ensuring that the first will in my country of domicile does not conflict with the foreign will becomes important. At a minimum, I should consider having my home country will make reference to any other wills that I might have. But this is not always the case, given that there may be reasons to retain confidentiality about the assets located in the other country.

Something that the laws of many countries provide for is that when one marries, previous wills become invalid; when one divorces, gifts to spouses specified in an earlier will are treated as if the spouse had pre-deceased. This may be a good thing, but there can sometimes be surprising results, meaning that the wealth owner needs to keep an eye on these things and be in a position to ask advisors the right questions. There are many examples of individuals who had set up careful estate plans, dividing their assets on death among their children and their spouse. Then the spouse passes away, and the widow or widower develops a new relationship that leads to remarriage. As the original will would commonly say that if the spouse pre-deceases, the children receive the entire estate, the surviving spouse may well think that all is as it should be when they remarry, the expectation being that the new spouse, who may have their own wealth or to whom specific gifts through trusts or otherwise may be made, would not benefit under the will. What many wealth owners do not realize is that the new marriage results in the carefully drafted will being considered to have been revoked, meaning that if the wealth owner dies without making a new will, the new spouse would now receive, in addition to what the wealth owner may otherwise transfer to her in trust or otherwise, a substantial share of his estate on his intestacy.

Even where one has a will that is valid, a number of issues can arise. One relates to whether the will meets the requirements of forced heirship rules that may have application to the estate of the deceased. In most common-law countries, like the USA, Canada, the UK, and others, there are no forced heirship rules (subject to some important exceptions such as Louisiana in relation to some heirs, Scotland for moveable assets, and Singapore for its Muslim citizens). As a result, if a wealth owner decides to leave all of his assets to one particular beneficiary, whether within or outside of the family, this is allowed. If dependent family members get nothing or very little, they may be entitled to apply for financial aid from the estate, but they have no particular right to any particular percentage of the assets involved. In other countries, particularly civil-law countries, like France, Germany, Switzerland, Indonesia, Taiwan, and Japan, "forced heirship" rules apply, meaning that specific family members are considered to be entitled to specific portions of the estate of someone who dies, with only a limited part of the estate being able to be freely transferred as the wealth owner wishes. The *Shari'a* law, applying to those living under Islamic law, similarly provides for a forced heirship approach.

Needless to say, forced heirship rules and how they apply vary from legal system to legal system, with, in some cases, there being an ability for family members to give up their forced heirship rights contractually. But this is not always the case, and in some forced heirship systems, an ability to contractually give up one's rights is not possible. Under some forced heirship systems, gifts can be given freely during life; in others, gifts may be invalidated so as to protect the forced heirs. And for today's wealth owner, great complexity can arise where one lives in a country with forced heirship, but owns assets in other countries that do not have such rules, or *vice versa*, where one lives in a country that does not have forced heirship rules, but assets may be owned in a country that does. There are some special rules that apply country by country in relation to the estates of foreigners, allowing them to opt out of forced heirship; there are also some multilateral agreements among countries that affect the issue of cross-border succession. All of these can be highly relevant to effective estate planning.

Trusts and other "tools" of wealth planning can sometimes help ensure that the wishes of wealth owners are achieved notwithstanding the complexities of forced heirship regimes. This is discussed in the next chapter, but most important for the wealth owner is to really understand the laws that apply to their succession. A wealth owner should always be considering the "what-ifs" – including the question *what if I die?* – and the effect of forced heirship and other rules on how assets will pass to the next generation.

When someone dies, also relevant is the question of how assets actually move from one person's name to another's, whether or not there is a valid will in place. When someone dies owning assets, this is not something that occurs automatically. In most countries procedures have to be undertaken to establish who has rights to the relevant assets, whether under a will or otherwise, and this procedure is often referred to as "probate" – the official proving of a will and the entitlements of beneficiaries thereunder, or in the event of an intestacy.

These procedures have a number of negatives for many wealth-owning families. First, the procedures are not necessarily quick and, depending on the circumstances, a family could find themselves in financially difficult circumstances given the delay between the death of the wealth owner and when they actually get hold of the assets. Probate procedures can also be expensive, with some countries even providing for lawyers who work on the probate to not be paid on the basis of the time they spend, but rather on a percentage of the value of the estate. And probate is usually a public procedure, meaning that information about assets and who gets what is not a private matter.

The problems of probate point to a need for wealth owners to address these issues, and some of the uses of the "tools" of wealth planning are to avoid probate in respect of assets, allowing immediate access to assets to those who are meant to benefit, and without the costs or delays (or public disclosures) that probate attracts. But even where a wealth owner has a trust, insurance, or other structure hold specific assets, a will is usually still needed, as it is almost inevitable that there will be other assets the wealth owner owns at death that will need to pass from his ownership to the ownership of those he wishes to benefit.

Of course, it is not only death that makes taking care of one's assets impossible; a variety of disabilities can affect the ability of a wealth owner to look after their affairs. Discussed later are changing demographics and the effect of living longer on wealth owners and their needs, but part of good succession planning is to consider who will be able to make decisions if you are unable to make them. Stress testing the succession plan also means considering what happens if you become disabled and unable to communicate; or if dementia or other disorders make it impossible for you to make decisions about your healthcare or financial situation. In the absence of clarity on these issues, decisions may fall to those in or out of the family who, under the relevant law, are able to apply for the ability to make decisions in your place – but is this always the right person to do this? Has the wealth owner considered that the nasty spouse they were about to divorce may be the one who ends up with the power to make decisions over not only their assets, but also whether or not they remain on life support?

"Living wills" are one way to deal with these issues, and where the laws of a country so permit, you can document your wishes as to who will make the decisions if you cannot. Some of the other tools of wealth planning, such as trusts and foundations, can also be used to set out who should be in a position to handle things in the event of disability.

But like with succession generally, it is usually not enough to just name one or more people to look after your affairs in times that you are unable to. On an ongoing basis, having discussions with those involved, and making sure the right "checks and balances" are in place, can be key. Just appointing one person to look after your financial affairs may be risky, with the person having more power than they should, and with little oversight. Perhaps decisions should be made by a committee, with governance and succession procedures that the committee must apply. Making sure that whoever is going to make decisions understands the decisions you would like to see made is also critical. A living will is, like any element of succession planning and asset protection, something that needs ongoing review, reflecting changes in relation to assets, the individuals to be involved in making decisions, and otherwise.

A couple without children appointed me under their living wills, together with another advisor, to make decisions regarding medical care in the event of their disability, once the other in the couple was not around or able to step in. They did this without having said much to me about what their wishes were, and I made sure, as an advisor, to ask for a meeting to discuss their thoughts on medical interventions and related matters, something that – given my responsibilities – I will do on an ongoing basis. Interestingly, one of the couple told me that it would be her wish that in almost any circumstance of serious illness, she would want me to make the decision to "pull the plug"... her husband had the opposite wish, that under pretty much no circumstances should such a decision be made.

Without clear ongoing communication and discussion, an advisor will not be able to make decisions that reflect what the wealth owner would really have wanted. A good advisor will insist on getting the information he needs – and a responsible wealth owner will make sure their advisors are kept up-to-date on what the wealth owner hopes for and will put mechanisms in place to help ensure that the right decisions are made.

Divorces (and Relationships Generally)

Another need relevant to virtually all wealth-owning families relates to the financial and other issues that divorce and relationships generally give rise to. I was giving a talk to a group of wealth-owning families, and made a statement that I believe in. I said *divorce is one of the world's biggest destroyers of wealth*. I had invited a friend of mine to join me for the talk, Sharon Ser, pretty much the top divorce lawyer in Hong Kong and Asia generally. Sharon, not a wallflower, jumped from her seat and shouted out *Philip is wrong! Divorce is not the biggest destroyer of wealth in the world. Divorce is the biggest CREATOR of wealth in the world.*

Sharon, of course, often acts for the person claiming assets in the event of a divorce, and is rightly proud of her record of getting the most out of hapless wealth owners (and their children) whose marriages are ending. While she certainly has helped many wealth owners protect themselves against claims where they are lucky enough to have her on their side, her disagreement with my comment helps emphasize the risk to wealth that divorce gives rise to. With up to 50% of marriages in many parts of the world ending in divorce, wealth owners need to understand the odds, and ensure that the divorces they suffer or that their children suffer do not end up destroying family wealth and businesses.

Divorce laws and the entitlements of spouses differ greatly country by country. In some countries the financial entitlements only arise where there is a real marriage, while in others co-habitation arrangements may also have meaningful financial consequences. A first step, therefore, is to try to figure out what laws will actually apply to a divorce – not always an easy matter. In the case of wealth-owning families, it is not uncommon for a couple to have married in one country, lived in several others, and to be maintaining homes in more than one place. Often, in the case of a divorce, there can be forum shopping in the sense that a spouse looking to achieve a particular financial result can try to get the courts of one or another country to take jurisdiction over a divorce. It is also often the case that whoever goes to court first might well find that their choice of court will govern the divorce.

English law is emerging as an increasingly problematic jurisdiction for wealthy spouses or ex-spouses. Even where a divorce has been completed in another country where a spouse, on divorce, may have received a modest award, there may be an option for the poorer spouse to then move to England and petition for a "top-up" award against the wealthier ex-spouse. Enforcement may be an issue, but this is an increasing danger to wealth owners with property interests in the UK or in jurisdictions that are likely to enforce English judgements.

Something that I believe wealth-owning families, and particularly the younger generation, need is an understanding about how these rules work, and how the steps they take in relation to a divorce can make a dramatic difference.

The Christian wife of a Muslim man may get nothing on death or divorce in certain *Shari'a*-law countries, given that they are not Muslim; the same wife, taking action in London, where the couple may have a house or flat, could end up with half her husband's assets. I sometimes tell friends of mine in Hong Kong, considering divorce and fretting over the financial consequences, to not go home and tell their wives that they are thinking of divorce; rather they should say, *I love you dearly... but we need to move to Shanghai for business.* Hong Kong often follows the UK approach of 50/50 divisions of marital assets. If the divorce takes place in mainland China rather than Hong Kong, the wife will get a fraction of what she would get under Hong Kong law.

A mistress in Hong Kong will get virtually nothing, as there is no formal marriage; a mistress in California or Vancouver may get a massive settlement, as co-habitation, and not just marriage, results in financial rights on a break-up of the relationship. Wealth owners need to understand how these things work, and in every family, education about the risks of divorce and relationships is a necessary part of effective asset protection.

There are planning approaches that can be undertaken to protect assets in the case of divorce, and particularly opportunities for the older generation to do things that will make it difficult for the spouses of their children to make claims against assets deriving from the older generation. But not all work, and it is interesting to see how many cases there are of families who have lost control of substantial businesses and wealth through a lack of attention to the risks involved.

Even discretionary trusts, discussed later, are often "looked through" when there are divorce claims – the focus being on what are "marital assets." In a simple example, mother may put the family business and assets in a trust of which her children are discretionary beneficiaries, thinking that this will protect the assets from a divorce claim in the younger generation. Over time, distributions from the trust are occasionally made to the younger generation, the relevant letter of wishes providing for discretionary allocation of a portion of the trust to one of the children. On a divorce, the spouse of the son or daughter will easily be able to say that the relevant portion of the trust, albeit discretionary, is a "marital asset" as the funds were used in the marriage and remained available to the spouse against whom claims are being made. And the idea of the child not disclosing the trust or other assets as a way of protecting these assets is not an option, as in most countries a spouse, on divorce, has to disclose all assets, including trust interests, and a failure to make such disclosure accurately might not only result in criminal and other penalties, but also enrage a judge who discovers the truth and who is then likely to be far from sympathetic.

But what if mother, in the example, puts the family business in a trust that the younger generation cannot access directly, and a smaller amount of wealth in another trust that the younger generation does receive distributions from? Might this reduce the risk of the family business being seen as a "marital asset" that might become part of a divorce claim?

Do wealth owners need to understand this in order to ask their advisors the right questions? Do wealth owners need planning if they trust their children? For me, the answers are yes, and yes – advisors may not always look at things in the holistic way that wealth owners need them to, and therefore the responsibility is back on the wealth owner to ask the right questions, and to seek the right advisors. And as to trusting your children, it is certainly often the case (but not always) that you can... but it is, sadly, less often the case that you can trust their spouses or near-spouses. And your children need to understand that how they use the money and other assets you make available to them will have an impact on whether their spouse can get hold of these assets in the event of a divorce.

Pre-nuptial and post-nuptial agreements play an increasing role in the protection of wealth in the case of a break-up of a marriage or other relationship. Not always a perfect fix, the laws of an increasing number of countries do pay attention to agreements entered into before a marriage (pre-nuptial) or after a marriage (post-nuptial) relating to the economics associated with a dissolution of the marriage. But there are many issues to consider in these arrangements, and good advice is usually needed given the many different ways in which countries view such agreements. A general rule is that for any agreement to work, the spouse signing the agreement needs to have had independent advice and full disclosure of the assets of the person they are about to marry or live with, factors that make it important to proceed carefully and in the right way.

In relation to the younger generation, I believe it is critical to discuss pre-nuptial agreements and their usefulness very, very early on in the process of discussing family finances and succession within a family. If Mom and Dad put off discussing pre-nuptial agreements until their son or daughter arrives home holding hands with *the* one, and on meeting him or her the parents then tell their son or daughter about the pre-nuptial agreements and their necessity – *um, son, can we speak in the kitchen?* – the younger generation will often perceive the discussion as a negative judgement on the specific person they have brought home for their parents to meet. Much more effective is to have the discussion about pre-nuptial agreements well before the younger generation introduces the man or woman of their dreams, and to make pre-nuptial arrangements a family requirement that is communicated to potential spouses as part of the overall family governance approach, and not something subjective and specifically related to them.

Relevant to not only divorce is the fact that a number of countries (and, in the case of the USA, this is a state-by-state issue) have "community property" rules that basically allocate assets to a spouse, in the absence of a pre- or post-nuptial agreement to the contrary, prior to any dissolution of the marriage or other relationship. It is one thing to find that on divorce a spouse is entitled to a portion of marital assets – but it is often a surprise for wealth owners to discover that assets they thought they owned are actually not owned by them at all, regardless of whether their marriage dissolves.

A typical fact pattern involves a family business that grows over the years as children become involved. Over time, the parents may decide to transfer all or part of the business to their children, and some of the children may move to different countries, continuing to work in the family business, and expanding its global reach. If a child moves to a jurisdiction where community property rules apply, such as would be the case in California, a spouse may become an owner of part of the business (or at least part of its value) without the family being aware of this. Say the family business grows in value during the time one of the children lives in California, working on expanding the business in the USA. The child, at some stage, may decide to transfer the business into a trust or other structure for the benefit of his children – but under community property rules, he cannot. The child may have good reasons for wanting the family business to be in a trust for his children and not for the benefit of his spouse – maybe the spouse has children from a previous marriage living with their other parent, or who are independent and who, in any event, have nothing to do with his family business which had been established by his own parents or grandparents.

The spouse will be considered to own half of the growth in the value of the business that was achieved during the time the couple lived in California, meaning that a transfer of the business by the child whose family established the business requires the consent of that spouse – consent the spouse may very well refuse to give without a significant financial settlement.

Community property rules may be sensible as a way of protecting a spouse or other partner co-habiting with a wealth owner. But is it right that community property rules can break up a family business and sometimes require that it be sold in order to comply with laws the family may not even have been aware of? The child may be planning to leave more than enough to his spouse after his passing or disability, to provide generously for her, keeping her in the lifestyle to which they have become accustomed. But the child may not want to provide a share of the family business, and to risk it then going to people outside his immediate family, such as the children of his wife's first marriage or otherwise.

Objectives such as these can become impossible to meet in an example such as this one. While living in California, and, say, tripling the value of the business, the wealth-owing child and his wife in the example mentioned above were living in a "community of property." As a result, half of the value created during their time of residence in California already legally belongs to the child's wife. Even in the absence of a divorce, the wife is an owner of assets registered in the name of her husband, and the only way he could legally transfer the assets to a trust in favor of his natural children, and restrict his wife's interests to lifetime distributions to maintain her lifestyle, would be with her written consent.

Could wealth planning help in these circumstances? Maybe. If the parents of the wealth-owning child do not transfer the business to the child, but rather put it in a trust for future generations, separating the business from other assets the child would have access to, this might well work.

In the case of divorce, community property, co-habitation, and otherwise, it is easy to say that the rights of the spouse or other party are there because they need to be protected. And this is often the case, and why laws are in place to provide this protection.

But for a wealth-owning family, and particularly where wealth is at the higher level, it is critical to understand how laws designed to protect a spouse can be abused to provide a spouse with rights to family businesses and wealth that by no stretch of the imagination should they have access to. And with lawyers charging on contingency, getting paid on the success of their efforts, is it fair that decisions on family wealth falls into the hands of those who fuel the flames of marital disputes?

Second Families

It is increasingly common to run across wealth owners on their second, third, or subsequent marriages or similar relationships, often involving children from more than one spouse, and a set of complex emotional and legal issues that arise. When a wealth-owning parent remarries or establishes a new or additional long-term relationship, there are many financial and psychological consequences, and it is rare to find families that actually manage to avoid all of the potential pitfalls.

The issue of second families does not affect every family, but is an example of a need that can be specific to a particular family, requiring special consideration.

One of the biggest issues that often arises in relation to new marriages and relationships is the consequences of the break-up of earlier relationships. While second (and further) marriages often arise after the passing of a spouse, when the widow or widower begins a new relationship, there are many cases where the earlier spouse is being effectively "replaced" by another.

A first clear lesson to be learned from the bad experiences of others is the vengeful way in which marriages can break up when a second relationship is looming. I have worked with several families where, in earlier and happier times, spouses were brought into family business and related meetings, were provided with full detail on family and business assets, and were, as a result, equipped with information and materials that helped them to make the divorce process both difficult and expensive.

While it sounds mean to think of the worst – that a relationship will break up – in today's world it is only prudent to help families consider minimizing the potential risks that come with spouses being too involved in what might rightfully be viewed as an inappropriate area. In-laws can and do have very important roles in wealth-owning families, and in many cases contribute hugely to the continuity of family businesses and otherwise. But where relationships are at an early (and more fragile) stage, giving thought to what a spouse should know and participate in is something that is at least worth some consideration and discussion.

The risks, in my experience, are even greater in the case of second, third, and further relationships, with these relationships all too often pretty clearly linked to economic motivations, as the "older model" is being traded in for the younger. Bringing the new spouse into knowing too much, and being too involved, can not only be dangerous in terms of what may happen if that relationship breaks up, but can be particularly destructive of family relationships given how the wealth owner's children will feel about the new partner of their parent, particularly when the other parent is still alive.

Second and further marriages often cause more issues within families than the wealth owner establishing the new relationship thinks. The wealth owner often ends up in a difficult situation that jeopardizes not only the well-being of his children, but also the chances of success in his new relationship. As a believer that money comes into the picture in every relationship (because everyone is a gold-digger, at least to some extent), recognizing this is a first step toward finding approaches to help the process not be a destructive one.

A very common pattern is where a wealth owner has a close relationship with his children, and his marriage comes to an end – either on divorce or the death of the wealth owner's spouse. The close relationship between the wealth owner and his children is challenged when the wealth owner begins to establish new relationships, and particularly as a new relationship moves to a second marriage or co-habitation. Money inevitably becomes an issue. Often the wealth owner doesn't really want or need to marry again, but the new companion is the one putting on pressure to formalize the relationship.

While there are many cases where children would want to see their widowed parent happy in a new relationship, unless the financial situation is clear, it is difficult for a new spouse to be accepted, particularly where the new spouse may be younger than the children of the wealth owner and where they may have a clearer perception of the financial objectives of the new spouse than their father or mother has. The wealth-owning parent likely has a different view of their new spouse, and faces difficult initial conflicts between their new spouse and the children of their previous marriage.

If financial issues are not clearly dealt with at the outset, there is huge potential for unhappiness, uncertainty, and danger. The relationship between the new spouse and the children will be strained, and this may cause the new spouse and the children to both focus on money more than they should. Over time, the new spouse will inevitably exercise more and more influence over the wealth owner, asking for gifts and insisting on provisions for the future that take up bigger and bigger shares of the family wealth. Family businesses may be at risk. Tensions increase, and families and relationships are destroyed.

The approach that I advocate is to ensure that financial arrangements and understandings in and around a new marriage or co-habitation relationship are made clear at the very outset. Depending on how this is done and when, it may be possible to engineer an approach that not only keeps everyone happy, but also provides a foundation for strong and supportive long-term relationships between all involved. Ideally, the discussions should take place before the marriage, so the new spouse goes into the relationship with clarity on what he or she should expect should the new marriage come to an end on divorce or death. For the wealth owner, having this discussion upfront and agreeing the arrangements may be unromantic and challenging, but it is a good way to make sure that the issue of money is dealt with in advance and in a way that hopefully avoids a lifetime of effort by the new spouse to worm his or her way into getting more. Quite common here would be a pre-nuptial agreement that might provide relatively modest amounts if the marriage lasts only a short time and increasing amounts otherwise, but the key here is for clarity upfront.

And the safest approach to benefit the children and protect their interests is to consider making arrangements for them clear as well, with at least some assets being transferred to them, if not at the time of the new marriage, then into trusts or other structures designed to assure that there are no circumstances under which the wealth owner, coming under pressure from their new spouse, could compromise what has been assured will go to the children. In other words, this does not necessarily mean that the children get a large amount right away or that the wealth owner is no longer able to make investment and other decisions. What it does mean is that the wealth owner makes an irrevocable commitment to what the children will eventually get, and what part of the assets should remain under the control and at the discretion of the wealth owner.

While this approach means that the wealth owner is giving up at least a portion, and perhaps a large portion, of their wealth (if not their administration of it), the upside is great. If the new spouse knows what he or she will be getting out of the deal upfront, money is off the table, and the new marriage can progress with a focus on the well-being of the couple and their long-term happiness. And as to the children of the wealth owner, knowing what they will be getting and that their new step-parent has no ability to affect this in the future, even if their parent becomes increasingly dependent on the new spouse, increases the chance of the relationship between the children and the new spouse developing in a positive way.

Whilst I cannot say that these steps will always address the bad feelings that can arise within families where there are second, third, fourth, and further marriages, I do believe that the approach can much reduce the unspoken concerns of the younger generation and avoid some of the bad feelings that can grow between children and their step-parents. As to the new spouse, I like to believe that clarity on what he or she will ultimately get will help move money "off the table" in the relationship – hopefully, with the economics clear, the new spouse will not be spending time "working" their new partner as he or she ages, trying to get more and more than was initially planned, a scenario which is all too often the case. And the upfront discussion of money allows the new spouse to evaluate whether they want to go ahead with the marriage under the terms on offer. If all works out, the wealth owner's children will understand the arrangements and weigh in on the marriage, and perhaps can celebrate that their parent has someone to spend their later years with and who, potentially, could help with the support of a parent they care deeply about.

There are many, many other issues that accompany the "second family" situation, and disability is one of them. If a wealth owner becomes disabled (including falling into dementia in old age), who will call the shots on his or her assets? In the case of an aging wealth owner who enters a new marriage, the new young spouse may be the one the law will put in charge. In the absence of the advance planning that I advocate, will this be a comfortable situation for the wealth owner's children? Could this fuel costly and destructive disputes?

In second and subsequent family situations, also relevant is who gets the personal effects – family photos, heirlooms, and other items. Should a new spouse get family albums that have childhood photos of step-children and a previous spouse? What if the albums are in the home the deceased wealth owner shares with his new spouse? Is the home and its contents, going under the control of the new spouse, creating potential friction? Asking all of the relevant "what-ifs" is crucial to an effective asset and succession plan, particularly where there is a new family.

Financial and psychological issues can be even more severe where the second family involves children – whether step-children given that the new spouse is also divorced or widowed, or a new set of natural children. Should all the children be treated equally, or are the children of the first marriage to be favored? There are no magic answers, as each family situation is different. For me, the crucial thing is for decisions to be made and reviewed on an ongoing basis, and ideally for the real wishes of the wealth owner to be implemented – not approaches to be developed over time based on who in the family puts the greater pressure on the wealth owner. And all too often, because little in the way of thinking takes place, the wealth owner dies or becomes disabled before they have put a well-thought-out plan in place, leaving it to the law of the relevant jurisdictions to work out who gets what.

Second and further families include relationships with mistresses and toy-boys, a topic discussed earlier, and which also brings into the picture the question of illegitimate children. Many surprises can emerge where there are illegitimate children. Some trusts exclude them from benefit; others include them. Does the wealth owner know what his trust provides? Is it what he intends? And under the laws of some places in the world, California being an example, an illegitimate child is actually entitled to get what his legitimate siblings get.

A wealth owner may leave everything to his two legitimate children and nothing to an illegitimate child, but this may only lead to costly and destructive litigation that the illegitimate child, if well advised, will undertake.

Multi-jurisdictional Families

The world is getting smaller, and it is increasingly common to find wealth-owning families whose members are living in different countries, holding a variety of citizenships, and coming under the tax and other laws of the various countries to which they are connected. It is very hard to predict where one's children will ultimately study, live, and work – and as a result, understanding the issues that multi-jurisdictional families face is another need that all wealth-owning families have.

A parent living in Singapore and holding Singaporean citizenship may have a daughter who is a US citizen and/or resident. Rather than fearing complexity, the cross-border world is one that allows for a number of tax and other benefits if carefully navigated. Because a US person can generally receive assets tax free (albeit with reporting requirements depending on the source of the assets and the amounts involved), there are many tax advantages that careful planning can result in when there are US taxpayers in the younger generation. And when some of the children live in yet another country, while this adds complexity, it may also add opportunity. One example is that income accumulated in certain foreign trusts can give rise to punitive tax rates when distributed to a US beneficiary; capitalizing that income and first distributing it to a Canadian-resident family member might allow for tax-free distributions from the relevant trust to both the Canadian resident and, subsequently, the US beneficiaries if properly handled. While the only thing to be sure of is that the tax and other rules constantly change, part of what a wealth owner needs is the ability to take advantage of a multi-jurisdictional family, and the benefits that diversification of residence and citizenship locations can provide.

The issues are not only tax related, and as discussed elsewhere in this book, places of residence and citizenship can affect everything from the ability of creditors to have access to assets, exposure to political risk, and many other things.

Of course, it is impossible to find any advisor who has all the answers, particularly if multiple countries are involved. An effective advisor, however, is one who is able to raise the right questions, helping to navigate complexity and recognizing that a multi-jurisdictional family may be able to find opportunity in their exposure to different legal and tax systems.

Changing Demographics

We are fortunate to benefit from the ability to live much longer than was the case in the past. Medical care is improving, and individuals are in a much better position than they used to be to understand the lifestyle and other choices that impact their lifespan. But when one lives to 80, 90, 100, or more, this has an impact on the succession process, and brings with it a number of issues that need consideration by all wealth-owning families.

The traditional approach to succession has and continues to be to arrange for a will, supplemented by other tools, such as trusts and insurance arrangements, all of which are oriented to passing wealth on at the death of the wealth owner. The wealth might move to a surviving spouse who lives for a further number of years, and on the second death moves to the "younger" generation. But with many living much longer than they used to, is this traditional approach really the right one, and is it safe?

One of the first important considerations is whether it makes sense for "children" to be inheriting at the age of 60 or 70, as may be the case if their parents live to 90 or 100. And if the younger generation pre-decease their parents, the planning done for grandchildren and further generations may not have adequately reflected the input of the parents of the beneficiaries, the generation below the aged wealth owner.

It may well be that the older generation would prefer to hold on to what they have for good reason and to not benefit their children – this is fine, and a personal choice, but it is a good thing to make the approach clear to your children so they know that they should not be waiting a lifetime for something to come to them. The difficult family situation of Brooke Astor, discussed at the beginning of this book, provides a good example of the problems that can happen. By the time Brooke Astor, a wealthy philanthropist, died, she was well over 100 years old. Her son, who was over 80 at the time of her death, had taken advantage of her growing dementia, making use of his mother's assets, and encouraging her to change her will when she did not have the mental capacity to do so. While the son, who was imprisoned for his actions, was clearly a wrong-doer, perhaps the problems of the family could have been reduced had there been greater dialogue between Brooke Astor and her son regarding her intentions in relation to her assets, and the need for her son to do more to make his own way. Had Brooke Astor gifted to her son, early on, part of the inheritance she did provide, might this not only have benefitted her son, but also encouraged him to take better care of his mother in her last years?

But if we give part of our assets to our children long before our death, will there be enough left to ensure a comfortable retirement, and provision for every eventuality? Can I trust my children to take care of me in my old age? Given that my philosophy is not to trust anyone, perhaps it is dangerous to give too much away to children or a younger spouse early on, as you never know what can happen. Even if your child can be trusted, which I optimistically assume to be the case, what if he dies without provision to protect you, resulting in the child's wealth passing to a spouse who then remarries and creates a new family? Living a long life is a good thing, but succession plans need to adapt to new realities. One family I know involved a wealth owner who remarried, and established a trust that provided for his new, younger wife to be protected financially on his death by receiving the trust income for her life, with the balance of trust assets, on the death of his wife, going to his children. A fair and appropriate approach, but in the circumstance, the younger wife, after the death of the wealth owner, is still alive and well at 92, and the wealth owner's children, some of whom are now in their 70s, and who could use some money, have still not inherited given that the arrangement does not benefit them until their stepmother passes away.

Using trusts and other structures, it is possible for a wealth owner to protect themselves, at least in part, from some of the issues that living longer give rise to. I can establish a trust that sets aside a portion of assets determined to be sufficient to cover my needs and more for my entire life, howsoever long I may live. The balance of assets might also be held in trust, with set conditions and times for access by my children, but with thought given to protecting against more coming out of the trust than my children should have, meaning that if a child pre-deceases me, for example, the remaining assets will not immediately go to a surviving spouse, but perhaps revert to be held for the older generation and eventually grandchildren or others who are intended to benefit.

Planning in view of the possibility of living much longer than was the case in the past is also important as a means of addressing some of the real issues aging wealth owners face. It is sadly common to see the elderly suffering from forms of dementia, first not remembering where they left their possessions, and soon developing a form of paranoia, suspecting staff and family of stealing their possessions. Money becomes something to hang on to, with a sense developing that it is the tie that keeps the younger generation coming to visit.

I encourage the families I work with to discuss these dynamics openly at an early stage of their planning, and to clarify the approach that works best for succession in the context of their family. For me, the objective should be to ensure that the last 20 years of a long life are as free as they can be from ongoing discussions about money and succession. There is always a need for review of the succession plan, and reflection of inevitable change in the regulatory world and within the family, but the more succession plans are discussed and agreed within the family very early on, the more likely that wealth will not become destructive.

Family Conflict Resolution

Most of the older generations I have worked with over the years wear rose-colored glasses, and believe that their children (and presumably grandchildren and further generations) will all love each other and get along famously, working together and looking after each other. Sadly, and this crosses all cultures I have run across, it is far from always the case that the younger generation get along, let alone look after each other's interests.

Developing mechanisms for the resolution of family conflict is clearly a need that all families have.

Where there is a family business, it is more often the case that governance approaches are put in place to deal with the disputes that can arise. But too often, where the assets do not involve an active business, little if any attention is paid to how to resolve a potential dispute.

Whatever the vehicle used for the succession of assets from one generation to the next, be it a trust, company, partnership, or otherwise, thought needs to be given to whether it is really important for the assets to remain together. Permitting a division of assets in specified circumstances can often avoid many problems.

It is a nice thing for families to invest together, and there can be significant benefits to them doing so, but if the relevant stakeholders cannot get along, is trying to keep them together going to do more harm than good? Given that splitting things up does not necessarily mean that each family member has immediate access to all the assets (such as where trusts are used), allowing family members to go their own way might be better than encouraging bad feeling and, possibly, costly litigation. But even before contemplating any sort of division of assets should be the establishment of procedures for how disputes might be resolved, and by whom. And, like virtually everything else in relation to succession, the more the dispute-resolution approach is discussed and agreed among family members, the more likely it will be respected by them and work.

Business Succession and Family Constitutions

While not all families are involved in active businesses, the succession issues business-owning families have to deal with are highly relevant to all families and bring to light areas of need that all families must address. And family constitutions, which are increasingly used as part of the succession process, are not only relevant to families that have businesses passing from one generation to the next.

Much more information and education on effective business succession is available to the wealth owner than is available on the many other issues wealth-owning families face. Business schools around the world provide training to the younger generation, and many advisors focus on the issues in and around family business governance and structures.

What I find, however, is that the education available to wealth-owning families tends to be focused on education of those who will succeed in the management of a family business. Insufficient education is available to those family members who may not become managers of the family business, but who need coaching on how to become an effective *owner* of a family business. And related to this is that for families that do not have a family business, but rather a portfolio of investment assets, there is again a lack of effective and thoughtful training and education available. But where assets are investment assets rather than ownership interests in a business, many of the issues involved are the same, given that real success comes from an approach that is akin to owning a business – being equipped with what it takes to ask the right questions of those managing the business or the assets, and understanding the rights and responsibilities of an owner. Succession in family businesses and family investment assets requires real preparation of the younger generation (and of spouses who may become successors), as well as ensuring that the right governance approaches are in place.

A key starting point in looking at family businesses and succession is to recognize that when the founder of the business is alive and well and running the business, there is less need for governance and structure than is the case as the business passes through the generations. The founder of the business knows almost everything that is going on, and has a tight rein on things. The founder is entrepreneurial and driven, and in control of the business. As the business moves to the second, third, and further generations, whether or not the same level of entrepreneurial drive exists as did during the founder's time will be an issue. Certainly the control of the founder is no longer there, and these factors make the need for family governance critical – the use of structures and approaches designed to allow a business to thrive as it navigates generational change.

One family that I worked with a number of years ago provides a good example to highlight some of the many issues that business-owning families face. Interestingly, as is sometimes the case, it was not the older generation of the family that had involved me and other advisors in their planning process, but rather members of the younger generation who realized that unless their parents would undertake more in the way of sophisticated planning, the business of the family, and the family itself, would be at risk. Three members of the younger generation, in their 40s and 50s, took the lead to try to sort things out for their family, something they ended up doing very successfully.

The business in issue was one that had been established by a single individual, the grandfather of the generation that had approached me. Grandfather started a manufacturing business, and successfully built it up. Grandfather had five sons, but died at a very early age, just before reaching 50. At the time of his death, only one of his five sons was over 20 years old, and that oldest son took over his father's business. As his four brothers reached an appropriate age, they joined the family business, and the five brothers eventually worked extraordinarily well together, building the manufacturing business into a global conglomerate, with operations in several countries and diversifying into a number of areas, ranging from banking to retail businesses and property development.

Trusting each other, the five brothers did not pay much attention to how the family business was owned, and given the political and other dynamics of their home country, went to some lengths to ensure that not all their business or personal assets were in one single structure or in the ownership of any one of the brothers. As the global business developed, particular businesses were owned by one brother, other businesses by another; there were bank accounts in Switzerland and elsewhere in the name of one of the brothers, and certain properties in the name of another. But the assets involved were considered to be the assets of all five, treated by them as part of one family business.

All five brothers themselves had children and many, but not all, of them were active in the family business. In some cases, the spouses of the children were employed by the business. The children, being in their 40s and 50s, themselves had children, making it clear that the question of business and asset succession was going to become more and more difficult, with the growing population of family members, particularly in the younger generation.

The wake-up call for the family came when the oldest brother of the five passed away. After his death, his children sought to clarify what they were about to inherit, and they put forward the legally valid position that they (and their surviving mother) were entitled to the assets that had been legally owned by their father. The four surviving brothers disagreed, and pointed out that while the five brothers had owned the business and other assets of the family in an unorganized way, the family always treated the assets as the assets of the family as a whole, and not as the assets of any one family member, despite how the assets were legally owned. Fortunately, the four brothers were able to convince their nieces and nephews that the family and the family business would benefit from a structured succession approach. The first step for the family was to develop a family constitution.

Family constitutions are increasingly used by families, not only those with a family business, to set out a framework for the more detailed planning that will subsequently take place. One of the biggest benefits of a family constitution is not the constitution itself, but the process of family engagement and discussion that implementing a family constitution results in. What a family constitution covers may vary significantly, but can include many items that are important for business-owning families to consider. And family constitutions, and the areas they cover, are very relevant to families who may only own passive assets, and not actually be in businesses that are to pass from one generation to the next.

In most cases, while family members sign the relevant family constitution, it is not a legally binding document. Rather, the constitution is then used as the basis for creating binding documents that can include partnership and shareholder agreements, trust or foundation structures, and other arrangements that do provide legal rights and responsibilities.

These are a few of the many items a well-thought-out family constitution might contain:

- *Background on the Family and Family Business.* While the family may know its own history well, thinking about how the family business started, the values of the founder of the business, and the family origins can be a useful starting point for the constitution and for the family discussions that putting the constitution in place will require.
- *Mission and Vision.* Drawing on the history of the family business, the objectives of the family can be laid out, covering what the family hopes to achieve for the benefit of the family, the family business, the employees, and the communities in which the family lives and operates.
- *Family Governance.* While related to the governance of businesses and assets, apart from the structures used to own assets, families can consider how the family itself will be involved in its own governance. Typically, a family council or similar body will be established, and procedures set out for who in the family will populate the council, how decisions will be made, and how family council members can be appointed and replaced. Often the family council is elected by a family assembly, and issues relating to assembly meetings, votes, and other matters will be covered as part of the governance approach. A key issue for families is the question of the extent to which spouses participate in family meetings and overall governance. If this is not made clear, difficulties can arise later, as the discussion of the issue of whether spouses should attend family meetings can become personal in the sense that the discussion becomes about a particular spouse, affecting family relationships and otherwise. If Dad remarries, should he be able to bring along his

new, young wife to a family meeting despite the fact that the children and grandchildren are disturbed about the divorce of their parents, and Dad's choice of new partner? Should a son or daughter-in-law be excluded from participating despite the fact that they are successfully involved in and contributing to the family business, and are clearly responsible for raising the next generation of family members?

- *Who are Family Members?* Apart from spouses, upfront consideration of how the family views step-children, adopted children, and others is important, and ideally the issues should be discussed before specific questions arise about specific family members, a potentially emotional and divisive issue.
- *Family Assets and Who Really Owns Them.* A critical issue for families to consider is the extent to which members of the younger generation are meant to be owners of assets or custodians of assets for further generations. Often, when I ask the younger generation about this, they think they are the owners of the assets they inherit, and that they are free to do with those assets what they want. When I ask the older generation, they are often much more oriented toward viewing their children as stewards of family assets and the family business – taking over their management, helping to preserve and grow the business for the benefit of further generations of the family. If assets pass to the younger generation before the question of stewardship versus ownership is addressed, it is often too late to ensure that the values and expectations of the older generation are respected. Can your daughter sell the Picasso that your father left to you, and which you hoped would stay in the family? Or should she enjoy it and live within her means, leaving the painting to the next generation to also enjoy?
- *Family Values.* While family values have to be part of the upbringing of children, setting out the values of the family in writing is often a good way of cementing the approach to business and wealth that the family is committed to. In the media and elsewhere, wealth owners are looked at as the "rich" and there is a caricature of the wealth owner living a lavish lifestyle, splashing money around and with the younger generation in the families involved living a spoiled and pampered life, getting all the material things they want and spending apace. There are certainly many who fit the caricature, but in my experience

there are many, many more wealth owners who take responsibility for the wealth and businesses they own, and who understand that material possessions and a lavish lifestyle do not bring happiness and harmony to them or to their families. I work with a number of families at the more extreme levels of wealth who live surprisingly modest lifestyles, and happily so, and whose children are brought up to understand that an upper-middle-class, comfortable lifestyle may be more appropriate and fulfilling than a life of private jets and yachts. Discussing family values and reflecting them in the family constitution is part of the process of helping the family to agree on the principles they wish to live by.

- *Family Education.* There are many elements of education that are important for wealth-owning families to consider, including the background that might be needed for those family members who want to join the family business. The constitution can also lay out how the family will support educational costs, and not only for university and otherwise, but also for specialized programs offered by business schools and others which are designed to prepare the younger generation for their responsibilities as wealth and business owners. In a number of families (and also in the education programs offered by many universities to business-owning families) there is not enough emphasis on training not only those who will be involved in managing a family business, but also those who will become owners of a family business. How to read a balance sheet, be an effective board member, ask the right questions of executives running a business... these are some of the many skills that need to be learned by those who will be effective owners of a family business.

- *Employment Policies.* Should every member of the family (and maybe their spouses) have a right to work in the family business? Addressing the employment policies associated with family members working in the family business is a key area for a family to address, recognizing that the question of who is right to work in a family business will give rise to much in the way of potential unhappiness. Successful family businesses have clear guidelines as to expectations regarding the backgrounds of those family members who want to work in the family business, including educational requirements and, often, minimum levels of experience working outside of the family business. The issue of employment of family members can be so difficult for family businesses that have passed through several generations, that some families adopt the policy of having *no* family members managing their businesses, using only professional managers who are not family members. Instead, the focus of the family is on preparing the younger generation to be effective owners of the family business, and on governance structures to deal with issues in and around ownership of the family business.

- *Expenses and Use of Family Assets.* The constitution should also consider the extent to which some expenses of the family may be communalized, and related to this is the extent to which communally owned assets, such as a family house, boat, or otherwise, will be used and paid for. Can family members use a ski chalet owned by the family freely? Can they offer it to their friends? What are the financial arrangements? If none of these things are considered and discussed, there is much room for dispute as one family member makes more use than another of a family asset, and incurs expenses that the overall family is responsible for.

- *Social Responsibility and Philanthropy.* The family constitution is a good place to set out the family's views on responsible investing and philanthropy, and family values in relation to the family business, and its importance to non-family stakeholders, such as employees and the communities in which they live and work.

- *Entrepreneurial Children, Competition, and the Role of a Family "Bank."* Where there is a family business, families often focus on the many issues they need to consider in ensuring that the younger generation are well prepared to be involved in the business. What many families are less well prepared for are the challenges that having a particularly entrepreneurial child can raise, and how to encourage and develop the entrepreneurial objectives of the younger generation. I worked with a family where one of the children, supported by his father both emotionally and financially, started an online business in the same area as the "bricks-and-mortar" family business. Over the years, online activities became very important for the future growth of the family business, and the fact that a close family member was competing with the family business became both problematic for the business and divisive for the family as siblings and others adopted the view that their brother had built a valuable business using family resources, contacts, and more. Eventually the problem was addressed through a buyout of the son's online business, and bringing him back into the family business, but the example shows the need to address whether the younger generation can compete with the family business, and also who should own new businesses that the younger generation may develop on their own, but with financial support from the family. A family "bank" might be a good approach to consider as a means of providing financing to the younger generation for a venture they want to undertake on their own. This does not require the establishment of a formal bank, but would involve setting out how decisions will be made on whether or not to fund a venture someone in the family wants to undertake and, if so, on what terms. This can be by way of a loan, where the entrepreneur owns the new business they establish, but repays the family, with interest, for the help. But what if the business fails? And if the loan is unsecured and the business succeeds, should the return to the family be more than just a low interest rate? Perhaps more fair would be that the family obtains a minority stake in the new business or investment. Having a "family bank" approach allows for a structured path to make decisions about supporting family members in their efforts to establish new businesses outside the framework of the original family business, and what is meant to be kept together. Less critical than the actual formula used is to ensure that the issues are discussed, and that there is a perception of fairness to the approach that the family buys into. Perhaps the family can invest in a business a child wants to get involved in by lending 80% of the funds needed, and investing the other 20% as equity. If the business succeeds, the family owns 20% and the child 80%, and the child repays the debt. If the business fails, the family loses the 20% equity investment and, while the loan is not repaid, the amount involved comes out of the future share of family wealth the child would have ultimately received.

- *Compensating Family Members Involved in the Family Business.* A thorny issue that business-owning families face, and which the family constitution should discuss, is how family members will be rewarded for the work they do in a family business. How should a daughter be rewarded if she takes on the leadership of a family business that she inherits 50/50 with her brother, a successful doctor, who, while supportive of his sister, is not directly involved in the business? I usually advise families to consider treating their children equally, so would support the idea of the 50/50 share split in relation to the family business, and for the daughter running the business, her being compensated as she would be if she were working outside the family business in a similar role. This might require discussions with compensation specialists, and agreements on bonus and phantom stock arrangements to reflect the success she achieves. But this does not always work. In one family I was advising, the reaction to my proposed approach of the older son, who had begun to take things over from his father, was that if he did not directly own a meaningful stake of the company disproportionate to his siblings not leading the business, he would leave. His view was that he did not want to work for his siblings, and as an entrepreneur, wanted an entrepreneur's return for his efforts. So there are no magic answers on how to make this work, but it is best to have discussions and arrangements broadly in place upfront, and here developing the language to be used in a family constitution can be helpful in directing the attention of the family to this important area.

- *Family Mentors.* Through the family constitution or otherwise, considering formally appointing mentors to the younger generation can be most useful whether a family business is involved or not. The work that parents do in guiding their children can be enhanced by others, in or out of the family, being involved as mentors as children move into family business management or ownership roles. Where the dynamics of the family permits, uncles, aunts, and others can be a part of this. Having a formal approach to mentorships can be important and beneficial.

- *Expectations Regarding Pre-nuptial Agreements and Trust Arrangements.* Divorces in the younger generation can have a dramatically negative impact on a family business and family assets generally. Among the planning approaches wealth-owning families can take are well-structured discretionary trusts and, where they are respected under the relevant law, pre-nuptial and post-nuptial agreements. Having the family constitution lay out expectations regarding such arrangements and their being a condition to inheritance is important. Where pre-nuptial planning strategies are agreed upfront within a family, the discussion is unrelated to any particular potential spouse, avoiding the bad feelings that can otherwise result. When the need for pre-nuptial agreements is provided for in a family constitution, and a member of the family is able to explain to a potential spouse that the pre-nuptial arrangement is a prerequisite to being able to participate in the family business and wealth, the pre-nuptial arrangement is an easier one to discuss and put in place.

- *Pruning the Family Tree.* Families that manage to keep their businesses intact over the generations tend to be families that accept that it is almost inevitable that not everyone in the younger generation will see things the same way. Allowing for the likelihood that there will be family members who will not want to participate in and support the family business, and having clear procedures for how to buy out their interests and at what price, has been a key way successful families have managed to keep their businesses in family hands over the generations. While I like to see clear exit procedures, I also like to anticipate the ability of a return to the family business, with procedures that allow members of further generations of a family branch that may have sold out to buy their way back in. Valuations and procedures on this front can be tricky, but are well worth thinking about.

- *Harvesting the Family Business.* I have run across business owners, usually the founders, who sometimes say that they want the business to stay in the family "forever." Well, forever is a very long time, and it is clear that a business that is valuable today may not be particularly valuable in the future. Technologies change, economies change, and businesses change. Effective succession of a family business is often reflected by flexibility in what the family business is seen to be. Governance arrangements that are put in place should provide for procedures to determine when and how elements of the family business can be "harvested" – sold when it makes strategic sense to sell the business, likely with a view to reinvesting the proceeds in new businesses that form the constantly evolving "family business." Businesses and families are dynamic, and the constitution, and background family thinking and discussions, should best accommodate this.

- *Family Retreats.* Connected to the family constitution are usually arrangements for regular, perhaps annual or more frequent, family meetings, involving the "family assembly" or other body, or a more informal get-together of the family to allow the family to not only review its business and wealth, but also work on connecting the family and keeping it connected. As families grow, and businesses move to subsequent generations, more work is needed to keep a family together, and the family retreat becomes a key element of this. Families that hold successful retreats put much thought into their agenda, and many have some sessions that only family members attend, and others where advisors, such as lawyers and trustees, also participate. There are many things that an effective family retreat can achieve, and for families whose assets are simpler than those families seeking to preserve significant family businesses, family retreats are still an important thing to consider to help communicate the succession and asset-protection plan with family members, and to keep them up-to-date on where things are and what to do if the wealth owner dies or becomes disabled.
- *The Family Legacy and Individual Legacies.* The family constitution will often start out with a discussion of the family history and, combined with its focus on the family business and on the family's thinking on philanthropy and social impact, will represent the family legacy. It is often useful to consider, in the preparation of a family constitution and in discussions with family members, what "legacy" really means, and the need for all family members to have the ability to achieve their goals and to be proud of doing so. Success should not be measured by the past business success of the business founder, and for each generation, consideration should be given to what "legacy" really means. The founder of the business sometimes views his or her legacy as the business itself, not always a healthy thing, as this may make it difficult for the founder to let go and transition the business to the younger generation. In some cases, the founder may find himself lost on retiring, staying at the helm of the business until the very last moment, and through his dominance, not adequately preparing the younger generation and

professional managers for the roles that they will have to assume once the founder is no longer around. A founder who feels his legacy is the family business may also be less flexible about "harvesting" the business – selling it at the right strategic time to allow the family business to evolve into other businesses in the future. Here the family constitution and the surrounding discussions can seek to encourage a leading role in the family's philanthropic and related work, and in areas including the mentoring and coaching of the younger generation that help make the concept of legacy a broader one than just the family business the founder established. For family members who did not found the business, having the constitution and family assets permit them develop their own legacies can be important. For the younger generation, it is hard to compete with past success in their family, particularly if the success that the family celebrates is linked to money and not much more. Having the ability to establish their own businesses, art collections, and charitable endeavors can afford the younger generation the opportunity to create their own legacies, with success measured in any number of important ways, including contribution to family reputation, contribution to the community, and otherwise.

Even where a family does not use a family constitution, just thinking about and discussing the issues a typical family constitution covers can be useful.

Doing Good – Philanthropy and Families

Another need of all families relates to philanthropy, and other means of helping others.

Many wealth owners, at one point or another, consider what they can do to help the world, and philanthropy is often the way they achieve this. Related, but different, is a focus on ensuring that investments have a positive impact on society, and an increasing number of investors focus on not only the investment return, but also the impact their investments have on all stakeholders – employees, communities, and more. Blended-value investing, which focuses on bringing value not only to the investor but also to others, is an area of increasing interest for wealth owners.

But doing good is not always easy, and philanthropy, and impact investing, are by no means areas where a wealth owner can just assume that everything will work out right. Sad stories in the area of philanthropy abound, just as they do in relation to the many families destroyed by wealth.

A friend of mine, the head of a trust company in Asia, told me of her involvement, after the fact, with a foundation that had been established by a woman with significant funds she had inherited from her husband. The couple had been childless, and the woman had suffered from cancer, which eventually took her life. Before her passing she arranged for her trusted advisor, an Austrian lawyer, to establish a foundation that he would run and which would receive her assets on her death. The foundation was established to contribute to cancer research. After the death of the woman involved, her assets moved to the foundation and to the control of her Austrian lawyer. The foundation was eventually depleted of all its assets, none of which ever went to cancer research or for any use other than meeting the costs of the Austrian lawyer himself. The foundation funded many luxurious trips the Austrian lawyer and his wife took. While the lawyer occasionally visited cancer research facilities, he never used any of the funds for anything other than his own personal expenditures.

The lesson is not that philanthropy cannot be achieved, or that foundations or Austrian lawyers are bad. Rather, the lesson is that no one should be trusted – not because they are not trustworthy, but because there should always be "checks and balances" in place that limit the ability of someone in a trusted position to abuse the trust placed in them. The wealth owner whose funds went into the foundation had choices when she created the foundation, and among these choices were to take approaches that would ensure that her trusted Austrian lawyer would not have the power to abuse his position the way he did. And that at a minimum, there would be a third party with the job of ensuring that the foundation did what it was meant to do.

Philanthropy has the potential to be a binding force for families, and can also be an important way to establish family legacy apart from a family business or family wealth. It is sometimes difficult to get the younger generation to work together on a family business or family investments. Where the focus is on helping others, getting family members together can be easier to achieve, particularly if work on this is done early on, involving children in philanthropy and its importance when they are young. I sometimes encourage families to consider setting aside a small amount of money for the younger generation to use as part of learning how to be responsible wealth owners. At a family retreat, it can be fun to get the younger generation together – say children between 10 and 15 years old – letting them know that a sum of money has been allocated to them that they are responsible for investing. Discussions then take place on investments and how they work, but in a way that the younger generation can relate to. Why does McDonald's do better when there are difficult economies and people have to save money? Why are restaurant chains focusing on healthy food showing success? I ask a group of children about PlayStations as against the Nintendo Wii, or more current new products. Inevitably, imaginations are captured, and with the help of investment specialists we can discuss companies that the younger generation can relate to, helping them come to choices on how to invest the money that has been allocated for the purpose.

A year later, when the family gets together again, we look at the investment performance. Why has Sony increased in value? Why has McDonald's struggled? We look at how much money the investment strategy earned, and now the group has to work together to figure out who to give the profits to. We bring in speakers from various charities – someone can speak about UNICEF and the needs of children in different parts of the world; the World Wildlife Fund and its efforts to save endangered animals; the Make-a-Wish Foundation, and examples of children whose lives they have enhanced. The younger generation learn that there are many, many in need, and limited resources that can be made available to help, and together the younger generation in the family decide how to give money away.

All too often there is strife among the siblings in wealth-owning families, but the difficulties do not, at least yet, extend to their children, cousins who have an opportunity to learn how to work together as a family. A focus on the outside world rather than on the wealth they will keep themselves is a great way to learn responsibility and how to cooperate, and also to learn about investing and many other important skills that will serve them in the future.

Philanthropy can also be a key part of family legacy, itself a difficult and important topic for many wealth-owning families. Mom may have established a successful business, but as she ages, is she obsessed with the business becoming her and her family's legacy? Maybe the business is a great one, but one that at some point should be sold to achieve the best result for the family and the business itself. Will

Mom be lost once the business is sold? If the business passes to the next generation, and one of the sons runs it, is the business his legacy or that of his mother? Will the son have a sense of fulfillment even if he manages to not only be an effective steward of the business but also to grow it substantially? For Mom, getting involved in philanthropy in a serious way can be a means to establish a family legacy that is apart from the family business, and one which she can continue to build and be proud of regardless of whether the family business is sold, or if she hands on the business to her children or others to run. And for a son taking charge of a family business that he did not create, his own philanthropic endeavors can become his personal legacy and represent achievements of his own.

But like other areas of family wealth and businesses, it is not always the case that having family members work together will be successful. There have been many families where philanthropic projects the younger generation have been forced to work on together have been the cause of strife and litigation. And the philanthropic passion of the older generation may not be the passion of the younger. Dad may want to support schools in the village in China that his own father grew up in – how relevant will this be to Dad's children, who may have grown up in the USA or elsewhere, detached from the community Dad's philanthropic venture focuses on?

An interesting approach to philanthropy was taken by the Sainsbury family in England, where a common platform was established to support the philanthropic efforts of the younger generation. Children in the family were given the resources to establish their own charitable structures, focusing on their own passions, but with opportunities to work together with their siblings and other family members arising through their sharing of legal, tax, accounting, implementation, and other resources key to making philanthropic ideas become a reality. The Sainsbury approach shows a way of keeping the younger generation together; doing good in a professional way while encouraging the individual initiatives of the younger generation.

Like all elements of wealth ownership, philanthropy is not easy, and takes work and commitment. There are many philanthropic endeavors that languish, with the younger generation neglecting the opportunity to focus on what can be achieved, leaving funds that could be made available to make a difference sitting passively. There are also many abuses in the world of philanthropy, and perhaps too many examples of families trying to do things on their own.

Sometimes it is much, much more effective to cooperate with others in philanthropic efforts, and using advisors who have experience and who know the right questions to ask can be key.

A group of advisors that I work with mentioned to me one of their clients who wanted to establish a health clinic in Peru as part of their charitable endeavor. The advisors, hired by the family, traveled to the relevant community and found that there was a public clinic pretty much across the street from the clinic that was to be established by their client. When they asked the family why they were setting up a "competing" clinic so close by, they were told that the family found the public clinic inadequate. The advisors explored the management of the public clinic and ended up recommending that more good would be achieved if the family contributed to the public clinic, and helped it up its game – something that was ultimately done for the good of the community involved in Peru, and which facilitated an easier and more effective approach to doing good.

Tax also comes into the charitable world, and tax laws around the world are not yet where they need to be to reflect the reality that our world is getting smaller and smaller. In many countries, tax deductions are provided where there is charitable giving, but those deductions properly focus on giving to real charities, and controls are established to ensure that this is the case. All too often, though, tax laws require that charities be based in the same country to be easily approved, meaning that a wealth owner resident in one country may find it difficult to give to a charity in the country of origin of, say, their parents. Cross-border giving is a complex area, and while solutions are emerging, careful navigation of the tax laws is necessary to ensure that tax deductions are maximized, permitting more to go to the charitable destination the family has in mind. The King Baudouin Foundation in Belgium is one of the players working on encouraging cross-border giving and lobbying for change in tax laws to facilitate the reality that need is not only in the country in which wealth owners may reside.

On the tax front, there are also some interesting bigger-picture issues for wealth-owning families to consider. Where the wealth owner lives in a country with a significant inheritance tax, leaving money to children may come at a significant tax cost. $100,000 left to a child may leave the child with, say, $60,000 to give to charity if a 40% inheritance tax applies. But if donations to charity are exempt from inheritance tax, as they often are, instead of leaving the

$100,000 to her daughter, Mom can ask her daughter to administer a charitable fund Mom sets up with the $100,000 – now making considerably more available for the charitable endeavor.

Where there is a family business, more in the way of tax efficiencies can be achieved. If the wealth owner lives in a low or no-tax country, giving money away may not achieve much in the way of tax deductions. But if the same wealth owner owns a business that operates in various countries and includes subsidiaries in higher-tax countries, maybe having one of the companies in a higher-tax country make the charitable contribution will allow for a significant tax deduction, again allowing more funds to be available to do good. Maybe paying tax is also a form of doing good, but it is a less direct way of orienting funds to where they need to go.

Thomas Piketty is a French economist and major advocate of high inheritance taxes to address, among others, wealth and income inequality. I agree with the notion that those with wealth have a responsibility to make the world a fairer place. But I am more comfortable with the wealth owner having the ability to drive the philanthropic process themselves… giving money away directly rather than giving the money to governments in the form of higher taxes, hoping that the governments will be efficient in their use of higher tax collections. I am not a believer that governments will always get it right.

Creative tax thinking in the charity area can be a beneficial thing. Another example of tax-efficient giving would be a family that invests internationally and reviews what taxes are "left on the table." The family may be one that gives meaningful amounts without tax benefit being obtained, possibly because the family is resident in a country with low or no taxation, such as would be the case for a family based in a number of countries in the Middle East. Tax may not form part of their thinking, but if they review their global investment portfolio, there may be withholding taxes on, say, dividends from high-tax countries that are incurred on a regular basis. Withholding taxes on dividends, in the absence of tax treaties having application, can be high – in Canada, withholding taxes are imposed at the rate of 25% of dividends; in the USA, at the rate of 30% and in Switzerland, at the rate of 35%. What if the family involved creates a structure, such as a partnership, which allocates dividend flows to charities? If properly structured, withholding taxes can be eliminated given charitable exemptions from the withholding tax, meaning that the amount available to be given to charity will be substantially increased.

Blended value and impact investing are not charity, but involve focusing on investments that are not only responsible investments, but which provide returns that go beyond investment returns to the wealth-owning family. All stakeholders, from employees to the communities in which a business operates, can be beneficiaries of well-thought-out investments, and more and more thinking is being done in this area. It is not always easy to measure returns beyond investment returns, but work is being done on this, and there are many, including Jed Emerson in the USA – one of the leading thinkers on blended value – who are working on it.

Blended value can also relate to venture philanthropy that benefits a business, not new thinking, but thinking that has, to some extent, been lost. There was a time, in Chinese traditional family businesses, for example, when the business worried about the education, health, and further care of its workers. A factory would be built in a new community, and as part of the project, the business would establish homes for workers, schools, hospitals, and would take care of the workers in their retirement. Has the world moved too far in businesses focusing only on short-term profits and lining the pockets of managers and shareholders, leaving it to the vagaries of governments to look after their workers and communities? Has the US healthcare system prior to the Obama government shown an example of success in caring for all stakeholders? Is the US education system, with its costly private universities that limit access to those without resources, the best way to encourage upward mobility? Wealth-owning families can, should, and do think about these things, and also how doing good can actually be good for their businesses in the long term.

Privacy and Confidentiality

It is sad (and dangerous) to see how moves to tax transparency, driven by abuses of bank secrecy and otherwise, are compromising the human right to privacy and the ability of wealth-owning families to keep their affairs confidential. It is a pity that countries that were once the champions of privacy have been shown to have abused their positions, permitting the misuse of bank secrecy and other regimes to facilitate tax evasion and to shield the identities of, among others, corrupt politicians and other criminals.

The world now lacks a real champion of the human right to privacy, and this leaves the wealth-owning family to its own devices to find the right investment and asset-ownership structures that allow for full tax and other legal compliance while retaining the privacy and confidentiality that wealth owners need and deserve.

Privacy is a need that all families share, and apart from the question of tax-related reporting obligations comes the question of whether and to what extent how families themselves operate and act affects the ability of a family to maintain privacy in relation to family assets and approaches to asset protection and succession.

Privacy is a human right, and for all wealth-owning families can be essential to the family's safety and security. This is certainly the case where families are connected to countries with significant political risk, or where corruption and other dangers are rife. But even where the countries to which a family is connected are developed and relatively "safe," privacy remains an important and legitimate need. Is it ever safe for a wealth-owning family to have information about their wealth available to the public and for access to be provided on the location of homes and other personal details?

As covered earlier, the tax landscape is fast changing, and automatic exchange of information and other initiatives are transforming the ability of governments to have information on the income and assets of wealth owners connected to their countries. Tax compliance for today's families is critical, and as a result, your government being aware of your income and assets should not be a problem. If it is, a family should be considering what steps to take to ensure that they can maintain privacy while being compliant. This might involve use of ownership structures for assets and businesses that legally avoid reporting or taking advantage of mobility and the ability of some or all of the family to relocate, and to be based in countries where governments can be trusted to not misuse the information they have. And while there are many initiatives developing that contemplate public ownership registers, there are, fortunately, a number of reasonable voices cautioning against information being made available other than to those who need to know. Tax authorities knowing about one's assets and income is one thing – having the press or other "interested parties" having the ability to access information is not only unsafe, it is simply not right.

So, for wealth-owning families, having a privacy "audit" is increasingly an important need. Understanding who has what information on the family and its assets, and what the family can do to legally ensure that information only goes where it is necessary to go, is essential.

Apart from the world of taxation and related reporting requirements, there are many other issues relevant to privacy that families need to consider and address. This includes the development of policies within a family about the use of social media and also how family members act in public, including in relation to their consumption and other habits. Educating the younger generation about keeping a low profile and the dangers of information falling into the wrong hands is important, and in an increasingly complex and challenging world, a critical part of helping families to avoid wealth being a destructive force.

Investments, Liquidity, and the Diversification of Ownership Structures

A clear need of every wealth-owning family is to have the right structures in place to permit investments to be made, something that requires thought and reflection on a number of issues.

Tax efficiency is clearly important, and understanding the tax systems relevant to an investment is key. Getting into an investment may be easy, but care needs to be taken to work out the eventual exit, and the possible tax costs that may arise.

The first step is always to look at the tax system relevant to the wealth owner personally, and how this affects taxes arising at every step of the investment process, as well as on realization of the investment or on transfer of the investment on death or by way of gift to family members or others. Tax exposures in the country or countries where the investment structure may itself be located will also be relevant and, of course, taxes in the country in which the investment is made. Finding the right investment approach requires looking at the rules in all relevant jurisdictions, and the starting point is almost always the home country of the investor. Access to tax treaties, maintaining the ability to take advantage of tax exemptions, foreign tax credits, and otherwise all come into the mix.

With increasing tax transparency, rules are fast developing in relation to information exchange, much of which will be automatic. Intermediaries such as banks and trustees have the responsibility to exchange information, making countries aware of who the beneficial owners of assets are. Other forms of exchange of information are extending to information on how profits are allocated between jurisdictions, allowing each to capture what their rules consider to be that country's fair share of taxation.

While wealth owners need to become comfortable with the notion that governments will know what they are doing, a key need of families is to have a clear understanding of which governments get what information. In a world where not every country has tax and legal systems that can be trusted, knowing where one's financial details are going is vital. Something I often suggest to families is that they determine how the investment and asset-holding structures they use will impact information disclosure, noting that keeping assets in separate baskets can sometimes help manage the risks associated with more information flowing than actually needs to flow.

Most wealth owners understand very well the need to diversify investments in order to reduce risk; fewer understand the value of diversifying ownership structures. The reality is that information disclosure and risk can also be managed through a diversification of ownership structures. A simple example can be made in relation to protecting assets from divorce claims in the younger generation. As mentioned earlier, in many legal systems, a spouse may have a claim over assets that are considered to be "marital assets" – assets available to the married couple and used by them. A wealth owner who has all their assets in a single trust, for example, may allow children to benefit from the trust either before or after the wealth owner's death. Use of the assets by children can well expose the entire trust to being considered a "marital asset." Safer might well be to have a separate trust or other structure as the vehicle from which children receive funds, allowing larger amounts to be set aside for further generations and for other purposes in structures that are more likely to protect against marital and other claims.

For wealth owners investing in a variety of asset classes and in investments in different countries, having specially designed approaches for each asset class and investment destination can make sense, and bring efficiency (and speed) to the investment process. And of increasing importance is having a quick way to deal with the burden of compliance, and the many questions that have to be answered when bank accounts are opened or where funds are being dedicated to specific collective or individual investments.

Liquidity is a related need, and the structures adopted by families can affect how quickly assets can be mobilized for whatever purpose they are needed. Having funds tied up in complex structures that do not provide ready access may not be ideal if the investment objectives of the family suggest a need for quick decisions and ready access to funds.

Important in thinking about the diversification of asset-ownership structures is the question of whether it is also important to diversify who in the family owns the wealth of the family. This will depend on the circumstances, but diversifying ultimate ownership is also often a prudent thing to consider. If a wealth owner is sued for any reason, assets not owned by the wealth owner may be protected. If the wealth owner separated himself from ownership early on, by way of a gift or other transfer to the younger generation, or to a properly established trust or insurance structure, perhaps real ownership diversification and asset protection can be achieved.

Tax-Advantaged Investing

Tax is only one of many needs that families have, and is an example of a need that is affected by countries of residence, citizenship, and investment. An understanding of a family's tax position, and the effect on tax exposures of where residence and citizenship is maintained and how investments are structured and located, is critical. And in an increasingly transparent world, and one in which it is difficult to achieve meaningful and safe investment returns, tax-advantaged investing is becoming more and more important.

There are many facets to what tax-advantaged investing means, but in the simplest terms, to invest on a tax-advantaged basis means focusing on the after-tax and not the pre-tax return on an investment. It is very easy to get into an investment, but often not enough attention is paid to the question of how one will exit from the investment, and what the tax consequences of this might be.

In measuring risk and return, the tax result will be highly relevant. Uncertainty as to how a country may tax investments is part of the evaluation of risk. Today, a number of emerging markets, including India and China, have been focusing on taxing the returns of foreign investors, and enforcing tax approaches that were not previously thought to apply. This uncertainty in tax treatment is clearly a risk factor that a well-advised wealth owner should be taking into account in working out what investments to make.

A good general example that can be made to highlight what tax-advantaged investing involves relates to investments that may be made in real estate. In the context of the USA, a non-US investor who is considering buying real estate can do this in any number of ways. They can buy the property in their individual name, they can set up a US company to own the property, they can use a non-US company to own the property, or use a number of other structures including trusts, foundations, or partnerships, and can even combine ownership approaches, perhaps having a non-US company that owns a US company make the investment. Financing of the purchase and how this is effected can also be one of the planning opportunities the investor has. All of these choices can dramatically impact the after-tax return, and relevant here will be not only how the USA taxes income generated from the real estate and any gains on a future sale, but also how the investor's home country will treat the investment, something touched on in an earlier chapter of this book.

So where does the wealth owner begin in developing a tax-advantaged investing approach to a contemplated investment, say a real-estate project as in the example set out above? The first step is to understand the home-country tax position. If the wealth owner lives in a country that taxes on the basis of residence, and this tax is imposed on a worldwide basis, then a relevant question will be whether there is a credit or exemption for any foreign taxes that may arise given that the investment is being made in another country. Most countries that tax on a worldwide basis will provide such a credit for foreign tax arising on a real-estate investment, but obtaining the credit may require that the investors own the real-estate investment directly. In other words, if the investor owns a company that owns another company that owns the real estate, will the home country provide a tax credit on a dividend the wealth owner receives from proceeds of the investment if the actual tax paid to the country in which the real estate is located was paid by a holding company that is two tiers down the ownership chain?

Rather than tax credits, some countries provide exemptions for the foreign income involved, and while tax treaties can be important, in relation to real estate a treaty will usually confirm that the country in which the real estate is located (the USA in the example) has a first right to tax, with the country of residence of the investor having to provide a tax credit or other relief against possible double taxation.

Other differences in how the home country may tax the foreign investment will also be relevant, however, including whether there are CFC rules that would affect corporate ownership of the real estate, and whether there are other rules, at the home-country level, that dictate one form of ownership over another.

From the home-country perspective, the simplest scenario will be where the wealth owner lives in a country that does not impose tax, or which does not tax foreign income at all. In this case, the only focus in tax-advantaged investing will be the country of investment, in the example, the USA. Focusing only on the rules of the USA, it might be easiest to have the individual own the property directly. But in the USA, in the case of foreigners owning US assets, such as real estate, exposure to US estate tax can arise, with significant potential tax on the value of the US assets owned by the individual at the date of death.

The US estate tax, which applies to all assets of US citizens and domiciliaries on death, only applies to US assets in respect of foreigners, but is a potentially expensive tax in that it does not focus on the profits from an investment, but on the entire value of the investment itself. And while US citizens and domiciliaries enjoy large exemptions, meaning that only reasonably wealthy families actually pay the tax, for non-US persons not eligible for additional treaty benefits, the exemption available is limited to $60,000 of US assets, a relatively small figure. With rates of inheritance tax that can, at the Federal level, reach as high as 40% of the value of the investment (2016 rates), the "after-tax" cost of the investment, taking into account estate tax alone, can be huge.

So clearly for the investor, if the real estate to be purchased will be held for the longer term, the risk of estate tax arising because of the death of the investor has to come into the mix. Given the high rates of tax involved, avoiding, in a legal way, exposure to estate tax can be a key element of tax-advantaged investing. And this, in relation to the USA, is an issue not only for real estate, but also in respect of other US "situs" assets, such as classic car collections kept physically in the USA, jewelry in safe deposit boxes in the USA, and, most importantly, shares of US companies, including portfolio holdings of publicly listed US companies. With regard to the latter, estate-tax treaties between countries can sometimes protect against US estate tax, but there are many circumstances where such treaties do not apply. And where investors own US shares in their portfolios, asset managers have been slow to remind the investors of their exposure to estate tax, a matter that will come under increasing focus and enforcement as the world moves to tax transparency and the USA is able to take action against banks and others who are involved in managing the assets of global wealth owners and who fail to encourage tax compliance.

So, avoiding estate tax in relation to the real-estate investment may be an important objective for the wealth owner in the example. One possibility might be to consider leveraging the investment – and thereby ensuring that on death the value of the property is reduced by the mortgage outstanding on the property. This is a simple technique that many wealth owners use, and not just in relation to US real-estate investments. Another possibility would be to not own the real estate directly, but through a non-US company. On death, the wealth owner would not die owning US real estate, which attracts the US estate tax, but rather would die owning the shares of, say, a British Virgin Islands company that owns the US real estate. In this case, as the British Virgin Islands does not tax on the death of an owner of BVI company shares, no tax should arise. But for this to work, the BVI company has to be "real," in the sense that it is not a sham. It is not enough to just "wrap" the real estate in corporate ownership – the company needs to be respected as the real owner, and proper governance is therefore important, full and proper documentation at the corporate level of how the company obtained its funding, minutes of board and shareholder meetings showing the reality of the company, and much more. Ensuring the proper substance of the company is key to achieving the legal avoidance of US estate tax that is sought.

But in the context of the USA, corporate ownership, by a BVI or other offshore company, may carry with it some negatives. If the real estate being invested in is income producing, the BVI company may be considered to have established a branch in the USA, attracting exposure to a 30% withholding tax on net profits (the "branch tax"), even if those net profits are not remitted outside the USA. And unlike an individual owner of the property, who when selling the property at a profit is able to take advantage of substantially lower capital gains taxes that apply to individuals, a company pays the highest possible rates of capital gains taxes. So these exposures also come into the mix in working out the best approach to use for the investment. Perhaps other structures, involving intermediate US holding companies that the BVI company owns, the possible use of trusts or partnerships instead of corporate structures (given that they retain the possibility of individual tax rates), and otherwise, may need to be considered.

No question that it is, at the time the investment is made, easiest and cheapest to just invest and worry about tax issues later. The reality, however, is that once the real estate has been purchased, it becomes more costly to restructure ownership later. And the tax costs of not having considered the after-tax return and how this can be maximized can easily wipe out any gains, and possibly more, particularly if inheritance-type taxes come into the picture.

A simpler example of tax-advantaged investing involves focusing on withholding and capital gains taxes on portfolio investments, and the possible tax savings that can be achieved through reliance on a tax treaty. If I invest in a publicly listed company that is a US or Swiss company, and I am not a US resident for tax purposes (and not a US citizen), I can sell the shares at a profit with no tax as neither Switzerland nor the USA tax capital gains on a sale of shares owned by foreigners. However, if I invest in companies that produce part of their return through dividends, I need to be mindful that both the USA and Switzerland (like many other countries) tax dividends paid to foreign shareholders by way of a withholding tax – in the case of the USA, at the rate of 30% and in the case of Switzerland, at the rate of 35% (at the time of writing). Similarly, if I invest in an interest-producing investment in Switzerland, I may be subject to a 35% withholding tax on the interest I receive, such as on a corporate bond. This withholding tax can have a significant impact on my after-tax return, even if I am living in a jurisdiction, say Hong Kong, that does not itself tax me on my foreign income.

If I use an intermediate company to own the investment, say in the BVI or elsewhere, the withholding tax is a certainty, as the BVI does not have any favorable tax treaties with the USA or Switzerland, the countries of investment in my example. If I am, however, a resident of Hong Kong, a tax treaty between Hong Kong and Switzerland can provide substantial tax savings. No equivalent treaty with the USA is in place, meaning that unlike my Swiss dividend and interest returns, which under the treaty could decline from 35% to 15% in the case of dividends and 0% in the case of interest, the withholding tax in the USA would remain at its 30% level, where it applies. Given the significant tax savings and enhancement of my after-tax return, it is critical for me to understand the after-tax position of investments in either the USA or Switzerland in order to make an informed choice as to which of the two countries to invest in. Looking at the after-tax return has to be added to the elements that make up the overall investment decision, including industry sector, currencies, and other factors.

Importantly, coming out of the opaque world of hidden money, many asset managers do not pay attention to tax-advantaged investing, particularly where the wealth owner is a cross-border investor. To achieve the most tax-efficient means of investing, it is critical to take into account home-country tax exposures, tax exposures in the country in which investment structures are located, and tax issues in the country of investment. This process is not one that many are able to effectively manage, and it is up to the wealth owner to raise the right questions in relation to investments to make sure that the after-tax return is what it can and should be.

Linked to an understanding of tax-advantaged investing is the ability of an asset manager to report investments and performance in a way that facilitates tax filings in relevant countries, including the home country of the investor. A major failing of many wealth managers is their inability to either provide a true tax-advantaged investing service, lacking the understanding of the three levels of tax that are often involved – the home country, the country in which an investment vehicle is located, and the country of investment – and linked to this, lacking the ability to handle the compliance involved, including tax reporting and applying for relevant withholding and other tax refunds. Global custodians holding shares for wealth owners offer a commodity business, at low margins, and do not generally do the work that has the potential to significantly add to returns.

Wealth management is a knowledge business, but sadly run by many who are more focused on their own interests rather than on the need to invest in and manage knowledge for the benefit of their clients. A wealth owner has little choice but to get a handle on what is relevant to their own situation, and be in a position to ask the right questions that will lead them to the right advisors. And for the wealth manager who gets it right, the opportunity to excel and attract clients is significant.

Asset Protection and Preservation

The term "asset protection" is a very broad one, and covers many areas of need of all wealth-owning families. Dealing with tax efficiencies, protecting against the risks of divorce in the younger generation, and many other areas already discussed involve asset protection. But another more specific area relates to creditor protection – keeping assets safe in the case of litigation and claims from potential creditors.

There are moral issues in and around the area of asset protection. Should a doctor who makes a mistake be able to protect some of his assets from claims by a patient who has been wronged? Should an owner of a chemical factory be able to shelter assets from claims if the chemicals end up polluting a river and affect the health of those living close by? Should a ship owner be able to protect himself against claims associated with an environmental disaster created by leakage from an oil tanker?

The world is increasingly litigious. In the USA and elsewhere, lawyers can work on contingency, meaning that they do not get paid unless they win. Ambulance chasers advertise freely and widely, soliciting clients and encouraging them to *sue, sue, sue*. Directors of public companies are increasingly at risk of lawsuits from investors and others. Can and should a prudent wealth owner seek to protect himself?

There are a variety of ways that wealth owners can use structures, including trusts, insurance policies, and other approaches, to help limit the risk that litigation will reach all assets. The main thing about asset-protection trusts and other structures is that they only really work if, after the structure is established, the founder remains solvent despite the transfers of assets that have been effected. What this generally means is that the asset-protection structure needs to be set up before and not after legal claims arise. As an example, suppose a wealth owner has assets with a value of $2,000,000, including investments in real estate, liquid assets in banks, and otherwise. The wealth owner also owes money under mortgages and business loans that have been taken out, and debts total $800,000. The wealth owner's net worth is therefore $1,200,000, being the total of the assets owned, less amounts that are owed. If the wealth owner makes a transfer to an asset-protection structure of less than $1,200,000, after the transfer, the wealth owner remains solvent; if the transfer is more than $1,200,000, the wealth owner has become insolvent through the transfer, and the asset-protection structure can easily be challenged as a fraud on creditors. More importantly, if the wealth owner in the example has not done any planning, and has discovered that there is a possible claim against him, it may well be too late to avoid any transfers being considered as fraudulent and subject to challenge. In other words, if the asset-protection structure is set up after there is reason for a claim to arise, it is much easier for the structure to be challenged by a claimant.

There is much more to effective asset protection, and this includes ensuring that the structure used, whether a trust or otherwise, is truly irrevocable and legally distances the wealth owner from the assets that have been transferred. Ideally, the wealth owner cannot himself benefit from the assets in future, though a variety of approaches can allow ongoing influence over the assets involved and the possibility of the assets being used for his benefit at some point. But again, in simple terms, if a wealth owner has truly given assets away while solvent and before there are any claims, such as by way of an irrevocable gift to a trust that only his children can benefit from, the assets are no longer his, and in the event of a future claim, they may well be protected.

There are also practical issues that a well-thought-out asset-protection structure will take advantage of. If assets are located outside the country in which claims may arise, this in and of itself may make it more difficult for a future creditor to access them. Further protection may be afforded by laws in the country in which the asset-protection structure is located, such as rules that require any claims to be made within particularly short time frames if a creditor is arguing that a transfer has been fraudulent. Some jurisdictions, like the Cook Islands, actively promote the asset-protection benefits of trusts created under their laws by making it difficult for foreign claimants to take action and by not enforcing a judgement that may be obtained in another country against the wealth owner involved, even in the case of bankruptcy. High burdens of proof for claimants apply, and as a result the Cook Islands, and some other jurisdictions, have created an industry offering asset protection to those involved in high-risk professions or businesses.

While the notion of aggressive asset protection may well have a dark moral side, asset protection as a general matter is a need all wealth owners have. When dealing with succession planning, it is always good to also have an eye on asset protection, not only at the level of the wealth owner, but also at the level of the wealth owner's children and other successors, a much easier task. Again, we consider a simple example. A wealth owner may have funds they plan to leave to their son, a surgeon practicing in the USA. The wealth owner has grandchildren, but feels that it is easiest and best to just leave their assets to their son, and have him take care of how he would like to pass these assets on to his children. Once the wealth owner has passed away, the assets come into the ownership of the son. If a lawsuit arises and a valid claim is made against the son for malpractice, the assets will certainly be at risk, and any benefit to the grandchildren will be lost. If the wealth owner, instead, leaves part of their assets to their son, and another part to a structure, perhaps a trust, for the benefit of grandchildren only, then the assets at risk in the event of a claim against the son will only be the assets the son actually has. Even if the trust set up for the grandchildren leaves it to the son to decide at what ages the grandchildren might benefit, so long as the assets clearly cannot fall into the son's ownership, asset protection has been achieved.

It is certainly easier not to think about all the possible risks to wealth that can arise, and just leave things to the younger generation to sort out. But in a complex world, this is not always the best way to go.

Art, Jewelry, Classic Cars, and Other Valuable Special Assets

Almost all wealth-owning families have a need to address the specifics of the assets they have and which will form part of what moves from one generation to the next.

Particular thought needs to be given by wealth owners to how assets such as jewelry, art, and similar items are dealt with as part of an effective succession and asset-protection plan. There are many reasons why assets such as these need special attention, and among them is the reality that values, the location of assets, and other issues can all be particularly problematic. This area represents a need of wealth-owning families that differs from one family to the next, the succession and asset-protection process having to adapt to the particular assets of an individual family.

When there is a liquid portfolio of assets under management, there is usually custody with a bank, and when there is a need for assets to pass to the next generation, while planning is needed, at least there is usually not a huge amount of difficulty finding the assets or knowing their value. But when Mom has an important collection of jewelry she is passionate about, her children (or spouse) may or may not know which of her pieces have what value, or even where they are. On death or disability, pieces may be stolen or lost, and often are.

Also problematic is where valuable items are physically located. In a number of countries, inheritance taxes arise if valuable moveable items, such as cars, art, or jewelry, are located in the country involved. A wealth-owning family may live in a country that has no inheritance taxes, but if they keep valuables in the UK, the USA, Canada, or many other countries, inheritance taxes can arise based on the fact that the assets involved are physically in a country that imposes an inheritance tax. Varying exemptions arise, but for valuable assets, the problem can be a very real one. Careful planning is important, and this sometimes involves ensuring that the asset is not in individual ownership, but rather held through some sort of structure, such as a properly established and administered company set up in a country that itself does not impose a tax on death.

If Mom, who is not a US citizen or domiciliary, owns valuable jewelry kept in a safety deposit box in the USA, estate tax will arise if on Mom's death the value of all her US assets exceeds US$60,000 (with some variations of the relevant amount depending on applicable estate-tax treaties). Mom can avoid this tax by either keeping her jewelry in a safe box in a country that does not impose inheritance tax on the moveable assets of foreigners, such as would be the case in Switzerland, or by having the jewelry owned by a properly administered company formed outside the USA, perhaps in the British Virgin Islands or elsewhere, such that on her death the jewelry is not owned by her, but rather by the company, meaning that the assets passing on death are the shares of the company, a British Virgin Islands, rather than a US, asset. US estate tax is thereby avoided. With a tax as high as 40% of the value of the assets involved at the Federal level (state taxes, where they apply, can add to this), a meaningful amount of tax is involved.

Not thinking carefully through where valuables are kept can result in expensive mistakes, and for wealth-owning families that have homes in various places, the ownership of the homes may well have been well structured, with good advice obtained at the time of acquisition. But once the family begins furnishing the property, and bringing their artwork, jewelry, and other collectibles into the homes, less thought may be given to the consequences, tax and otherwise, of this in the event of the passing of the wealth owner.

A number of other tax issues arise in relation to valuable items such as art and jewelry. Value-added taxes can be high, and when art, as an example, is brought into a country that charges such taxes on imports, this can be a significant cost. Lots of planning comes into addressing value-added taxes, including the type of entity that is used to own the art. There are also sometimes surprising other taxes that arise, including "use" taxes in some US states. These excise taxes are similar to value-added taxes, and can be a problem when, for example, art is brought to a home a family may maintain in a state that imposes such taxes.

As with everything, there is much more to be considered than just tax. The distribution of family heirlooms, regardless of value, on the death of a wealth owner can be an extraordinarily emotional and divisive issue. If a parent has not made it clear who gets what when they pass away, how the children will work it out may be a difficult process. Even worse is where the actual ownership of a family heirloom is not clear. Mom and Dad may have retired, and now spend time visiting their grandchildren, with regular visits to the homes of each child. Over time, they may leave family heirlooms and collectibles at the homes of their children – jewelry, art, or whatever. On death, questions may arise as to whether the parent gave the item to the child in whose home the asset has been left. One child may think they own the item – the other may think the item should be considered part of all the assets of their parent left to both children to divide. Something of relatively little value may become the cause of bad feelings and disputes.

It is much safer for wealth owners to consider, early on, how best to deal with special assets, taking into account tax and other issues and considering carefully what might happen if the wealth owner dies or becomes disabled. If whoever is intended to come into the ownership of the assets involved is unaware of their existence, value, or location, real problems may well arise, including theft of the assets by staff or others, sales at significant undervalues, and confusion as to the intention of the wealth owner in relation to how those meant to succeed to the ownership of the assets are meant to divide things up. It is certainly easier to just leave the problem to the younger generation to sort out, but this is not always a great thing to do if the objective is to help preserve values and family relationships.

I have had many clients with important family heirlooms that they have specific ideas about in terms of who should end up with them. Mother may have inherited jewelry from her own mother, and her intention may well be that only her granddaughters will get the jewelry – often thinking *certainly not any of my daughters-in-law.* Mother may then die prematurely, and under the approach taken by her in her estate planning, or under the relevant law if she has not done any planning, the jewelry comes into the ownership of her surviving husband. After a time, he falls into the clutches of a pretty young thing who ends up with all the jewelry on his death (if not well before), leaving out not only daughters-in-law from benefit (who likely would have treasured the jewelry, protecting it for their own daughters), but everyone else in the family, including granddaughters.

Political Risk

Political risk is an example of a need that is driven by the laws that impact a family, something that can arise through the residential or citizenship connections of the family, or by virtue of where investments owned by the family are maintained.

A first-generation Canadian, my parents had moved to Canada from Europe, escaping the destruction of the Second World War and the asset confiscations and other trials they had endured. Growing up in Canada, I saw political risk as a very distant and historical danger. In my legal studies, and in my initial work as a lawyer in New York, political risk was not something that formed part of what I was exposed to.

When I moved to Hong Kong in the early 1980s, I became aware of the underlying political risk that was a concern to wealth owners in Hong Kong and elsewhere in the region. In the run up to 1997, the year in which Hong Kong was handed back to China by the UK, political risk came to the forefront in the thinking of wealth owners in Hong Kong and the international business community. One of the most capitalist places in the world, Hong Kong, was going to become part of one of the most communist places in the world, China. It was at this time that I began to become very involved in the asset-protection planning those exposed to political risk consider undertaking.

But what is "political risk?" In fact, there are many risks that a wealth owner is subject to that can fall under the heading of "political" risk, including changes in the tax landscape, perhaps in part as a result of a new focus on income and wealth inequality. In the context of Hong Kong in the run up to 1997, however, the main political risk that was most focused on was the question of whether private ownership of assets would be respected by China, which in the 1980s did not have much concept of such ownership in its own communist system.

Under international law, a country is viewed as being legally able to expropriate assets located within its borders. This relates to the sovereignty of countries, and the general principle is that a country can make its own rules regarding who owns what. Expropriation of domestic assets is therefore something a country can validly do. As a general principle of international law, however, if the expropriation relates to assets owned by nationals of another country, compensation should be paid. The extent to which this general principle can be enforced, however, may be limited and will very much depend on the circumstances.

So in the context of Hong Kong, the general legal position under international law supported the main fear of wealth owners in the run up to the handover of Hong Kong to China – as Chinese nationals, a wealth owner could find themselves subject to rules forbidding private ownership of assets, effectively resulting in expropriation. And if the assets expropriated were not owned by foreigners, there would be no rights of compensation. Even where foreign ownership existed (say the ownership of Hong Kong assets through a non-Hong Kong company, or direct ownership by a wealth owner with foreign citizenship), it was by no means clear that compensation would be paid in the event of an asset expropriation or whether such compensation would be fair if paid.

Because of the fear of expropriation, many international businesses restructured themselves, often using a corporate "inversion." The Jardine Matheson group, the Hong Kong and Shanghai Banking Corporation (now known as "HSBC"), and many others undertook this form of planning (interestingly, at the time of writing this book, HSBC considered, but decided against, a return to Hong Kong as a corporate base given regulatory and tax advantages. Political risk, however, likely remained a barrier to this).

Historically, many Hong Kong-based businesses began as Hong Kong companies. As the business expanded, global subsidiaries would appear beneath a Hong Kong holding company, and eventually complex global structures developed with Hong Kong parent companies owning many subsidiaries and affiliates both in and outside Hong Kong. For public companies, the Hong Kong parent company would be the listed vehicle; for private companies, the Hong Kong parent company would be a holding vehicle owned by the wealth-owning family.

If China were to expropriate assets in Hong Kong, the fear was that the Hong Kong holding companies would themselves be expropriated and that the expropriating government would then control all the global subsidiaries and other assets involved, the expropriation thereby extending beyond Hong Kong's borders.

Through corporate "inversions," this risk was, supposedly, addressed. In the case of the Hong Kong and Shanghai Banking Corporation, the new holding company of HSBC became a UK company, with the Hong Kong operations of the bank becoming a subsidiary, theoretically limiting the risk of an expropriation in Hong Kong to only the Hong Kong operations. In the case of the Jardine Matheson group and many others, the new holding company became a Bermudan company with, again, all the foreign operations of the group owned through that holding company rather than suffering the risk of being owned by a Hong Kong parent company.

Corporate inversions are, however, only part of effective political-risk-minimization planning. Given that a country is, under international law, effectively allowed to expropriate the assets of its own nationals, if the individual owner of a corporate group established outside the risk country, again, say Hong Kong, is himself living in Hong Kong, could the government not expropriate the shares of the overseas holding company the wealth owner has an interest in? While the foreign country in which the holding company is based may not recognize an expropriation, the answer is generally yes, meaning that for real protection, the ownership of companies outside the risk country should be set up in a way that reduces risks. Ideally, after the corporate inversion, the wealth owner will transfer his interest in the foreign holding company to a structure that cuts off his ownership, thereby making it difficult for an expropriation to be achieved. In simple terms, the wealth owner no longer owns the foreign holding company, and now its shareholder is an appropriately formulated trust, foundation, insurance policy, or other structure outside the risk country, which is designed to cut off the ownership of assets by someone living in a country that may be subject to an expropriation order.

Planning of this kind can be very sophisticated, but achievable, and surprisingly, in a world where political risk features, very little attention is actually paid to this area by wealth owners, despite the fact that they often invest or live in troubled countries.

There is also another level of political risk that is even less well considered than the risk of asset expropriation. In some countries, like the USA, there are rules that allow action to be taken against "enemies" of the country. This action can include freezing or vesting orders that can either tie up the assets of an "enemy," or actually allow the US government to take them away. When the US-supported Shah of Iran fell, the USA froze the assets of Iran and of Iranian citizens in the USA. Wealthy Iranians who had put assets in the USA with American banks, thinking that this was a way to increase the safety of their assets, found their assets frozen, and were forced to go through difficult and costly litigation to recover them. During the Noriega crisis, when the USA was seeking to arrest Manuel Noriega, the drug-dealing leader of Panama, President George Bush (the older, smarter one) threatened to freeze the assets of Panama and Panamanians if Noriega was not caught. At the time, I had several clients in the shipping industry, many of whom used Panamanian companies to own not only their ships, but also their personal real estate in the USA. I had a number of frantic calls from clients asking if their home in California or their apartment in Manhattan, owned by a Panamanian company, might be frozen if the crisis continued. The answer was yes.

The younger President George Bush (the less clever one), at the time of the Iraqi crisis, used his powers to vest, or take away, the US assets of Iraq and Saddam Hussein and his family.

Today, sanctions come and go over perceived "enemies" of the USA and other countries, affecting a wealth owner's access to assets. While these sanctions may often be appropriate, the assets of innocent wealth owners seeking to protect their wealth from an unstable government can also be caught in the net.

The ability of a country to freeze or vest assets belonging to "enemies" is another level of political risk. In my example of the concerns of Hong Kong wealth owners in the run up to 1997, the year of the handover of Hong Kong to China, had China actually expropriated privately owned assets in Hong Kong, what would the consequence have been of an expropriation of the Citibank building on Garden Road, or of any other US-owned assets? Could the USA have retaliated by seizing a Chinese-owned airplane landing in Los Angeles? Could the USA have frozen the US assets of Hong Kong families and businesses? The answer is possibly, and from a planning perspective, using approaches designed to cut off ownership by family members who may be in states subject to freezing or vesting orders is another element of good political-risk planning.

But what of assets located in a country that itself may be troubled? One approach that can sometimes be taken is to leverage the assets involved – borrowing on the security of the assets, effectively passing the risk of expropriation or other actions to the lender. Usually this is not overly practical, however, as in situations of political unrest, lenders are aware of the risk, and insist on personal guarantees and other security. Other steps can, however, be taken in a similar vein, such as avoiding cash accumulations at the corporate level, and otherwise. Political risk insurance is also an option, and this is sometimes available privately or in combination with public variations of such insurance, the latter largely designed to encourage investment in developing countries. Adopting investment structures that allow access to such protection, where it exists, can be important as publicly available political-risk insurance may be restricted to policy owners from particular countries or who make use of particular investment approaches.

Investment protection agreements, and their use, also suffer from insufficient attention. Investment-protection agreements are usually bilateral agreements between countries, and what they provide for are clear rules that require compensation in the event of an expropriation. While one may have uncertainty as to whether a treaty of this kind would be respected, it is worth considering that certain countries, such as the USA, may be in a particularly strong position to enforce such agreements given the American assets most countries own, including US treasury bills and other financial instruments. So, if I am not an American, and am investing in a country with political risk, should I do so using a British Virgin Islands or other offshore company given that the entity is tax free? Or should I ask whether the British Virgin Islands has an investment-protection agreement with the country in which I am investing? And not surprisingly, many of the "pure" offshore tax havens, like the British Virgin Islands, have very few, if any, investment-protection agreements. But if I use a US company, say a Limited Liability Company or "LLC," to make the investment, I may well be able to avoid any US tax arising, given the "flow-through" treatment of an LLC, while accessing the US investment-protection agreement with the country I am investing in. Singapore, and many other "midshore" (as opposed to offshore) tax havens can also provide benefits of this kind.

It is generally easy to make an investment, but all too often not enough attention is paid to the risks of the investment, and how one will eventually exit. The time to think about this is in advance, as it is cheaper and easier to address tax, political risk, and other issues when setting things up for the acquisition, rather than later in the process.

Also relevant in any investment is the governing law of the contracts used. When capital levies were imposed in Cyprus, bonds of Cypriot banks lost their value... but those bonds that were issued under UK law rather than under Cypriot law fared much better, with those holders being favored. Ensuring that a foreign court with a solid and dependable judicial system will deal with any potential political-risk event can be critical to managing things.

Capital levies imposed by Cyprus, a clear form of expropriation, were actually branded "taxes" by many. In my thinking, a tax is something you know about in advance, and which can form part of a decision on whether and where to invest. It is a clear form of political risk where a country imposes an unexpected tax without warning, and it is interesting that the notion of capital levies is one that has received attention from commentators focused on ways of addressing the debt levels of countries and the perceived growing inequality of income and wealth. Thomas Piketty, in his writings, refers to capital levies as a means of collecting revenues from those who should pay, and his suggestion of this form of "tax" (again, nothing more than an expropriation of assets) was picked up by commentators including the International Monetary Fund (which then backed down on the reference to capital levies as an appropriate fiscal tool) and the German Bundesbank.

Tax changes, however, are a clear form of political risk, and it is unfortunate to see countries not appreciating that constant changes in the tax laws affect how investors evaluate the risk of investing in the country involved. As an investor, I want to be able to know upfront how much tax an exit from the investment will result in. India and many other countries have, of late, created great uncertainty among foreign investors, given changing interpretations and enforcement of tax laws. Even the UK, given the constant changes to how foreigners are taxed in respect of their UK real-estate interests, is clearly a country of political risk for wealth owners who need certainty in order to plan their affairs.

Addressing political risk will be an increasing need of wealth-owning families. The current focus on income and wealth inequality, increasing populism in the political sphere, and the difficult financial position of many countries is increasing risk, and not only in parts of the world one normally thinks of as unstable.

Security and Kidnapping Risks

Depending on the countries to which a family is connected, as well as other factors, security and kidnapping risks may be of particular relevance. Safety and security are, of course, issues relevant to all families, but geography and circumstances will certainly have an impact on the priority with which the area needs to be considered.

A very wealthy family invited me to their family home for a meeting. Living about 90 minutes from the airport I had traveled to, I was picked up by the family chauffeur in a lovely, comfortable car. I settled myself into the back seat, opened my briefcase, and removed my papers, getting ready to do some work during the journey. I chatted with my driver, and soon became so engrossed in our conversation that I put all my papers away and spent the entire journey learning about the security world.

My driver was actually not only the family chauffeur, but also the head of security for the family. A retired member of the UK security forces, my driver explained to me that he was a member of a small group of specialists, most with similar backgrounds, working for families at the higher end of the wealth spectrum. We had a wide-ranging discussion, and among the many things he shared with me was the fact that kidnapping is not something that only takes place in developing countries, but is actually an ongoing problem in many more unexpected places in the world, including the UK, Japan, and elsewhere. He explained that one of the biggest challenges for those involved with ensuring the security of the families they serve is where kidnappers are not professionally organized, his view being that at least with "professional" kidnappers, there is an ability to go through an almost accepted routine in the event of a kidnap. First, he explained, is to require "proof of life" – evidence that the person you are negotiating the return of is actually still alive. Second, demands for ransoms are often way out of proportion to what will actually be accepted, and there is a process of negotiation that precedes coming to the right figure. And in many, many cases, at least according to the person I was having the discussion with, the authorities are either not involved or are very much on the sidelines of the process, the decision on whether to bring the authorities into the picture very much depending on the country involved. In some, it is the authorities who are themselves potentially linked to the kidnappers.

Our discussion covered many areas, including the important training security consultants can provide to family members about how they should act, and how they can stay out of trouble. In the case of one family that I worked with a number of years ago, they brought security specialists into a family retreat – a meeting of the family designed to review financial, succession, and other matters.

The security specialists led a discussion on security, and how family members could avoid danger – and for the relevant family this included coverage of danger in England, where some of the children were studying, dangers in Pakistan, where the family owned businesses and spent time, and in other locations to which the family had ties. In Pakistan, the family was warned to take different routes from their home to their places of business, staying away from routine journeys that could be monitored and form part of a kidnap plan; the younger generation studying in England were warned about keeping a low profile – how to dress, how to interact with others, and how to deal with problems if they arose. For many families, reviewing issues in and around personal safety and security in advance of anything happening is most worthwhile.

Over the years, a question I have often asked myself is what happens when there is a kidnapping, and the family does not have any pre-existing understanding of what to do and who to call. And what if the person kidnapped is the matriarch or patriarch, who her or himself knows where the available funds are and otherwise is in a position to make decisions. If an unprepared spouse or child is contacted by a kidnapper and told *if you want to see your husband alive, we want $5 million by tomorrow, and if you call the police, he will die...* what does the recipient of the call do? Will the threat regarding what happens if the authorities are contacted be acted upon? How will the $5 million be obtained if the wealth owner is himself the one kidnapped?

What I encourage families to consider is hiring security consultants as part of their overall review of asset protection and succession. With the right expertise upfront, the family is better equipped to know how to avoid problems and, importantly, how to react and who to call if there are problems. And sometimes related to this is ensuring that there are funds available, perhaps in trust or otherwise, that can be accessed if needed in relation to a ransom request. Kidnapping insurance is another option, though one that some families evidence concern about given the disclosure of information that obtaining the insurance can require.

Do I Need Separate Structures for All These Things?

Wealth-owning families have many needs, and my summary of some of these reflects only a portion of the needs families have given the special issues that arise in particular families, and the needs driven by the nature of their businesses and investments, where they live and invest, and much more. But does this mean that the family should have separate planning and structures to address each of their needs? The answer is that how assets are held, and succession and asset protection is planned, should ideally be holistic, with each structure reflecting all the needs of the family.

The same trust that is used to achieve a tax benefit for the family should be the trust that achieves political risk and asset protection, and provides for the governance that is set out in the family constitution, if there is one in place. Interestingly, when a structure is designed to address more than one objective, the structure becomes a stronger one from many perspectives. In a number of jurisdictions, tax laws may allow for a challenge to favorable tax results where an ownership structure has been designed specifically to obtain tax benefits. Where a structure is set up with the sole purpose of protecting assets from creditors, this may make it easier for the structure to be challenged in the event of claims being made. Where the structure can be shown to have been set up for many valid reasons, this may well help the structure achieve the asset-protection and tax benefits sought.

This said, as part of good planning in today's world, I am a believer in some diversification of ownership structures and approaches.

There is one thing pretty much every good investment advisor will say: The investment world is an uncertain one, and diversification in investments is key to long-term safety and growth of assets. In the case of the structures families use to own their assets, there is often little thought given to diversification. In some families, all assets are simply owned by Dad, and the expectation is that Dad will do the right thing and eventually pass the assets to Mom if he pre-deceases, and to the next generation otherwise. But what if Dad is sued – the entirety of the assets are then at risk. What if Mom pre-deceases, and Dad ends up in the clutches of a new, gold-digging spouse? Would Mom have wanted her share of the family assets to end up going to the new spouse's children from her previous marriage rather than to her own children? If all the assets of the family are in one single trust, and distributions are made, the tax authorities in a number of countries have the right to see everything that is in the trust.

Where assets are divided in different, well-thought-through ownership structures, the benefits of ownership diversification can be achieved, something that in my experience is usually not sufficiently discussed or considered.

6

The Tools of Wealth Planning

If, while reading this book, you suddenly hear a rush of water, and find that a pipe in your home has burst, you will call a plumber. The plumber will arrive at your home not with just one tool, say a wrench, but with an entire toolbox containing screwdrivers, wrenches, hammers, pliers, and many others. In succession and asset-protection planning, there is also a toolbox, and there is no one tool that addresses the needs of every family. It is often the case that many of the tools of wealth planning are used for the same wealth-owning family, and some of the tools might be mixed together to bring the best result.

This chapter discusses only some of the many wealth-planning tools that are commonly used. Effective planning requires that the family understand the tools that are in place in relation to their wealth, at least such as to allow them to be in a position to ask the right questions of their advisors and other service providers.

Wills

The laws of most countries provide for some form of will, or testament, that can be used by a wealth owner to set out how their assets will pass on in the event of their death. If a wealth owner dies without a will, something will still happen to their assets, but here the succession will be determined by the relevant law, which may or may not be the law of the deceased's residence, domicile, or nationality, particularly if some of the assets are located outside of that country.

Wills are useful, as no matter what additional approaches are taken in the succession plan, it is inevitable that there will remain assets in the personal ownership of the wealth owner at the time of his death.

For a will to be valid, care must be taken that the formalities for executing a will are properly followed pursuant to the law that is relevant. Many countries require that wills have at least two witnesses who are in each other's presence at the time of execution. This said, a will that is not witnessed is, in a number of countries, valid if it is a "holographic" will – a will that is in handwriting, and not typed.

If the wealth owner has an interest in assets outside of his home country, consideration might be given to having a further will that is drafted under the law of the country where the assets are located. But here care needs to be taken to ensure that the two wills, that of the home country and that of the country where the investment is located, fit together, something often achieved by having each will reference the other, and having the home country will cover all assets other than those covered by the second will, which specifically covers the assets in the country of investment.

Where a home-country will covers assets outside the home jurisdiction, after the will is proven to be the deceased's last will, usually under a procedure known as probate, the will can then be proven as valid in other countries in which the deceased may have owned assets. These procedures can take time and be costly, and it is for this reason that some of the other tools of wealth planning can come into the picture, such as trusts, foundations, insurance policies, and others. In most cases, wills provide for immediate distribution of assets, and for the appointment of an executor, the person responsible to follow through and ensure that the instructions contained in the will are followed. An executor has a high level of responsibility, and this includes, in many cases, responsibility to ensure that any taxes due are properly paid, sometimes including past income taxes the deceased may have failed to pay. Being an executor is something that should not be taken lightly, and when drafting a will and choosing an executor, understanding the personal liability that an executor has is important for the wealth owner, who may not have in mind that the executor will, to protect himself, declare to the tax authorities taxes that the wealth owner had decided to illegally evade.

But as with any involvement of advisors, friends, or family members who may be appointed to look after things if the wealth owner is unable to, there is a need to consider whether there is appropriate oversight in place in relation to the executor, and an ability for the family to ensure that the executor is not abusing their position. At the time of writing this book, a dispute was in progress in relation to the will of Leona Helmsley, the widow of New York real-estate tycoon, Harry Helmsley. The New York State Attorney General argued, on behalf of charities benefitting under Leona Helmsley's will, that the fees charged by four executors, two of her grandchildren from her first marriage, and her lawyer and a business advisor, were out of line – a reported US$100 million, representing an hourly rate of US$6437 for their work, which the executors argued was extraordinarily complex.

As mentioned earlier in this book, there is no client better than a dead client. For Leona Helmsley, widely reported as being a particularly unpleasant individual, her executors seem to have been given more power than they should have been in relation to their ability to charge – and this is only one element of the "checks and balances" that any appointment of an executor under a will should be subject to.

In the case of younger wealth owners, particularly those with children, there are questions they should be considering in the use of wills given that in the event of death, the beneficiaries may be of a very young age. At what age is it appropriate for the younger generation to receive a significant amount? Is it helpful for an 18-year-old to come into millions? And if there are younger children in the picture, who will look after the money until they come of age? A will can provide for a trust to be created to protect vulnerable beneficiaries, and often the trustee will be the person appointed as the executor. Particular care in choosing an executor and providing for succession in the role is needed if the will creates a trust. And if there is no one appointed to the role, or if there is no will, perhaps the relevant court will appoint close family members to take charge of assets. In the context of your family, is this what you want? Is it safe to rely on those who would come into this position of power? What if a trusted godparent or sibling who has the role of "looking after" the children of someone dying young gets into personal financial difficulty? Will they be tempted to abuse their position?

As with all the tools of wealth planning, checks and balances are key. It is possible to consider having more than one executor, and depending on the family, there are ways to ensure that there is at least one person in the family who knows what the deceased wealth owner had in mind, and can see that things are being done as intended, and as the will provides. And as with all wealth planning, wills need regular review as assets change, the regulatory world changes, and families change.

Marriage generally invalidates wills – not remembering this when starting a new life, and perhaps remarrying, can result in startlingly different results than expected. If I leave my assets to my children under my will, and then remarry, if I die without a new will, depending on the relevant law, my new wife may get far more in the way of a share of my assets than I would have wanted given the short time of our marriage.

In a typical will, the person making the will sets out specific assets they want to go to specific beneficiaries. This allows for clarity on who gets what family heirlooms, and can be an important element of planning that avoids the misunderstandings a lack of clarity of intention can result in. Remaining assets are then often divided in particular shares, and wills are fairly flexible in the detail that can be provided. In addition to directly benefitting family members, a will can also direct that certain assets pass to other wealth-planning structures, such as a trust that may already be in place or which may be created by the will itself.

Trusts

Trusts can be very confusing tools in the wealth-planning toolbox, given their flexibility and the many different kinds of trusts that can be established. But this variety and flexibility makes a trust a very useful succession and asset-protection tool.

Trusts are creatures of the common law, first developed in England and then adopted by most common-law countries, such as Canada, the USA, Hong Kong, and the many offshore centers whose laws track English law, for historical or other reasons. Adding to the confusion associated with trusts is that civil-law countries, like Switzerland, Liechtenstein, and others, seeking to compete with jurisdictions offering trusts, have developed laws that allow trusts to be established in their countries, despite the lack of a common-law legal system.

Common-law countries have generally been clear about the tax treatment of trusts. While the relevant rules are, like all tax rules, constantly changing, countries like the UK, Canada, the USA, and many others have long had tax and related reporting rules covering most uses of trusts. More recently, civil-law countries have joined in clarifying the tax treatment of trusts, for example Denmark, Italy, France, and Switzerland. Often the tax clarity treats trusts as transparent for tax purposes, but in many cases, trusts that are well thought out can provide meaningful tax benefits. In some cases, however, such as in relation to France, the use of trusts might be tax inefficient given the heavy-handed treatment accorded to them by the tax authorities.

An increased focus on trusts by tax authorities has led some to believe that trust use is on the decline, and some trust companies have even been sold by their bank owners because of a misguided notion that the main reason families use trusts is to hide money and illegally evade tax. The reality, however, is that trusts provide many important benefits in the succession and asset-protection process, and that even where no tax benefits are achieved, the trust may be at the center of a well-thought-out succession and asset-protection plan. And well-planned trusts can provide many legal and appropriate means of managing tax exposures, particularly in complex situations.

A trust is a relationship, not a legal entity. When I set up a company, that company is itself a legal person, and I can open a bank account, for example, in the name of the company. When I establish a trust, I am the settlor, or founder of the trust, and I transfer assets to a trustee, which can be an individual or a trust company. When I transfer my assets, I am taking advantage of something that the common law provides for (and which civil law generally does not), which is to reflect the divisibility of the ownership of an asset between its legal ownership and its beneficial ownership. If I own a pen, I am both its legal owner and its beneficial owner. This means that I can sell the pen or give it away, and I can also benefit from the pen, using it to write and consuming the ink it contains. If I transfer the pen to a trustee and provide that the trustee should hold the pen for my benefit during my lifetime and for the benefit of my children after my death, I am dividing the legal and beneficial ownership. The trustee becomes the legal owner of the pen, with the ability to sell or give the pen away, subject to what the trust arrangement provides. But the trustee is not allowed to benefit from the pen, as the trustee is not the beneficial owner. The beneficial owners of the pen, in my example, include me during my lifetime, and then my children. If the trustee benefits from the pen, the beneficial owners can sue and win unless the trust document allows the trustee to benefit, such as in relation to the fees the trustee charges, and which it can take from the trust assets to pay itself.

The division of legal and beneficial ownership is very useful in asset-protection and succession planning, and in relation to tax planning, as when I set up the trust, I separate myself from the legal ownership of the asset. But more on this a bit later.

Once legal ownership passes to the trustee, it is the trustee who owns the asset. Sometimes confusing is the fact that a trust is not a legal entity. This means that it is not the trust that owns the asset, but rather the trustee. I may have called the trust "The Pen Trust" – but there really is no such legal entity. If the trustee wants to open a bank account, the trustee cannot do so in the name of The Pen Trust, as there is no legal person with that name in existence. Rather, the bank account has to be opened in the name of the trustee, who can, but does not have to, reference The Pen Trust, having the account be in the name of the trustee as trustee of The Pen Trust.

The fact that no legal entity is created means that the liabilities of a trustee are high. While trust documentation is often designed by trustees to limit their liability, trustees are themselves the owners of the assets, and if there are lawsuits associated with them, the trustee will be in the firing line. Trustees also have a high level of responsibility to the beneficiaries of a trust, owing their primary responsibilities to them.

Technically, trusts, other than trusts involving land, do not need to be in writing. As a practical matter, the trusts used by wealth owners are always in writing, and can take a number of different forms in terms of how they are documented. Most common is a trust deed, a document that sets out the name of the creator of the trust, the settlor, and also the name of the trustee. An alternative is a declaration of trust – this is a document that reflects the declaration of a trust by a trustee, signed only by the trustee, and which does not necessarily name the settlor. It is less common to use a declaration of trust today, given the many reporting requirements associated with the use of trusts and the need to document those connected to them, but the declaration of trust is part of the flexibility associated with how trusts can be created and documented.

The parties to a trust include the settlor and the trustee, both already mentioned. But it is worth pointing out that the flexibility of trusts makes it possible for persons other than the settlor to also contribute assets to the trust. I can have a friend establish The Pen Trust by contributing US$5 to the trustee and signing the trust deed as settlor. The trustee then accepts the settlement monies, and in the relevant documentation provision is made for the trustee having the power to accept other assets from other people. I can then contribute my valuable pen to the trustee to hold, pursuant to the terms of The Pen Trust. I do not have to sign the trust deed, and my name may not appear as settlor. Broadly, what has occurred is that there is a nominee settlor, my friend who contributed the US$5 to establish the trust. I, however, am the "economic settlor," albeit not named. The tax laws of most countries understand the possibility of this approach, and focus on the economic settlor and the assets the economic settlor contributes to the trust.

In addition to the settlor and trustee, the other parties to the trust are the beneficiaries. The trustee, as mentioned, owes its primary duties to the beneficiaries, and this can sometimes be of concern to a settlor who thought that they could call the shots. Once the assets are transferred, unless the trust arrangement provides otherwise, the settlor will find that the trustee's focus is on his obligations to the beneficiaries – a good thing in the protection of trust assets, but an important thing for a control-freak settlor to understand before the trust is established.

There is also an optional additional party that many trust arrangements include, and that is a "protector" or "guardian," whose functions are usually provided for in the trust deed, and provide a check over the trustee. It is common for the protector to have the ability to remove and replace the trustee, and to provide input on certain actions of the trustee, such as a decision to make distributions.

There are many kinds of trusts, and much to be said about the rights of beneficiaries, the liabilities of trustees, trust documentation, and otherwise. Many resources are available to wealth owners and their advisors who seek to learn more about trusts, but I will focus on four characteristics of trusts that can be fundamental to understanding how trusts can and do work to address many of the needs of wealth-owning families. These characteristics are "revocable," "irrevocable," "fixed," and "discretionary." Understanding these terms and how they work can go a long way in helping to understand trusts and how they can be used.

When a settlor creates a trust, a first choice that the settlor has is to consider whether to have the trust be revocable or irrevocable. In the case of a revocable trust, the settlor has a legal right to revoke, or cancel, the trust, with the right to require the trustee to return the trust assets to the settlor. The opposite is an irrevocable trust, where the settlor does not retain the legal right to get the assets back. In the latter case, the settlor may be a potential beneficiary and still have an ability to benefit, but there would be no legal right to cancel the trust and force the trustee to return the trust assets.

If I ask a typical client whether they prefer a trust that they can cancel and require the return of assets from as against a trust where the trustee may or may not have to give the assets back if there is a change of mind, most clients will say they absolutely want a revocable trust. Not so fast. What if the wealth owner owns a chemical factory, and is concerned that future risks may arise from legal claims related to pollution associated with seepage of chemicals or otherwise? If the trust is revocable, and the wealth owner has a right to get the assets that he transferred to the trustee back, it will not be at all difficult for a claimant to access the trust assets in the event of a successful lawsuit. But if the trust were established on an irrevocable basis, with no legal right for the settlor to get the assets back, the position would be very different, particularly if at the time the trust was settled there were no legal claims against the settlor in the offing, and the settlor remained solvent after settling the trust.

Another choice that the settlor has is to have the trust provide for fixed beneficial interests or for the trust to be discretionary. For example, I can settle a trust and require that the trustee, when each of my children reaches the age of 21, divides the trust assets, and gives half to each. In the case of a fixed interest of this kind, if the trustee does not give my son half the trust assets when he reaches the age of 21, my son can sue the trustee, and succeed in recovering his share of the trust assets. The alternative to a fixed trust is a discretionary trust, where the trustee can decide who to give the assets to at the trustee's "discretion." In this kind of arrangement, the trust deed, which provides for the discretion the trustee has, is often accompanied by a non-binding record of the settlor's wishes, either in a letter of wishes from the settlor, in a memorandum the trustee makes of the settlor's wishes, or otherwise.

I can therefore create the trust and provide that the trustee has discretion regarding when and if any beneficiary will benefit, and then supplement this with a letter of wishes setting out my thinking. In my letter of wishes, I can confirm that the trustee has full discretion and that the expression of wishes is non-binding, but I can ask that the trustee, in exercising its discretion, consider distributing the trust assets to each of my children, in equal shares, when they reach the age of 21. In this case, if the trustee does not exercise its discretion in favor of my son when he reaches the age of 21, my son cannot generally force the trustee to hand over the assets, as the trustee has no fixed obligation to do so, having discretion as to whether to follow the letter of wishes.

If I ask trust settlors whether they want a trust under which their children can sue if the trustee does not hand assets over at a designated age, as against a trust where the trustee only pays out "if they feel like it," most will think that what they want is a fixed trust, where their child can sue to get the assets at the relevant time. Again, not so fast. What if my son marries the sleazy girl down the street and around the time of his coming of age to receive trust assets, the marriage is in difficulty and divorce claims may arise? The assets may well be much safer against a divorce claim if my son does not have a legal right to the trust assets – the same in relation to a claim for medical malpractice if my son is a doctor and in relation to other potential claims.

Tax laws, of course, differ country by country, and how trust interests and transactions are taxed depends on the law that has application. There are, however, some general approaches to the taxation of trusts that track, in a logical way, the legal and economic difference between a revocable and irrevocable trust and a fixed and discretionary trust.

If I own an asset that today has a very low value and live in a country that has both a tax on gifts and a tax that arises on my death, if I believe that the asset will increase in value over time, will my family benefit more from my creation of a revocable trust or from an irrevocable trust? Generally, a transfer of the asset to a revocable trust will not attract a tax as my right to revoke means that I have not made a completed gift – I have the right to get the asset back so, in effect, I still own the asset. While it may seem like good news that there is no tax on the transfer of the asset to the trust, my continued ownership of the asset may well mean that I am not only taxable on income generated by the asset, despite its being held in trust, but that when I die, and the asset is worth much more, inheritance tax will apply. Once I die, I lose my ability to revoke, and the transfer becomes complete. If, on the contrary, I transfer the asset to an irrevocable trust, the gift is complete, and gift tax will apply, but on the value of the asset today, which is much lower than the value it will have in the longer term. By the time I die, the asset may be worth much more, but no inheritance tax will apply as I gave the asset away a long time ago.

If the trust in my example is a fixed trust, then the ownership of the asset, from a tax perspective, is often attributed to the beneficiary or beneficiaries with the fixed right to the asset. This might mean that income from the asset is taxable to them and that if they pass away, an inheritance tax will arise. If the trust is discretionary, and the beneficiary has no direct legal interest in the asset, there may well be no income tax to the beneficiary on income from the asset, and no inheritance tax if the beneficiary dies. In some countries, tax is avoided unless and until there is a distribution to a beneficiary, and even then tax may be reduced or avoided. In other countries, rules may attribute the income to someone involved in the trust, perhaps the settlor, in order to provide for an ongoing tax charge. But the principles of revocable, irrevocable, fixed, and discretionary often go a long way to helping one understand how trust interests are taxed, and the planning that can take place, particularly where families are divided between countries.

Trusts can be beneficial when revocable and fixed, but often trusts that are irrevocable and discretionary are particularly useful. But if I have no right to revoke the trust as settlor and the beneficiaries (which can include me, the settlor) have no fixed legal right, does it not mean that we have to trust the trustee? How can I advise this when my advice is, always, don't trust anyone?

This is where the "checks and balances" necessary in relation to all succession and asset-protection planning comes into the picture. I can start off the process by limiting the trustee's discretion in the trust to choosing among a class of possible beneficiaries, rather than leaving this open-ended. For example, I can have the trust deed provide that while the trustee has discretion as to who might benefit from the trust, I can limit this to choices the trustee has among a set class of potential beneficiaries, such as members of my immediate family – perhaps me, my wife, my children, my grandchildren, and further issue. In this way, the trustee, in exercising its discretion, cannot make a distribution to a member of his own family, if the trustee is an individual. But is this enough protection?

What if I pass away, and my trustee, an individual, has discretion to make a distribution to anyone within my family? I may have provided, in a non-binding letter of wishes, that my wish was for the trustee to divide the trust assets between my two children at a particular age. My trustee, wanting to get his hands on the valuable pen that I may have settled into the trust, can see that he has discretion to choose among a class of beneficiaries that includes my wife. The protector starts up an affair with my wife, and distributes the pen to her as a beneficiary of the trust, and uses it to draw flowers on her arm. Is this what I intended when settling the trust?

An important control over a trustee of a trust is a *protector*, an optional party to a trust. If, in the trust in my example, I required the trustee, before an exercise of discretion in favor of any beneficiary, to first give 30 days' written notice to the protector, combined with a power to the protector to remove and replace the trustee, a decision of the trustee to benefit my wife would require the trustee to first notify the protector of his intention to do so. The protector, knowing that I had wished the benefit to go to my children, can point this out to the trustee who, if he fails to do the right thing and benefit my children, will be removed and replaced as trustee by the protector.

There are many important issues to consider in deciding on an appropriate protector, or committee of protectors, and particularly on how and who replaces them. In many standard trust deeds, it is the protector who can appoint their replacements... but is this safe from the wealth-owning family's perspective? Subject to the tax and other issues that need to be navigated, I like having the family itself have the ability to appoint or approve successor protectors, but the most important thing is that the family really understand their structure, and ask all the right "what-if" questions to ensure that the right checks and balances are in place. And a big danger is when the advisor to the family, perhaps the trustee or the protector, is the one providing recommendations that are blindly followed – there is a conflict of interest that is inevitable here, as many trustees would, of course, prefer not to have a protector keeping an eye on them and their fees or, at a minimum, would prefer to themselves appoint and control the protector. And in relation to protectors, they may have incentives to not want family members to be able to remove them.

On trustee fees, it is interesting that at the time of my writing of this book a dispute involving trustee fees relating to a trust created on the death of artist Robert Rauschenberg was ongoing, with a Florida court deciding that a US$24.6 million award to three trustees was appropriate. Robert Rauschenberg had left his estate to a revocable trust, the sole beneficiary of which was the Rauschenberg Foundation. The trustees managed the trust assets for several years while the assets were being transferred to the foundation. The trustees initially claimed US$60 million for administering the trust; the Rauschenberg

Foundation claimed they were owed no more than US$375,000 for their work.

Ultimately, the trustees were awarded fees based on the value of the trust, which was substantial. While they did not receive the amount they initially claimed, the fees were still extraordinary given the relatively few years of work involved. The lesson for wealth owners is that with trusts or any other arrangements, making it clear upfront what trustees or others involved can and should charge is critical. And also critical is to have oversight, through a protector or otherwise, allowing for someone to have the power to remove and replace a trustee who for any reason may work other than in the best interests of the beneficiaries and contrary to what the creator of the trust would have wished.

In relation to trusts, the question of jurisdiction, or the laws under which the trust should be established, often comes up. While there are sometimes good reasons to form a trust under the laws of one jurisdiction or another, such as to take advantage of strong laws that protect assets against creditors, or to address forced heirship rules or otherwise, generally I am fairly relaxed on the issue of jurisdiction, at least among the numerous countries with good trust laws, an effective judiciary, and clarity that trust assets will not be taxed on the basis of where the trustee is located. More important than jurisdiction from my perspective is the choice of trustee.

Trustees can range from individuals to corporate trustees, and among the latter are trust companies that are owned by banks and "independent" trust companies that are not linked to banks. Increasingly useful for some families are "private trust companies" or PTCs, trust companies established to be the trustees of only trusts for a particular family or group of families. It is tempting for a family to opt for having a PTC as the trustee of any trusts they establish, given the sense of control this provides. But for a trust to achieve its objectives, the trust has to be real, meaning that the trustee has to properly exercise its functions as a trustee. Where PTCs are used, it is critical to ensure that they actually perform their trustee roles as required, and that the governance of the PTC is effective and able to evolve over the time the relevant trust remains in place.

Many considerations come into deciding on an appropriate trustee, but one of the most important questions is whether the trustee is capable of really doing the job of a trustee and is willing to do so. A competent trustee needs to know what the trust assets are, given the trustee's responsibility to look after them for the benefit of the beneficiaries; a trustee needs to know the family in order to be there if there is death or disability in the older generation; a trustee needs to monitor tax and legal developments that will affect the trust, and the parties to the trust in terms of tax, reporting, and other obligations. This all seems obvious, but a reality is that there are many, many trustees who have been far more focused on the trust fees they receive and on volume business than on really doing even the basics of what a real trustee must do. It is also a reality that wealth owners, not knowing the right questions to ask, choose trustees for the wrong reasons – often based on cost and without adequate consideration of whether the trustee is really able to perform the functions the family needs, both now and when the creator of the trust is no longer able or alive.

Individuals can be effective trustees, but there are issues given the succession that is necessary to provide for given that individuals are not around for more than a lifetime. Trust taxation may also be affected by where the trustee resides, and an individual may move from one country to another. And from a liability perspective, if my trustee steals from the trust, my children, as beneficiaries, can sue, but what if the trustee now claims to have dementia and is broke? Not to say that individuals cannot be good trustees, but asking the "what-ifs" can help ensure that the right checks and balances are in place to protect against what can go wrong.

There is much, much more that can be said about trusts, and wealth-owning families need to consider the benefits (and dangers) of trusts to determine whether a trust makes sense in their planning and, if so, how the trust should best be established. But the complexities of trusts arising from their flexibility and the many ways they can be established, and ever-changing tax and other laws, lead many wealth owners to think that it may be best to just leave their assets to their children, and let their children work out whether or not to establish trusts given their own circumstances. Just leaving it to the kids, however, may not be the best choice.

If mother lives in Hong Kong and has $10 million she plans to give to her son, also a resident of Hong Kong, should mother use a trust to make the transfer? Hong Kong does not have a gift or estate tax, meaning that if she gives her son the money, no tax will arise. So why not give him the money directly rather than thinking about using a trust and having to think through all the complexities? The son receives the $10 million – no tax – but is everything well protected?

The son becomes a plastic surgeon, and in his first operation he puts the ear where the nose should be and the nose where the ear should be. The son gets sued, and it is pretty clear that the $10 million will soon disappear. The son marries the sleazy girl from down the street, and well before anything to do with a breakdown of the marriage, she comes up with a hare-brained business idea and asks for some of the son's money to get her "business" started. He finds it hard to say no, and some of the money disappears.

The son, like many in Asia, decides to move to mainland China to take advantage of China's developing economy. At a certain point, he will be considered to be fully subject to not only worldwide taxation in China, resulting in his being taxed on earnings on investing the money received from his mother (which in the case of Hong Kong would have only been taxation on Hong Kong and not foreign-sourced income), but also in due course currency and foreign-investment controls.

If the son decides to move to Canada, he will freeze to death, and also be subject to worldwide taxation, meaning that tax will arise on the income he earns from investing the money received from his mother, regardless of the source of the income. Depending on the province in which he lives, tax rates can approach 45% or more, a not insignificant figure, and if the son dies, and wants to leave assets to his children, a deemed disposition on death will trigger more in the way of taxation, with capital gains taxes arising on any gains in value of assets owned, despite the fact that the assets are not actually sold.

A move to the USA and to many other countries would also result in worldwide taxation, and to potential exposure to inheritance and other taxes depending on the level of assets at death and other factors.

But what if mother, instead of giving her son the $10 million, transfers the money to a trust in respect of which her son is a discretionary beneficiary? Mother can retain the right to revoke the trust, keeping things simple and in her control, and many of the risks to wealth that would otherwise arise would be well managed.

A claim by a creditor against the son would, in many cases, not succeed in reaching the trust assets given that the son was not the one to transfer the assets to the trustee and is not accorded any legal right to the assets, being only a discretionary beneficiary. On this front, the retention of a power to revoke the trust in mother's favor will also be helpful, and a similar analysis would apply in the event of a divorce by the son.

If the son's new wife has a clever business idea and pressures the son into providing her with funds, he can simply refer his wife to the trustee who is in control of the trust assets and of any decision regarding distributions. Given the responsibilities a trustee has in relation to investment decisions and otherwise, it is unlikely the trustee would invest in the wife's business in the absence of good reasons to do so, allowing the son a face-saving way out of handing any of the money over.

If there is a change of residence to China, the assets remain outside of China's tax and foreign-exchange control net, simply not being owned by a resident of China. In certain circumstances, even a distribution from the trust to the son when resident in China may be tax free or tax advantaged.

A move to Canada will still result in the son freezing to death, but the assets and income in the trust will be free of Canadian tax and deemed disposition rules, meaning that investment income can accumulate on a tax-free basis. Both during and after mother's life, if income is properly capitalized within the trust, distributions to the son, when resident in Canada, can be achieved on a tax-free basis, despite the distributions being fully reported to the Canadian tax authorities, as they would need to be under Canadian law.

A move to the USA and to other countries could also take place without the trust income and assets coming into the income and estate-tax net, with distributions, in the case of the USA, being tax free during mother's life, given her right to revoke the trust (making the trust a "grantor" trust under US tax law) and limiting taxation after her death to the income on the trust that arises after her passing, to the extent that distributions take place. While complex, the US tax position can be managed in a number of favorable ways, providing significantly more in the way of tax benefits than would arise if there was a direct gift of the assets from mother to son.

In fact, around the world, from the UK to many other countries, trusts established by foreigners benefitting residents on a discretionary basis are not only favorable from a tax perspective, but also minimize reporting and other challenges to wealth owners.

So what if mother gives the money to her son, and he is the one to then set up the trust? The tax, reporting, and asset-protection profile of the trust is then completely different, with countries like Canada and the USA taxing the son on the income of the trust given that he was its settlor. In the case of creditor and other claims, the trust will be less protective, as the person being claimed against was the person who transferred the assets into the trust.

Trusts are not always the answer, but all wealth owners should consider the benefits that a mobile younger generation can achieve where a trust is in place. And unlike a will, which generally distributes assets on death, a trust allows assets to be held by a third party who can consider the right time to make distributions, and how best to achieve things in a way that is favorable to the family.

As with any succession and asset-protection plan, trusts should be subject to regular "stress tests" – reviews where the right "what-if" questions are asked and problems addressed. What if I pass away early, and my children are young – who will guide the trustee on making the right decisions in relation to how much my children should receive and when? What if the people I know at the trust company are all gone… who will keep an eye on the trustee and have the ability to replace the trustee if this is needed? What if my wife remarries, and her new husband is a gold-digger interested in the funds in the trust? Are the right controls there to ensure that I have made arrangements to protect my wife financially while being sure that there will be money left to take care of my children after her death, rather than going to her new husband?

Foundations

Foundations and trusts are increasingly interchangeable wealth-planning tools.

Foundations, unlike trusts, derive from the civil law, and traditionally were established under the laws of civil-law countries, like Liechtenstein, Panama, and others. However, common-law countries, such as the Bahamas and Jersey, now allow foundations to be established under their laws. Similarly, civil-law countries, such as Liechtenstein and Switzerland, provide for trusts to be administered in their countries and, in some cases, to be established under domestic trust legislation. These developments basically reflect the reality that jurisdictions compete for business, and look for ways to encourage wealth-owning families to establish structures under their laws.

Foundations, traditionally, were established in a very simple way, and historically all too often with privacy at the core. Assuming no one would find out about their existence, many traditional foundations in Liechtenstein and elsewhere were basic in their approach, providing for the creator, or founder, of the foundation retaining "founder's rights," basically allowing for a right of revocation and other rights against foundation assets, with a list of fixed beneficiaries entitled to the assets and income in particular circumstances or at particular times. Often the founder would him or herself be the "first" beneficiary, with "second" beneficiaries being the spouse and children after the passing of the first beneficiary. Basically, these foundations were akin to revocable, fixed trusts, and provided little in the way of asset protection and tax minimization given the legal right to assets that the founder and beneficiaries had.

Foundations can, however, feature similar flexibility to trusts, and it is possible to establish a foundation that is irrevocable and discretionary, with the approach taking a variety of forms. But foundations are different from trusts in a number of ways, and it is important for the wealth-owning family to understand some of these differences.

Foundations, unlike trusts, are legal entities. This means that if I set up a foundation, the foundation itself can own a bank account and own assets in its own name. This differs from a trust, where the legal owner of the assets becomes the trustee. Among other things, this has an impact on responsibility. In the case of a trust, a trustee, being the owner of the assets, has unlimited liability in the sense that the assets are the responsibility of the trustee. In the case of a risky asset, such as a leaky oil tanker delivering its cargo to the USA, a trustee will be very hesitant to take on legal ownership of the tanker given the potential liabilities involved. In the case of ownership by a foundation, being a separate entity, there is limited liability, meaning that claims, in a very general sense, can only be made against the assets of the foundation itself. This is a simplistic description, in that there are many exceptions that apply, including limitations of liability that a trust document may provide, and liabilities that often "pierce" the separate entity veil of a foundation. A foundation board, which makes the kind of decisions a trustee makes, may also incur liabilities, but in very general terms, the liability of a trustee is quite a bit more significant than that of a service provider involved with foundations. This is a reason that foundations are often cheaper to establish than trusts.

Being creatures of the civil law, foundation documents are often much simpler and shorter than trust documents. As the civil law involved sets out the rights and obligations of the various parties, the documentation of an individual foundation is often short and to the point when compared with the lengthy documents that trusts require, largely to ensure that trustees have the power they need to have to properly administer the trust assets. But unlike trusts, foundations do not generally have the same degree of responsibility to beneficiaries as is the case for trusts. In the case of a foundation, the founder is generally the main person the foundation owes its responsibilities to; in the case of the trust, it is the beneficiaries to whom the trustee owes its primary duties. These differences do not suggest that a foundation is better than a trust, or that a trust is better than a foundation. Rather, the differences mean that the wealth-owning family needs to ask the right questions, and understand the structure they have in place and what the responsibilities of those involved actually are.

Traditionally, an advantage of foundations over trusts is that foundations can, if the family so wishes, last "forever." In the case of trusts, the common law provides for the rule against perpetuities, the concept being that the ownership of assets cannot be kept in trust forever. Different trust jurisdictions feature different rules on how long a trust can last, but today more and more jurisdictions have eliminated the rule against perpetuities, allowing trusts to also last forever, if that is the way in which they are set up.

Control is another area of historical difference between trusts and foundations, with foundations, as separate entities, not having the risk of failing if the founder retains too much in the way of power. In the case of a trust, the trust can fail if the settlor retains too much control – in effect, there is no trust as the settlor has not given up his ownership of the assets. This said, in a number of trust jurisdictions, laws have been adapted to permit more and more control to a settlor, again, to at least some extent, making trusts and foundations increasingly interchangeable instruments.

To add to the possible confusion, the term "foundation" means different things in different circumstances. Under the laws of some countries, a foundation can only be established if the benefits go primarily to charity; in other countries, the term "foundation" can be mixed with trust use. For example, it is not uncommon to find a trust established that is called "The X Family Foundation" – technically a trust, but in its name referred to as a foundation.

As with trusts, key for any wealth-owning family is to really understand the structure they have in place and ensure that it not only achieves what they hope to achieve, but that the right people are involved, with appropriate oversight during the lifetime of not only the wealth owner, but also after the wealth owner's death or disability. In the case of a foundation, like in the case of a trust, the ability to make changes to those in charge and to ensure that there is appropriate governance in place is critical.

Partnerships

Partnerships are an increasingly valuable tool for wealth owners to use, and a variety of partnership structures can be used to address the planning needs of wealth-owning families. In basic terms, a partnership is not a distinct legal entity, but rather an arrangement to conduct business. But there are many ways that partnerships can be set up, and lots of variations on approaches under the laws of the many different countries where partnerships can be established.

While partners are generally responsible for the liabilities of the partnership, this can be managed by having the partners of the partnership be limited liability companies, or by using a "limited" partnership that allows for limited liability of individual partners.

Like trusts, partnerships can be very flexible tools, and this allows them to be used by wealth-owning families to address a number of needs. Partnerships can also be mixed with trusts and other wealth-planning "tools," and perhaps examples of how partnerships can be used can provide the best flavor of how attractive they can be as succession and asset-protection planning vehicles.

Mother, for example, has established a business that has a value of $5 million. Mother lives in a country that has both a tax on gifts she makes, as well as a tax on the value of her assets that pass on death. Mother is running the business, but has children who are involved in the business, and to whom she eventually envisions leaving the business. The business is going very well, and mother anticipates that by the time she passes away, the business is likely to be far more valuable than it is today.

If mother holds on to her interest in the business, and it passes to her children on her death, inheritance taxes will be imposed on the value of the business at that time. If the business has gone up in value to, say, $50 million, the tax that arises will be based on that value. Thinking about this might encourage mother to consider transferring her interest in the business to her children now. This would attract a gift tax, but at the current value of the business ($5 million). On the death of mother, there would be no further tax, because she would already have disposed of the asset involved.

While an early transfer of the business to the children could be attractive from a tax perspective, it would mean that the children own the business and control it, something mother may not be entirely comfortable with. Perhaps a family partnership can provide a better result.

Mother can transfer her business to a family partnership, and obtain in return an interest in the partnership that provides her with a priority right to receive, on sale of the business, the current value of the business, being $5 million, and to receive a fixed amount of profits while the business remains in the partnership. Mother's partnership interests can also carry all the voting rights in relation to the business being conducted, keeping control with mother, while "freezing" the value of her interest in the business. Mother can then give or sell partnership interests to her children, which interests can, for the moment, not provide any voting rights (or limit such rights).

In very broad terms, today the value of the partnership interests mother is transferring to her children is virtually nil, as all the value of the business as it stands today is with the partnership interest she retains. A gift of the partnership interests may therefore result in little or no gift tax. As the value of the business grows, the value of the partnership interest that mother holds is "frozen," in that it remains worth the $5 million that mother would receive were the business to be sold. If the business, when mother passes away, is worth $50 million, inheritance taxes might only apply to mother's interest in the partnership, the value of which is frozen at the $5 million figure. The children already own their partnership interests, which reflect the remaining value of the business ($45 million), and there is therefore no tax to pay on this. The children, through their inheritance of their mother's voting interests, now own the voting control of the business.

There are many variations on this theme that can be achieved through the flexibility of partnerships, and while in a number of countries there are specific tax rules and valuation principles associated with retention of voting control and other elements, the broad tax advantages can be achieved while also permitting the family to reflect the ownership approaches that are appropriate in the circumstances.

While similar benefits can be achieved through structures involving other than partnerships, variations of partnership approaches are commonly used to provide efficient ways to hold real estate. If a husband and wife are planning to purchase a holiday home in France, for example, despite not being residents of France, they would be subject to a variety of taxes, including wealth taxes, depending on the value of their property, as well as inheritance taxes that arise on death. If the property is put in the name of their children from the outset, inheritance taxes may be avoided, but control of the property falls into the hands of the children, which may not be ideal for a number of reasons. By having the family hold the property through a partnership, if there are two children, there are now four owners, and the value of each family member's interests may be below the threshold applicable for wealth tax to apply. Further, ownership of controlling interests, through a partnership approach, can assure the parents that they control decisions on use and sale of the property. On death, only the value of the parents' interests, now limited through the value already owned by the children, would be subject to inheritance tax.

Tax-wise, partnerships, unlike companies, are generally "flow-through" vehicles, meaning that it is not the partnership itself that is taxed, but rather the partners of the partnership. This can provide a number of advantages, including access to lower capital-gains tax rates applicable to individuals rather than corporations, as in the case of the USA. Using the USA as an example, the flow-through nature of partnerships means that if a partnership is set up and is owned by non-US partners, there is generally no tax if the partnership does not earn US-sourced income. And under US laws, there are LLCs that can be established and which can qualify for partnership treatment, meaning that the vehicle can be a hybrid between a company and a partnership.

But tax is not the main reason partnerships are often used in family succession and asset-protection structures. Rather, partnerships can be hugely flexible in terms of governance and economic arrangements that are put in place, and can even have "trust-like" elements to them, opening the door to even more possible planning uses. For example: mother can be the general partner of a partnership that provides for her, as general partner, to have a fixed interest in the value of the partnership, say again $5 million. Mother can have her two children hold partnership interests with a fixed value of $1 million each. As the general partner, mother can retain the ability, at her discretion, to allocate additional value to the limited partners (her children) or to new limited partners. If the partnership has a value of $10 million, $7 million is, in effect, "owned" by mother and her two children; the remaining $3 million is held in a manner that is similar to a discretionary trust or foundation, but which, depending on the country whose tax laws apply, attracts different, possibly better, reporting and tax consequences.

Like with trusts and foundations, the flexibility of partnerships makes it very important for wealth-owning families to really understand what they are getting into, and to ask the "what-ifs" that can help ensure the assets remain in the ownership and control expected and planned for.

Companies: Offshore, Onshore, and "Midshore"

Companies are common vehicles used to own assets and businesses, and there are many choices in how and where companies can be established.

Very commonly used have been tax-haven, or "offshore," companies. These are companies that are established in one of many offshore financial centers competing for business from investors and wealth owners looking for simple, tax-neutral approaches to asset ownership. Jurisdictions that come into the picture here range from the British Virgin Islands to the Bahamas and many others, all generally offering relative simplicity and low cost in the corporate formation process, and no tax exposure at all, particularly where no activity takes place in the offshore center itself.

This tax-free treatment, however, is only in the country in which the company is set up. The first question in relation to tax exposure is always the home country of the wealth owner himself – despite the fact that the company may not be taxed in its country of incorporation, the home country may have tax rules that impact things in a substantial way. These rules, as discussed earlier, can include taxing the company as if it were resident in the country of the wealth owner if the company is considered to be managed and controlled by the wealth owner in his country of residence. Anti-deferral rules, such as controlled foreign corporation rules, can cause immediate taxation of the income of the offshore company, and a number of other tax rules can come into the picture, including the home country simply ignoring the existence of the offshore company if it lacks substance and is considered to be a "sham."

Having a company own an asset rather than owning the asset directly can bring a number of advantages, though in some circumstances, there may be clear disadvantages. Advice is usually needed.

If, for example, I own a valuable classic car that I physically keep in the USA, and I am not a US citizen, resident or domiciliary, I may be exposed to US estate tax on my death given that on my death, there is a moveable asset that I own, the car, physically in the USA. If, in contrast, the car were owned by a non-US company, say a company in the British Virgin Islands, when I die it is not the asset in the USA that I own and which passes to my family (the car), but rather the shares of the British Virgin Islands company. Providing the company is "real" in the sense of my having respected it in all relevant transactions and appropriately documented things, I die owning shares of a non-US company, thereby avoiding US estate-tax exposure – and in the British Virgin Islands, no tax on my death arises. If my home country also has no tax that arises on death, tax exposures do not arise.

Some countries have rules that seek to limit the ability of wealth owners to "envelope" assets in companies, and an example of this is the UK, where using a foreign company to own domestic residential real estate not only does not provide protection against inheritance tax, but comes at additional tax costs.

Increased tax transparency and an overall focus by countries on collecting what they view to be their fair share of tax revenues is putting pressure on traditional offshore companies, which are generally established in locations where there is minimal substance in terms of employees, business activities, or otherwise. Various approaches can be used by countries to attack the use of offshore companies, including ignoring the existence of the company if it lacks substance, treating it as resident in the home country or elsewhere if the company is in reality "managed and controlled" from the home country (something that is a common taxing approach in countries including Canada, Switzerland, the UK, Hong Kong, Singapore, and others), or focusing on "transfer-pricing" rules to insist on income earned by the offshore company being reallocated to taxable entities more involved in generating the relevant profits.

While it is more than likely that a good number of traditional offshore centers will continue to not only survive, but also thrive, offshore centers are under challenge, and a good part of tax planning is moving both "onshore" and "midshore." Reporting and taxpaying are often simpler where the wealth owner uses onshore planning. The UK is an example, with relatively low tax rates for UK companies, and the USA another, with reporting and taxpaying being much simpler where US structures are used for US taxpayers. But there are still many cases where wealth owners benefit from using companies outside their home country, and this not only from a tax perspective, but also for confidentiality, asset protection, and other reasons.

Increasingly, "midshore" locations are attractive places for companies to be established. There is no real definition of what it means to be "midshore," but generally the term would describe locations for companies (and other structures) that are not traditional tax havens, but rather substantial financial centers whose tax and other laws provide incentives to establish structures there, and from where business and investment activities can be coordinated. Falling into this category would clearly be places like Hong Kong and Singapore, where territorial tax systems and low tax rates combine with solid tax-treaty networks and sophisticated infrastructures supporting the needs of investors and businesses. Also falling within this category are traditional "onshore" centers, like the USA and the UK, that offer a number of attractions to foreign investors making use of their financial and corporate centers.

Where companies are used, wealth owners need, as with all of the "tools" of wealth planning, to pay attention to governance, and understand what happens in the event of death or disability. In the case of a company, the shareholders are the owners of the company, and if the wealth owner is a shareholder and dies, those shares will pass, perhaps under their will. If the shares of the company are held in a trust or foundation, the trust or foundation will govern what happens to the ownership of the shares on death.

Shareholder agreements are a common and necessary tool setting out the rights and obligations of the shareholders of a company, and even where ownership is only within one family, such agreements are often necessary to avoid difficulties associated with exits from the business by family members, restricting transfers to people outside the family, dealing with capital raising, and many other issues. Like partnerships, companies, depending on where they are established, can also be quite flexible, and different share classes can permit voting rights to be retained by the older generation, while value is accorded to the younger.

Estate "freezes" as described earlier in relation to partnerships can also be achieved with companies. For example, Father can transfer a business to a company in exchange for redeemable preference shares that have voting rights. He can have a fixed right to the current value of his business, and perhaps a fixed return of, say, 5% on that value.

The common shares that reflect growth in the value of the company can go to the children, and these shares, worth nothing at the outset, would represent the future growth in value of the business, the shares of Father being "frozen" in value at the figure set as the redemption value of the shares, being the current value of the business.

Some families, at the more sophisticated end of planning, even use publicly listed companies as part of their family asset-holding structures. This is something that comes up where a family is in a third, fourth, or further generation, and where multiple shareholders create complexity in terms of permitting sales of shares and transparency on financial performance and other matters. By having the company that may hold a family business, for example, be publicly listed, family members can enter and exit the business, and obtain transparency on financial results. Through special classes of shares and otherwise, control can be retained with the family.

Investment funds are another similar vehicle that families can use, and these can also have elements of public listings in them. Like in the case of companies, the availability of favorable tax treaties and investment-protection agreements is a factor in the choice of location for such funds.

The Family "Bank"

The family "bank" is another wealth-planning tool, and was discussed in the previous chapter in my review of family constitutions. The family "bank" is more of a concept on how financial support for family members and their endeavors is accounted for, rather than being about the establishment of an actual bank.

Fairness is a key objective that wealth owners should have if they seek to avoid wealth being destructive of relationships. Where Mom or Dad provide funds to a child, whether to help them in establishing a business or to buy a home or otherwise, the question of fairness arises if there are other children who do not receive the same support. The family "bank" is a way of dealing with this.

It is the case that some families do consider establishing a bank, sometimes for political-risk protection given that banks have capital requirements, making it difficult for a home country to insist on the repatriation of funds where a family has the funds invested as the capital of a licensed bank in a foreign country. But this is not the type of family "bank" that I advocate all wealth-owning families consider creating in a notional way, perhaps as part of family trust arrangements or otherwise.

The objective of the family "bank" is to ensure a feeling of fairness in relation to the endeavors of the younger generation that are supported by family assets. The family bank can, for example, clarify what element of the support provided is a loan to the family member and what element is something else – perhaps a gift or an investment. A loan needs to be repaid at some point, possibly from the share of family assets that family member will eventually inherit. A gift does not have to be repaid. An investment by the family means that the family takes risks – if it is an investment into a business the child is establishing, and the business does well, the family benefits; if the business fails, the family takes the loss.

Key to success of the family bank concept is to develop fair approaches that are accepted by family members and which can adapt to the needs of the family. The family bank can also be used as an approach to deal with unequal consumption by the younger generation, whether for special advanced education, help with buying a home, or otherwise.

The more discussion that takes place within families on how the younger generation will be supported, the better, and parents who take into account the thinking of their children are more likely to avoid wealth being a destructive element within the family.

Insurance Products

A variety of insurance products are part of the wealth-planning toolbox, and insurance products are increasingly used by wealth-owning families to address not only tax minimization and management objectives, but asset protection and more.

There are many different kinds of insurance, including traditional insurance on a home against fire, earthquakes, and other threats, and coverage of loss of contents and potential liabilities of all kinds. For significant wealth owners, insurance needs in this area can already be complex, and can in some cases involve forms of "self-insurance," including the use of "captive" insurance companies that are wholly or partially owned by the family itself. In some cases, tax and other benefits can be achieved through such arrangements, but the more common wealth-planning uses of insurance come in the area of life insurance and life annuities.

In the case of insurance, like in the case of trusts or foundations, there are different parties involved. If I set up a trust, I am the settlor, and the person I transfer my assets to is the trustee. In the case of insurance, if I am establishing a life-insurance policy, and pay the relevant premiums and have the right to designate the beneficiaries, among other things, I am the policy owner. I pay the premiums to the insurance company, another party to the insurance arrangement. The life policy will designate one or more lives assured. This can be a life policy that I own which pays out on my death – in this case, I am both the policy owner and the life assured. I can also buy a life policy over the life of my wife, or over our lives jointly; in this case, either my wife or the both of us are the lives assured. When I establish the policy, I specify who will benefit from the policy upon the death of the life assured – and perhaps it is my children who I name as the beneficiaries.

In the tax area, insurance can provide interesting consequences, and this, of course, depends on the tax laws that apply to the wealth-owning family, and to the insurance structure itself. The first step in any tax analysis is to understand what happens when a premium is paid to the insurance company by the policy owner. Unlike a trust or foundation that is established, the transfer is not normally viewed as a gift, attracting a donation or similar tax if one applies in the country of the wealth owner. In fact, the policy owner is actually buying something – the policy providing the insurance coverage – and this is not generally a taxable event. In some countries a small excise or other tax may apply to the premium payment, but this is not a tax on a donation or on income. Reporting requirements for the policy owner may also be very different from those that might apply where a trust or foundation is established.

Once the insurance company receives the premiums, a further question will be the extent to which the insurance company itself pays tax, given that the amount the insurance company will eventually pay out to my family will be affected by the inside build-up of the policy, represented by the premiums paid, returns on the investment by the insurance company of the premiums, less the charges imposed by the insurance company and any taxes that apply. In a number of cases, insurance companies are established in countries where only the fees charged by the insurance company are taxable, and not the investment returns that form part of the inside build-up of the policy – this can be attractive, as it means that more money can be available for an eventual payout to my children. But do I, as the policy owner, get taxed on the inside build-up? Does the life assured?

In many countries, if the policy is a real life-insurance policy, the owner of the policy is not taxed on the inside build-up within the policy. And in the case of the life assured, there are almost never any tax issues that arise, as the life assured only provides the measurement of time during which the policy will remain in place; being a life assured does not necessarily involve any policy ownership or other interests.

What does it mean to be "real" life insurance? Generally, this revolves around the concept of mortality risk. In a traditional life-insurance arrangement, I may agree to pay the insurance company a premium of $5000 each year. Under the policy, if I die before the age of 75, the insurance company pays my family $50,000. If I die after paying two years of premiums, I win the bet – I may be dead, but I only paid $10,000 (two years of premiums) to have the beneficiaries of my life policy receive $50,000. The insurance company lost the bet – it took "mortality risk," believing that I would live long enough to more than cover the eventual payout, but was wrong. Because of the mortality risk that the insurance company assumes, it is common for insurers, before putting the policy in place, to review the health of the life assured, and at a certain age, life insurance may not even be available, or may be prohibitively expensive, because of the mortality risk involved.

What if I have a portfolio of assets worth $1 million, and instead of paying an annual premium to the insurance company, I agree on a single premium – I transfer the investment portfolio to the insurance company as the one premium for the life policy. And perhaps, as can be done, the insurance company places the portfolio in a unit-linked policy, where the investment portfolio is owned by the insurance company, but managed by the same asset manager that I used before I purchased the policy. Most importantly, how much will the insurance company pay the beneficiaries of the policy in the event of my death? If the policy is nothing more than an insurance "wrapper," perhaps the deal is that the insurance company will only pay out the investment portfolio – returns on the investment since the policy was established, less the charges of the insurance company. If I die soon after the policy is established, does the insurance company suffer any mortality risk? In my example, the answer is no.

In many countries, if there is insufficient mortality risk, the policy is not respected as being a life-insurance policy, meaning that the policy owner is still considered to own the assets that are in the policy. This results in the policy owner being taxed on the inside build-up of the policy on a current basis – the investment returns on the portfolio I transferred to the insurance company as a single premium would be taxed to me each year, as if I still owned the portfolio. But frequently, if there is sufficient mortality risk, the policy owner is not taxed on the inside build-up, a big tax advantage, particularly if the insurance company is located in a country that does not tax the insurance company on that build-up. How much in the way of mortality risk is needed for this favorable tax treatment? In some countries, this is clearly set out in the relevant tax rules. In other countries, the rules are less clear, and input from tax professionals is needed to be sure that the tax results are as expected.

Still on tax, there are other tax issues that life insurance involves. If I am the policy owner, what happens on my death? The ownership of the policy may transfer, and depending on whether or not I am the life assured, the beneficiaries may receive a payout. In some countries, such as the USA, the policy owner is considered to have something of value when he dies, and the transfer of the ownership of the policy will result in the potential of estate taxes applying. For this reason, it is relatively common for large life policies to be owned by trusts designed to avoid estate taxes applying, and minimizing any gift taxes associated with premium payments.

The death benefit of life-insurance policies is often tax free. In some countries taxes do apply to the beneficiaries, but at lower rates than on other receipts.

Life policies can also be structured to permit the policy owner access to funds during their lifetime, this through borrowings on the security of the policy or otherwise. Here too tax issues arise, and in a number of countries, limited borrowings can permit tax-free access to funds held in the insurance structure.

Apart from life insurance, a variety of annuity products can also provide interesting tax and other benefits. In some countries, like the USA, annuity products can be designed to provide retirement benefits, as is the case for deferred variable annuities. In very simple terms, tax laws facilitate the use of approaches that permit someone to place money in a deferred variable annuity, avoid taxation during the period over which the insurance company invests the premiums, and then be taxed only on receiving retirement benefits from the fund. This approach provides the tax advantages associated with tax deferral, or a delay in taxation until such time as the proceeds are paid out. The advantage here is that 100% of the income in a particular year can be fully reinvested, without any deduction for tax, meaning that there will be more money that accumulates than would be the case were tax paid each year.

The tax benefits of a retirement product along the lines of a deferred variable annuity can be even more interesting where the approach is used for someone who is not initially a US taxpayer, but who moves to the USA on a temporary basis. If, for example, an individual is living outside the USA and is not a US citizen, a move to the USA on a temporary basis would result in the individual being taxable in the USA on worldwide income during his period of residence in the USA. If, immediately before a move to the USA, the individual transfers an investment portfolio to a trust or foundation, US tax rules would require tax to be paid on the earnings of the trust, even if the trust is outside the USA. A variety of reporting requirements would also be triggered. If, in contrast, the individual, before a move to the USA, purchased a deferred variable annuity, and if all is properly handled, then there would be no US taxpaying or reporting requirements associated with the purchase of the annuity given that this takes place before US residence is established, and no taxation during the period of residence in the USA given that there is full tax deferral on the inside build-up within the annuity. If the individual leaves the USA before retirement and the triggering of annuity payments, no tax arises.

Of course, strategies such as this one always require careful review of the tax and reporting rules at the relevant time, and tax laws are always changing. But creative cross-border use of insurance and annuity strategies is part of the wealth-planning toolbox.

Insurance products are not only about tax. There are many other potential benefits to wealth-owning families, including clarity about how assets pass on death and, as well, asset protection and other benefits. On the asset-protection front, once assets are in a well-structured life policy, if properly planned, the assets in the policy can be protected against spousal and creditor claims. From a political-risk perspective, ownership of the assets is now with the insurance company rather than with the wealth owner, and if the insurance company is in a more secure country than that of the residence of the wealth owner, political risk protection may be meaningful. And increasingly, insurance approaches are available that facilitate not only the holding in policies of liquid assets, but also the shares of family businesses and other assets.

Insurance is an area where the costs associated with the policy may not be anywhere as transparent as they should be. While things are changing from a regulatory perspective, requiring a much higher degree of clarity to the wealth owner on the actual costs of insurance, it is very important for the wealth-owning family to really understand who is getting what where an insurance policy is being put in place. Not only are commissions sometimes much higher than one would expect, but hidden costs and kickbacks are part of what is seen as fairly standard. Conflicts of interest are also common, and this is an area discussed in the next chapter in relation to not only insurance.

Derivatives and More

There are many other "tools" in the wealth-planning toolbox, and addressing the real needs of wealth owners means identifying the right tools and using them in the right way to achieve objectives that will help families navigate an increasingly complex world. Derivative products, in simple terms, involve contracts that provide for benefits that track underlying securities – providing a return that mimics the return that a security would otherwise provide.

A number of years ago, I was involved in helping a family deal with an inheritance-tax issue arising in a country whose laws imposed an inheritance tax where ownership of a company exceeded a certain percentage, say 5%. The wealth owner owned slightly higher than this percentage of a publicly listed company that had been a family business, and that he did not want to sell shares of. Seeking to achieve avoidance, in a legal way, of the inheritance tax, the wealth owner sold enough shares to a bank in order to come below the 5% ownership threshold, but entered into a derivative contract with the bank under which payment to the bank was made from the proceeds of sale to obtain a derivative providing the same economic returns as the shares that had been disposed of and a right to the holder of the derivative, after a set number of years (designed to take place after the death of the wealth owner), to reacquire the shares that had been disposed of. In simple terms, while economically the family was in the same position that they would have been had no shares been sold, the use of the derivative allowed for inheritance taxes to be minimized.

7

Advisors – We Need Them but Need to Control Them

Advisors are almost always necessary, but it is important to understand their role, and to manage them in an appropriate way. And an effective advisor is one who has the interests of their clients at the forefront, and positions themselves as a true trusted advisor.

For the wealth owner, it is not just a question of negotiating fees, but of really understanding how bankers, lawyers, and accountants work and charge, and, importantly, the hidden ways they can profit from their clients' wealth – and from disputes that arise in the family.

Letting an advisor "kidnap" the succession process is very dangerous, and all too common in a complex world where "leaving it to the experts" seems to be the way to go. It is, after all, the wealth of the family involved – not the wealth of the advisor – but there are many situations of advisors becoming the "gatekeepers" to the family's wealth, using wealth that is not that of the advisor to benefit themselves in a number of ways. This chapter focuses on advisors – who they are, how to choose them, and how they charge.

It is important to understand that for many advisors there is no client better than a dead client. A client of a private bank, trust company, or law firm may, depending on the mechanisms in place in relation to succession, become extraordinarily valuable once dead, given the limited ability of surviving family members to provide an appropriate check on fee charging and discretionary decision-making. Dead clients cannot question fees or fire advisors – so it is critical to ensure that the right checks and balances are in place in relation to structures that may have been established during the lifetime of the wealth owner.

Even the most honest and reliable individual or organization can abuse their position if there is a lack of oversight. A good rule of thumb is to simply operate on the basis of *trusting no one* in developing the right succession plan. This is not to say that no one, whether in or out of the family, can be trusted. Rather, if too much trust is accorded to anyone, there is a risk that such trust may be abused. It is critical for appropriate family members, such as the spouse and children of the wealth owner, to be prepared to take on an oversight role in relation to advisors, and to help manage the transition that can otherwise risk having the advisors end up being the ones in control. A good advisor is one who proactively helps their client understand the need to have the right oversight. There is no better way to sell your services than by *not selling*, but telling the truth.

The more the wealth owner understands their real needs, and the roles of advisors, the more the right controls can be put in place. To really understand their own affairs, a wealth owner does not need to know all the answers – in fact, the world is so complex that there is no one who has all the answers. But the more the wealth owner is able to ask the right questions and admit to not understanding elements of the structures in place in relation to their family's wealth ownership and succession plans, the closer he can get to meeting his responsibilities to his family.

This book is also for advisors to wealth-owning families, and particularly for those at an early stage of their careers. My view is that the more an advisor is able to align their interests with the interests of their clients, the more successful they will be and the more rewarding their career will be, not only financially, but also in terms of allowing the advisor to enjoy the knowledge that they are really helping the client families they serve. Transparency on fees is one part of being a real trusted advisor, and in the education and development of those in the financial services industry, much more needs to be done to develop a sense of ethics and high standards that focus more on long-term relationships than on short-term revenues.

Where and when should the wealth owner start the process of understanding their succession structure? The answer is that it is never too early to begin the process, and for the younger generation or others with an expectation of inheriting or otherwise receiving benefits, the more they understand, the more the family will be protected.

Lawyers and Accountants

Things on the legal, tax, and accounting front are increasingly complex and ever-changing, and there is little chance for any wealth owner to be able to navigate safely without the help of the right advisors.

The first key step is to find the right advisors, and one of the biggest dangers is running across a lawyer or accountant who does not acknowledge what they do *not* know. It is not at all uncommon to find wealth owners who have turned to their business lawyers or accountants for help in succession and asset-protection planning, only to find that the advisor took on the job without having the experience or knowledge needed to do it properly. A superbly competent commercial lawyer may well *not* have the experience and knowledge needed to put together a will or trust, but may turn their hand to it, making a mess of things for the family involved. A good, trusted advisor will acknowledge where they need help, and most effective for the family is for their long-standing commercial lawyer or accountant to stay in the picture, liaising with specialists who can provide the input the family really needs.

Tax has been a driver of much of the planning that wealth-owning families undertake, and another failing is overreliance on a tax specialist who may not be best placed to provide the holistic input that a family really needs. A US, UK, or other tax specialist may well provide solid advice on tax-minimization approaches relevant to their country of expertise, but they may not have the human and other skills needed to help the wealth-owning family develop a holistic succession plan. Something I have seen many times in my career are trust and other structures that have been implemented by tax advisors whose sole focus was addressing a particular tax issue. The wealth-owning family, not knowing the right questions to ask, only later discovers, to their detriment, that the structure in place failed to serve them on many other fronts, including in relation to asset protection, good succession planning for the younger generation, and even the tax laws of other countries relevant to the situation of the family and their investments.

Among the many examples I have seen of such failed planning include many trust structures established for Hong Kong-connected wealth owners during a time at which Hong Kong had an estate duty, a tax on death that no longer applies. Complicated trust structures were used to avoid the tax, and often the wealth owner did not fully understand the limited power retained once the assets were put in trust. An over-focus by advisors on the estate-duty elements of the structures often resulted in insufficient attention being paid to other issues, such as when family members and others would have access to assets, and tax issues relevant to their own countries of citizenship or residence. Despite Hong Kong having eliminated estate duty, many historical structures remain in place, with the succession of assets within families following approaches that were not designed around thinking about what would be best for the family, but rather around avoiding a tax that no longer exists.

Another very common failing in planning is the over-emphasis on US taxation that international families sometimes fall into, in part from fear of the heavy-handed enforcement of US tax laws and from the approach of some US advisors who fail to consider that the tax and other laws of other countries are also of relevance to the families they serve. Non-US families buying real estate in the USA, or who have children who live in the USA or who hold US citizenship, sometimes find themselves victims of expensive and complex structures that may well address US tax issues, but which fail to take into account more important needs relevant in their home country, both tax and non-tax. A revocable trust, for example, can be a very good approach for a foreign wealth owner to take with a view to benefitting a US citizen child in a tax-effective way given the US "grantor trust" rules that would allow tax-free benefit to the US child on the death of the non-US grantor. But what if the creator of the trust is sued or gets divorced? And what of the tax issues in the creator's home country? Having the right to revoke the trust may not be ideal.

One of the worst problems I have run across are approaches adopted by families who have been misled by advisors, whether lawyers, bankers, or others, about the protections afforded by bank secrecy. This was a huge problem in Switzerland, where I was based for many years, and despite the many changes that have taken place to encourage tax transparency, there remain advisors in Switzerland and elsewhere who mislead families into thinking that hiding their assets and income is a way to go.

Countless wealth owners were told by their bankers, lawyers, accountants, and other advisors that no one would find out about their hidden structures and accounts. With growing transparency, families are discovering that they not only have more in the way of tax to pay than they would have done had they complied with the tax laws relevant to them, but also may now suffer criminal and/or civil penalties and other costs that compliance could have avoided.

In some cases, families, thinking that hiding the money was the best solution, neglected to do the work necessary to plan for their succession in the right way. I worry that increased enforcement of tax laws is resulting in some families putting all or part of their wealth in assets that are outside of the banking system, where tax compliance is increasingly having to be demonstrated, and through approaches where the assets involved, be they diamonds or gold, are not maintained in structures that properly protect the assets through the succession process. Is it worth breaking the law and risking your assets as a means of paying less tax? I recently learned of one wealth-owning family going through a name change as a means of supposedly evading tax liabilities – an approach which is not only illegal, but gives rise to many risks associated with the succession process.

The more the wealth owner is able to understand their real needs, the more they can help ask the right questions, and assemble a team of advisors who can work together efficiently and look at things holistically.

A first step for the wealth owner is to understand that no accountant or lawyer will be an expert on everything, and particularly not when matters cross borders, which they almost always do. But too many lawyers and accountants that families work with pretend to know what they do not, a real problem given the complexities that need to be navigated. An effective advisor is one who knows what they know, and knows what they don't. But for the wealth owner, it is ideal if a trusted advisor can coordinate input from the various advisors who may need to be involved to address a complex situation. Tax laws may come into the picture, as may trust rules, and the impact of both in more than one country. This alone may require a team approach.

The results, the costs, and the whole process will depend on how the project is managed, and how well the initial work is executed and then updated and adjusted to adapt to changes in the law, the family, and their assets, changes which are inevitable.

Large global law and accounting firms can be an answer given that, at least theoretically, they should have the experience and capability to handle multi-jurisdictional and disciplinary issues. But they have their limitations, and it is important for the wealth owner to understand how some of these firms work (and charge). I spent my legal career in a large global law firm, and while I am a big believer in what they can achieve for clients, I am also a believer that results can be achieved in as or a more cost-effective way by smaller, single-jurisdiction professional firms providing that the advisor the family is working with understands their own limitations, and knows the right questions to ask, and to whom.

The reality is that professional services are extraordinarily expensive, something that is lamentable, but which is a product of an increasingly complex world, the high cost of running a professional firm, and what are sometimes unjust income expectations of the professionals involved.

Personally, when I use a lawyer or accountant, I like to first ensure that I am using the right person for the right job – I want to know that the lawyer or accountant I am working with has experience and knowledge in the area that I need help with. Given that many professionals charge based on the time they spend, I certainly do not want to pay for the time my advisor takes to learn an area they are unfamiliar with. I am much better off with an advisor who charges a higher hourly rate, but who has done the same or similar work many, many times before. Also important to me is to develop a reasonable budget for the work I anticipate needing to have done. Open-ended arrangements can only lead to unhappy surprises, and the way lawyers and accountants are often incentivized in their own firms is to involve many more junior people in the job, and maximize the revenue generated.

I may see a partner of a law firm who is super-experienced and knowledgeable, and who "sells" me his ability to handle what I need to have done. They agree to take me on as a client and to move forward. When I leave the office of the lawyer, the partner calls in two members of his junior team, briefs them on my matter, and asks them to write a memo. The junior lawyers are themselves under financial incentives that require them to bill as many hours as possible – in some law firms, bonuses are not paid before lawyers bill 1800 and often more hours a year. With a month's holiday a year, this works out to more than eight billable hours a day, assuming a five-day week. And it is absolutely common for the successful young lawyer to be billing 2000 or 2200 or more hours a year. How can this really work, if during the working day the lawyer is also going to the washroom, eating lunch, reading up on legal developments, attending internal management and other meetings, going to the dentist, or doing whatever else they need to do? There are many cases of abuse and overbilling, but even where time recording is honest, does this really work out to the benefit of the client?

The young lawyers run off to the library, research things in areas they are not familiar with, look at previous work product, and draft a memorandum for the partner to review. He reads it, spends hours correcting it, finally gives up, tears it in two, and dictates a letter to me, his client, that is to the point and reflects his knowledge and maybe a bit of the research his young lawyers spent hours and hours putting together. The result may be good, but the bill I get reflects a massive number of billable hours that I should not be paying for.

Clarity on a budget in advance of work done is the right way to keep a check on how lawyers and accountants work, and where possible, a fixed cost for a fixed outcome is the way to go. But this does not always work, as there will be circumstances where a budget or fixed fee will not be appropriate, as what needs to be done may include negotiations or other steps that are not easy to predict at the outset. Here, huge transparency on how the lawyer or accountant will work, and who will be involved, will be key, as will getting very regular updates on work done, costs, and progress.

I remember a client once telling me that his preferred choice of lawyer was to find a hardworking, busy, and experienced sole prac- titioner very familiar with the area of law that was involved. The lawyer would then not have the ability to involve young lawyers in the project, creating the "leverage" that larger firms use to enhance profits, with partners of the firm earning from not only their own time spent, but also from the time spent by their juniors. I am not sure that this is necessarily the right solution in every case – to me the key is transparency on costs and the anticipated outcome, and not being afraid to discuss money at every stage of the process.

Over the years I had many clients who asked for discounts, and most law and accounting firms will offer these. But more important than a discount on hourly rates is to have an agreed fee for an agreed deliverable. I do not really care how high the hourly rate is if the outcome is delivered at the right price. If I pay $200 an hour to a lawyer who will spend 50 hours on the job, learning the law, involving colleagues with even less knowledge, is this better than using a lawyer who charges $1000 an hour, but who only spends five hours adapting something they recently did to my circumstances, and who addresses my needs based on their solid experience?

Managing the advisor is important, and while it can be boring work for the wealth-owning family, the reality is that the outcomes will be better and cheaper the more they understand their own situation, and are able to ask the right questions. There is now much in the way of information available from many sources, without cost, on virtually any issue one faces. Doing a bit of advance reading and narrowing the question to the lawyer or accountant can both help manage costs and focus the response to what it needs to be. And where the wealth owner does not want to do this themselves, using an intermediary, whether from a family office the family maintains or perhaps from a private bank or otherwise, can make a big difference. Someone who is an experienced consumer of legal and accounting services can be of big help to wealth-owning families.

And for the private banker or other intermediary, equipping yourself to be able to help families work with legal and tax advisors efficiently helps make *you* the trusted advisor – you don't need all the answers to be able to play this critical role, but you do need to know how to ask the right questions, and to leverage your contacts and experience to the benefit of your clients.

If I plan to move to a certain country and invest there, I will hunt around for an advisor from that country who looks like they know what they are doing. I will let them know my plans, and hopefully the advice I get will be the advice I need and at a price that is reasonable. If I am already working with a private bank or other organization that operates in a number of countries, maybe that private bank has resources, in the form of wealth planners or others, who work with clients of the bank who have similar needs to mine. If this is the case, they will, given their constant work on the issues, know who the main advisors are with experience in the area; they will know the right questions I should be asking; they will know the right price I should be paying for advice – and may even have better negotiating power than me to get the right advice at the right price given that they are important clients of the advisors involved, referring work regularly given their involvement with similarly placed families. Making use of intermediaries in the right way can be of real value to the wealth owner, and within private banks and other organizations providing services to wealth owners, understanding what clients really need, and how to help them by making effective use of networks of internal and external experts, can be key to success.

Private Banking and the Wealth-Management Industry

I became exposed to the wealth-management industry many years ago when I began working with families in Hong Kong in the early 1980s. The handover of Hong Kong to China was being negotiated in the run up to 1997, and wealth owners in Hong Kong were beginning to focus on political risk. Families and businesses began to restructure, and many wealth owners began diversifying their investment, residence, and citizenship destinations to the USA, Canada, Australia, Europe, and elsewhere. Providing advice to affected families, I began working with private banks, trust companies, and others in the industry, but learned very quickly that many private banks and others servicing wealth owners were simply not meeting the real needs of their clients.

Private banking and wealth management is a big, global business. Private banks generally make their money from managing the liquid assets of their clients, charging a percentage of assets under management (AUM). But what wealth-owning families need is much, much more than help with the management of their assets. And for private banks and others, I think it is important to understand that asset management is increasingly a commodity, and one where pricing challenges will increase significantly. The reality is that markets are ones that all asset managers are dealing with, and while it may be possible to outperform the competition from one year to the next, broadly when markets go up, portfolios do well, and when they go down, they do not. Index funds and automated "robo-advice" are permitting dramatic cost savings, making what many financial advisors charge for commodity services unsustainable in even the medium term.

Typically, a client of a private bank would have assets managed by the private bank. If the wealth owner has $5 million in liquid assets, the bank would seek to provide discretionary asset-management services, charging, say, 1% of the assets involved as their fee. The bank would thereby earn $50,000 a year from the family involved, but the assets would simply be managed in the same way the bank manages the assets of other clients of the bank with similar risk profiles, meaning that not much is actually tailored to the individual family involved.

Today, around the world, there are increasing regulations that require asset managers to provide transparency on charges to their clients, but there continue to be many circumstances of hidden charges that asset managers, such as private banks, impose on their clients. In my example, the private bank earns 1% on the AUM involved; but is the client aware that the bank may have made arrangements to receive "retrocessions" or kickbacks from investment funds in which they may invest the client money they have under discretionary management? Relatively recent court decisions in Switzerland require banks to refund retrocessions they historically received in a number of circumstances, but unsurprisingly the industry is pretty quiet about the rights their clients may have to obtain refunds of amounts their advisors secretly received.

Hidden commissions and other benefits are by no means confined to Swiss private banking, and it is fortunate that regulation is increasingly protecting wealth owners from abuses that have been rife in the industry. But are wealth owners reading the small print in the documents private banks and other asset managers provide them? Are they signing away their rights and consenting to practices that they would object to if they read the documents in front of them more carefully? I believe that it is critical to really understand how your asset manager charges, and for a successful private bank or other advisor to provide *genuine* transparency on fees.

But how many financial services providers really align themselves with the interests of their clients? How often are fees charged for asset management more than once through a fee being charged to the client for a service, and then the investment made into a product offered by the same bank or other asset manager, with further fees arising that are not disclosed to the client or even to the relationship manager of the bank involved, helping to keep actual costs murky to the client family?

For wealth owners, there is no choice but to be very critical in review of how banks charge, and to consider, where one has negotiating power given the level of assets involved, *not* signing the standard documents that banks put in front of you, but rather to set out your own terms, mandating your advisors to work in a way that makes sense for the wealth-owning family itself. Even where the amount of wealth involved is not enough to dictate your terms to the banks you work with, my suggestion is to agree in writing the actual service you expect to receive, and to make it clear what your expectations are. You may well have signed all the standard documents that your bank has required, the small print of which is generally all looking to protect the interests of the bank, not yours. But this does not mean that you cannot separately have a letter of agreement with the bank that lays out in detail exactly what services the bank will be providing, and how these will be delivered.

Private banks often offer a range of services other than asset management, but where they make their money is still from assets under management and the charges they impose on AUM. But as mentioned above, I believe that asset management is increasingly a commodity, and that pricing is and will continue to be under serious pressure in the years to come. The reality is that all asset managers are dealing with the same markets. Markets go up, and markets go down, and it is therefore not easy for an asset manager to consistently outperform their peers. As the world becomes more and more complex, those asset managers who can outperform their peers tend to be those who are very specialized, perhaps operating through a hedge fund or otherwise. So for a private bank, can they really sustain the charges that they currently impose on the asset management they perform, given that technology increasingly allows for investment performance that can match or exceed the performance of typical private banks at a much lower cost? It is interesting to compare the results of investing in indexes with the traditional stock picking of discretionary asset managers, and to also compare the costs involved.

Warren Buffett, famously, wrote in relation to advice to his heirs:

> My advice to the trustee couldn't be more simple: Put 10% of the cash in short-term government bonds and 90% in a very low-cost S&P 500 index fund. (I suggest Vanguard's.) I believe the trust's long-term results from this policy will be superior to those attained by most investors—whether pension funds, institutions or individuals—who employ high-fee managers.

But there is much more than just asset management that an effective private bank can and should provide. A wealth-owning family needs a trusted advisor that is not only able to take charge of asset management in relation to liquid assets, but who is also able to help the family in relation to investments in real estate, art, and anything else the family is interested in. There may also be a family business in the picture, and certainly asset protection, succession planning, and tax minimization will be topics of interest to the family. But if the private bank is focused on the income it earns on AUM, will it really be able to help the family in all the other areas of need?

There are many private banks today that offer a variety of services to families. Asset management is usually the cornerstone, but the bank may have, in addition to the *relationship manager* the family deals with, specialists, such as *wealth planners*, a trust company with *trust officers*, and a variety of others who can help address the needs of wealth-owning families. These resources, if properly used, can be of enormous help to a family, and can be much more valuable than the asset management the bank may provide. But in many private banks, how wealth planners and trust-company representatives charge and what their role should be is far from clear. In a number of cases, there is confusion about whether these functions are *profit centers* or *cost centers*, and the reality is that when the CEO or other manager looks at the figures, it is all too tempting to think that where the bank really makes its money is based on AUM and nothing more, with the high salaries of good wealth planners being a cost to be cut rather than a function to be focused on and built.

In times when private banks abused bank secrecy, and basically said to the wealth owners they worked with *we don't need to care about the tax or other laws of your home country – no one will find out about the assets we hold for you – let's go for lunch* the services and charges of the bank involved were not something the clients really focused on. If a client of a private bank was evading a tax imposed at 40% or more of the income that they earned, and was also evading inheritance and other taxes that could absorb a large percentage of the assets, the client did not really focus on the 1% or higher charge the bank was imposing on AUM, or the retrocessions and other kickbacks the bank was receiving, or on the high transaction costs the bank added to the bill, together with charging the client for the nice lunch they took the client to.

And where assets were just hidden from view, the banks involved did not need to invest in really understanding the tax and legal systems of their clients, or in software permitting them to provide clients with the tax reports the clients need to fill in their tax returns. And rather than investing for clients in a way that legally minimizes taxation through tax-advantaged investing reflecting the specific tax rules of their clients, banks invested for all their clients in exactly the same way, a cheap and easy way of doing business. Many of the clients of private banks historically had *hold mail* arrangements – the money being hidden from home-country authorities, the client did not want to have any mail come from the bank to their home.

Instead, bank statements would be held by the bank, and on an annual visit to the bank the relationship manager would point to three large boxes of unopened bank statements and ask, *do you want to go through all these?* Many clients would not, and the banker and client would go to lunch, leaving the bank statements unopened, with little review of bank charges, performance on asset management, or otherwise, the client happy with the savings enjoyed through the illegal evasion of tax, the high charges of the bank and the poor performance on investments being worth it.

But in a world of transparency and tax compliance, there is a huge shift that many private banks will not be able to cope with. It is no longer possible for a private bank to proudly serve clients from around the world – to be effective, a private bank needs to understand the real needs of their clients, and this requires knowledge of the home-country tax and legal systems, the ability to provide tax reporting and tax-advantaged investing, and the licensing of the private bank enabling them to legally provide services to clients from the country involved. Even the largest of private banks can therefore not really service clients from all over the world – there is a need for specialization. And clients who are fully compliant with their tax obligations are much more focused on the costs they incur in using a private bank, and on investment performance. In relation to costs, it is key to see that the client is actually receiving value, meaning that sustaining high fees on AUM will be increasingly difficult for a successful private bank.

An effective private bank needs to understand the real needs of their clients, and to align themselves with the interests of their clients. But all too often the wealth-management function in banks has fallen into the leadership of investment bankers who tend to think in a very short-term and transactional way. More interested in the earnings of the bank in the next quarter than in what is in the best interests of their clients, the boss focuses on assets under management, where the bank earns most of its income, and the incentives are on increasing these, rewarding those bankers who manage to bring new money into the bank to manage.

I have often debated with the CEOs of private banks the question of whether a private bank needs more *hunters* (most CEOs arguing that what they need are effective salespeople) – bankers who can *hunt* for new clients, bringing AUM to the bank. I argue, usually unsuccessfully, that private banking is not a business for hunters, but rather a business for *farmers* – those who get to know the family they work with, meet the in-laws, develop long-term relationships that lead to growth not only in AUM, but also in the long-term retention of the family as a client of the bank.

What clients of private banks really need is a trusted family advisor, and continuity in relationships that avoids the family having to re-educate relationship managers given the turnover in staffing suffered (or encouraged) by the industry today. If I meet a relationship manager of a private bank and discuss with them holistic issues affecting my family, I will be hoping that the relationship manager will remain with the private bank for the longer term, and ideally after my own passing or disability, enabling them, with their colleagues, to look after my affairs for the benefit of my family. But compensation systems within private banks, and how staff are managed generally, work against this alignment of interests, and increasingly relationship managers in private banks move all too frequently from one bank to the next.

The first question to an experienced relationship manager exploring the possibility of changing banks they work for is not what their name is, but rather how much in the way of AUM they might be able to bring with them when moving banks. The turnover in the industry, combined with the idea that clients belong to the relationship manager rather than the bank, fuels a disincentive to relationship managers institutionalizing clients. Even where a private bank has excellent wealth planners and trust officers able to help in providing holistic input to a family, the relationship manager may decide against introducing a client to his or her colleagues for fear that the client may *like* the wealth planner or trust officer. If the relationship manager then leaves the bank, they will have more difficulty dragging the client with them to a new bank, hence the disincentive of institutionalizing the client.

The wealth owner needs to understand how the industry really works, and the failings of those running private banks to truly align their businesses with the interests of their clients. I share more of my thinking on how private banks can get it *right* in the next chapter, but for the wealth owner, taking charge of the relationship is key.

The wealth-management industry is a huge business in chaos. Change is happening on many fronts, with the business models of the past falling away as tax and related transparency becomes the norm. Banks have and will continue to bear enormous compliance-related costs, in part due to the abuses of the past. Enormous fines have been paid to the USA and to other countries in and around abuses of tax and other laws, and these will continue for some time to come. Some banks are pulling out of elements of the wealth-management industry as a result, and others are closing down operations in traditional wealth-management centers, such as Switzerland. Smaller private banks are finding it difficult to survive, and new entrants to wealth management are likely to come from the technology sector, where new thinking and approaches may be better placed to serve wealth-owning families.

I worry that we are coming into a period of greater and greater danger for families, of fraud and other risks that increase when those involved in the industry see little security for their own futures.

Independent Asset Managers, Multi- and Single-Family Offices

The failings of private banks have led to the creation of independent asset managers (IAMs) and the multi- and single-family office, and variations on a theme. Pricing abuse, high turnover of relationship managers, misalignment of focus, and poor service generally have resulted in many families fleeing the private bank, turning to individuals who were sometimes previously with a private bank to offer them what they do not get from banks.

The typical IAM is a successful relationship manager with a private bank who develops good relationships with his clients, but who sees the inability to provide what the clients really need within the environment of a private bank that focuses more on short-term profits than on long-term relationships. The relationship manager resigns from the bank, and convinces some of his better clients to continue to work with him. The relationship manager is now working independently, providing his clients with asset-management and related services, while leaving the portfolio of assets with either their former bank or another bank, which now acts only as a custodian of the assets.

In very basic terms, the exit of the banker from a bank and the conversion of the bank from being an asset manager into being nothing more than a custodian of assets results in a meaningful loss of income to the bank, with the example of a 1% fee on AUM now going down to 20 or 30 basis points (and often much less) for the custody the bank continues to provide. The IAM charges the client the 70 basis point difference, meaning that the client is still paying an overall 1%, but now has an IAM more committed to providing the continuity of relationship that the client really wants, and which the private bank failed to deliver.

I believe that family offices, both the single-family office and the multi-family office, are also products of the failings of the wealth-management industry to serve the real needs of families.

Defining the term "family office" is not easy, and there are many versions of family offices that bear little resemblance to each other. Today, private banks, law firms, accounting firms, trust companies, and others market "family-office" services, further confusing the term.

The reality is that every wealth-owning family has a family office, whether they know it or not, and that it is difficult to find any two family offices that are the same. Someone, in every family, is taking care of the things that a typical family office would deal with. A family involved in a family business may have the chief financial officer, or whoever is handling the books for the business, also keep an eye on personal investments, perhaps liaising with asset managers, and also pay bills on real estate and otherwise manage the private assets the family holds. In effect, the individual involved is the family office, but not being well structured, the function may or may not be managed in a way that is best for the family.

The family office, or part of it, may also be handled by one or more people in the family – perhaps one of the children looks after a property in a particular country, while the wealth owner's spouse handles private bank accounts and the underlying investments. Typically, the "family office" is a disorganized collection of functions that may partially be handled within the family, partially handled by staff of the family business, and partially handled by external advisors, including lawyers, accountants, trustees, and private banks, but with no overall coordination and supervision, resulting in a more expensive and less effective structure than the family could put in place.

The more formal family office is where a family sets up a "single"-family office – a function put in place just for their family. Here, there is no one model that families adopt, or which is the "right" one. A senior accountant with the family business coming to retirement might be appointed as the head of the family-office function, coordinating the external advisors providing support to the family in relation to assets and succession and asset-protection structures. This would be the start of a simple family office, the idea being to have someone keeping an eye on things in a coordinated way.

Family offices can be very sophisticated, even where the family office is representing the interests of only one family. Some family offices bring in their own asset managers, replacing external asset managers, or acting in the role of determining asset allocation and supervising external asset managers. In some cases, the family office can include the trust function, with private trust companies administered for the benefit of the family involved. Looking after the "toys," which can include cars, airplanes, boats, holiday homes, and more, can also occupy the time of family offices.

For many families, the cost of a family office, and the distraction of running it, makes the idea of a multi-family office of interest. Here the services involved are being provided not just to a single family, but to many families. As the multi-family office grows, it begins to look more and more like a private bank – albeit without the custody of financial assets. Some of the failings of private banks can develop, as the focus moves away from alignment with the interests of the single family involved to the interests of those working or owning the multi-family office. But if there is a real focus on aligning interests, the multi-family office can be an effective way for the wealth owner to get what they need.

Interesting to observe is that the IAM and single and multi-family offices usually come into the picture when the wealth-owning family gets fed up with the poor service they get from their traditional private bank. And while the private bank ends up being nothing more than a custodian, the IAM or family office begins to focus on negotiating even these fees on behalf of the wealth owner, putting more pressure on the private banks.

Can any of the private banks get it right? I believe they can, and must. And that, given the continuity and financial resources they can bring to the table, families can be *better* served by private banks than by IAMs or multi-family offices.

Conflicts of Interest – Everyone Has Them!

Typical private banks have many conflicts of interest, and one of the challenges the industry faces is that clients have increasingly become aware of these. If I have an account with a private bank, they have an interest not only in managing my money, but also in directing me to investments in products they have a financial interest in. These may include internal investment products where the bank earns further fees, or third-party products where the bank gets some form of benefit, whether a retrocession or otherwise. Transactions may give rise to revenue for the bank, and this may create an incentive to "churn" the account. If I use a trust company that is owned by a bank, does the trust company have an incentive to keep assets under management with the bank as a means of enhancing overall revenue? For some banks, the trust function has traditionally been a cost center, specifically for the purposes of expanding assets under management.

But if I turn to an independent asset manager or independent trust company, or to an independent lawyer or accountant, am I assured of freedom from conflicts of interest? In my view, the answer is *always* no. *Everybody* has conflicts of interest of some kind, and for the wealth owner, the best thing is to accept that this is the case, and to be aware of what the conflicts of interest are, so that these can be managed.

The lawyer or accountant I work with may or may not be getting a financial benefit by introducing me to an asset manager or other specialist. In the end, it doesn't really matter so long as I know and understand what the benefit they may be receiving is. Most lawyers will not accept financial benefits given the ethical issues involved, though some will – but even where there are no financial benefits in the picture, is there a conflict of interest when a lawyer refers me to a trust company that in turn hires that lawyer on a regular basis? Is the lawyer referring me to the trust company that is best placed to meet my needs, or is he referring me to a trust company that will give him more business because of the referral?

There are many other conflicts of interest that wealth owners need to be aware of, and these include the growing regulatory and other burdens that are placed on advisors to wealth-owning families. Banks are increasingly required to document their clients for anti-money-laundering purposes, and need to understand the origin of assets and, increasingly, the tax compliance of those owning the assets involved. With obligations to file suspicious activity reports without tipping off the wealth owners involved, "trusted" advisors, which can include, in many countries, lawyers, accountants, real-estate agents, and others, may well have their own interests ahead of those of their clients, something that the wealth owner certainly needs to be aware of.

Tax authorities globally are increasingly putting responsibilities on tax and other advisors to monitor abuses of tax systems, requiring reporting and other steps where certain strategies or structures are implemented. Automatic exchange of information, through the US FATCA system and the OECD's common reporting standard, are requiring a broad range of intermediaries, including trustees, insurance companies, and banks, to confirm the tax residences of their clients and to provide the relevant tax authorities with information that includes not only income and gains, but also bank balances and more. The growing compliance burdens are certainly increasing costs, which will be passed on to wealth-owning families, but are also discouraging some from continuing to provide services to sectors of wealth owners. Americans are an example, with a number of banks outside the USA having restricted the services they provide to families with US residential or citizenship connections.

Given the risks to financial intermediaries of getting it wrong, there is a shift to hyper-compliance – some intermediaries going overboard in terms of intrusive questions and documentation – something well-advised wealth owners can try to manage and resist. Also increasingly problematic will be that information exchange will include significant information that has no taxing impact, but which may well give rise to complex discussions with tax authorities and others. I may live in a country where there is a tax on interest income, but no wealth tax – does the relevant tax authority need information, which they will now get, about my bank balance? I may be the protector of a trust that benefits a family in another country, but as a "controlling person," information on the trust income and assets may be sent to my country of residence. Will I have difficulties explaining to my tax authority that the assets and income should not be taxable to me? Will these discussions require explanations and documentation that will hugely increase the costs to the family with an interest in the trust? Will my country of residence trigger information finding its way to other countries, which may use the information not only for tax enforcement, but also perhaps corruptly against the interests of the family with an interest in the trust assets?

There is no replacement for the wealth owner and his or her family really understanding how advisors work. The wealth owner needs them – but needs to manage them, and to prepare the family for the work they need to do to keep an eye on them, and to make sure that they get what they pay for, and know what they are paying and why.

And with growing transparency and information exchange, it is key to know who will be getting what information, and to ensure that intermediaries make this clear.

And for advisors, understanding what their clients really need, and aligning their interests with the interests of their clients, is key to being the trusted family advisor – an advisor who is not measured by how markets perform and who is a commodity, but an advisor who is valued for telling the truth, and always having the client's interests at heart.

CHAPTER 8

Getting it Right

I t is possible to get it right. For families, for banks, for trustees, and for others involved in and affected by issues in and around asset management and protection, and succession planning. And wealth can and should be something that is a positive thing for wealth-owning families and the societies they live in.

But getting it right and avoiding having wealth destroy a family do take thought and effort on an ongoing basis given that things are always changing, both in the external world and within families.

Stress Tests and Understanding That No Plan *is* a Plan

It is never too early to begin thinking about the succession process and to work out what would happen to your assets if you were to become disabled or to pass away prematurely. A "stress test" basically means asking the "what-ifs"... *what happens to my assets if I pass away, and is whatever plan I have in place appropriate to my current circumstances and what I would like to see happen? Most importantly, will what I have put in place in terms of planning be destructive of my family and wealth?*

If you were to pass away suddenly, what would happen to your assets? This will, of course, depend on what structures may be in place to deal with the transition of wealth, including trusts and other vehicles. If there are wills that have been validly executed, these will also come into the picture, and the laws relevant to where assets are located will also be key. But who will make sure that the right things are done, and that assets are actually tracked down and properly looked after and transferred? Is there an inventory of assets that has been kept up-to-date, and do family members or others who are meant to benefit know where they should go to get information about what to do if something happens to the wealth owner? In my experience, it is actually pretty rare for things to be smooth, and stress testing succession may well mean thinking through exactly what will happen in the event of death, and making sure that what is intended is what will really take place. Part of the stress testing is also to review whether what has been put in place will not create problems in terms of those who may have expected to benefit not benefitting, or otherwise. And if excluding or limiting the benefit of family members or others is actually intended, would it be better to clarify this before the death of the wealth owner or not?

Wealth owners often worry about the cost of putting the right succession plan in place, and of regular health checks on the plan. But the cost of getting it wrong is almost always multiples of what it would have cost to get it right. And the costs of getting it wrong are not only financial costs.

There are no black-and-white answers to what is the right way to deal with all the intricacies of succession, but the key is to review what is in place on an ongoing basis. Given changes in assets, in family dynamics, and the external legal and tax environment, reviewing things on an annual basis makes sense, at every level of wealth.

The approach of stress testing the structures and approaches in place is not limited to considering what happens on death, but also what would happen in the event of disability, divorce, and a number of other sudden or not so sudden things that can affect the assets within the family.

Knowing What You Have and Where the Assets Are

It is terribly common for assets to get lost and stolen as wealth owners age and in the process of succession. Asking yourself how family members or others are meant to track assets down in the event of your passing or disability is important, as it is to ensure that those who will be dealing with your assets actually know their value and what your intentions are in relation to them in the event of death. Where there are valuables kept at home or in safety deposit boxes or elsewhere, will the right people find them and do the right thing with them? The best protection is to make sure that those who are intended to benefit know what they should be looking for, but this is not always possible or appropriate given the ages or positions of those involved. Here, using trusts or foundations may be the best approach, but the general guidance is to make sure to think about these things – not doing so is almost surely problematic.

Advisors, the "Family Office," and Who Will be Doing What

Every wealth-owning family has, in effect, a "family office" – one or more people who handle things in and around the assets of the wealth owner. Often, the wealth owner takes care of the assets while the wealth owner is around, but is attention paid to who will take over this function in the event of death or disability?

There may be excellent tax and succession advice that has been obtained, but are the lawyers and accountants who were involved at the outset now in the picture on an ongoing basis? Very often, the legal or tax advisor is transactional, in the sense that they may have been involved in drafting a will or setting up a trust, but as the years go by their files are out-of-date or lost as they retire or move on to other careers or firms. How to pick up the trail may be very difficult after the passing or disability of the wealth owner. Even the most sophisticated of families, and ones who have professionally run family offices, may not have everything set as it should be. Spending a day going through exactly what would happen in the event of death or disability, and thinking this through, is something that wealth owners should be doing regularly, as it is pretty inevitable that not everything will be arranged as it should be, given the constant changes in assets, in family circumstances, and in the regulatory and tax world.

Communication and Avoiding Surprises

I may be idealistic, but I am a believer that much in the way of bad feeling and risk in relation to succession planning can be avoided through ongoing communication and openness within families regarding how the succession process will proceed. As children get older, getting their input on the succession process is valuable, and the more those who are to receive assets know about what they are meant to get and where the assets are, the safer the succession process can be.

In complex situations involving second and subsequent marriages and otherwise, avoiding surprises is part of effective planning. The destruction of relationships, the litigation that follows the death or disability of the wealth owner, and associated problems are more likely to occur when there are surprises that emerge when the wealth owner is gone. When everyone knows what to expect, and has been given every opportunity to provide input into the process, there is much less danger of bad feeling and disputes later on. Hoping no one will find out about your mistress is less effective than having a clear financial arrangement with your mistress that discourages her from causing problems when you are not around.

Most effective in communication is to set up family retreats, ideally annually, covering age-appropriate issues and allowing for good discussion within families about the assets of the family and how transitions are meant to take place. Medical and dental check-ups are something we should all undertake regularly, and ideally comprehensively. As we age, medical check-ups become even more important. In the case of asset protection and succession, looking at things comprehensively and regularly, and involving those who will benefit from our assets, is exceptionally important.

How Far Do We Go to Minimize Tax and to Protect Assets from Claims of Creditors, Spouses, and Others?

As a tax lawyer, my job has been to work with wealth owners and help them legally plan their affairs such as to minimize tax exposures. But how far should one go to pay the least amount of tax possible? Is it an ethical obligation of wealth owners to pay headline rates of tax to help address wealth and income inequality and to not take steps to reduce tax exposures? Where is the line between legal tax planning and illegal tax evasion... and what of tax avoidance, something that used to be considered legal and appropriate, but which is increasingly condemned by tax authorities and others?

These are issues families need to consider and which often require good advice and input from professionals who are able to help wealth owners understand the risks and where the moving line of what is legal and what is not actually is. I am a strong believer that wealth owners have a responsibility to society to pay their taxes and to help in addressing inequality. I am not, however, a believer that tax systems and governments always have it right or that tax systems are always fair in how they work. Wealth owners have choices on where and how they invest, where they live and hold citizenship, and when and how to transfer assets to family members and others they wish to benefit with their wealth. Whatever the view of the wealth owner on how ambitious to be in their tax planning, the key is to make informed decisions, and to understand the choices that one has.

I have seen many, many wealth owners who have created much in the way of unhappiness by trying too hard to pay less tax, this through assets that were lost by being so well hidden from tax authorities, that they ended up being hidden from those intended to benefit from them. I have seen assets that have fallen into the hands of corrupt governments, lawyers, accountants, and others, and have also seen families miserable at being forced to stay away from their country of origin to avoid being taxed there. Is it worth living alone in a tax haven, away from family, friends, and one's culture and heritage in order to pay less tax? Can you take it with you when you die?

I have worked with many wealth owners who have delighted in having more wealth available to do good in the world and to expand their businesses, benefitting their communities, employees, and others, through careful, proper tax planning, and through adopting a lifestyle that allows them to spend time in a variety of countries, but with taxable residence being maintained in countries with fair and reasonable tax systems. So getting it right is a balance – an informed and well-considered decision on what matters and how to both enjoy life and family, and legally minimize tax exposures.

I am not a believer in Thomas Piketty's view that governments are best positioned to decide how much to take away from wealth-owning families through taxation and to redistribute that wealth. I am much more of a believer that wealth owners are better placed than governments to ensure that money made available to help others is properly and effectively applied. But there are no rights and wrongs – wealth owners need to make informed decisions, and also need to get more involved in how the world addresses the needs of those who need help, something that too many wealth owners have ignored. And laws have to be respected, including tax laws.

And is it right and ethical to protect assets from a claim of creditors, or from a claim of a spouse on divorce? Should a wealth owner consider all his sons and daughters-in-law to be gold-diggers, as I have suggested they are? Again, there is, to me, no right or wrong here. The wealth owner should simply make sure they understand how things work and how they can go wrong, and then make informed decisions on how best to try to have things work out the way they want them to work out.

And I stick by my view that one should hope for the best, but certainly plan for the worst.

Women and Wealth

With all the considerable moves toward gender equality, I lament the difficulties that often arise given the lack of knowledge about money that women in families sometimes suffer. Whether in marriages or otherwise, women, like men, need to know and understand things having to do with money to protect themselves and their families.

When it comes to mechanical things, men often pretend to know more than they do, and women less than they do. Changing the light-bulb, installing a computer or television set, putting up a picture – it seems that women often leave this to men who pretend they know what they are doing before they finally call an electrician or plumber to fix the mess they have made in trying to do it themselves. Sadly, when it comes to money, this is sometimes also the case.

In a marriage or other relationship, a woman should be asking herself whether she knows exactly what would happen if her partner died or became disabled, or if the marriage otherwise came to an end. I have come across many situations of women with no idea of how much money their husband actually has, and where the money is. In a divorce or on the death of their husband, there is a mess to sort out, and the possibility of the widow or divorced wife being left in very difficult financial circumstances.

A woman does not need to know how to fix a computer (and neither does a man), but she does need to know who to call if her computer stops working. And in the case of money and the ownership of assets, a spouse has every right to know who owns what and who to call and what to do if things go wrong.

There is one very important reality about women and wealth. The chances are that they will end up with the money, one way or another – so they had better know where it is and how to deal with it. Women live longer than men, and in a marriage, it is likely that they will outlive their husband. And if the marriage fails, which many do, the wife will and should end up with something – so everyone needs to be prepared, and all too often, women are not.

For wealth owners, educating their children to understand what they need to know about wealth and marriage, and the inevitable risks, is very important. Not only daughters need to know how to protect themselves, and how to make sure that they are financially independent in their relationships, allowing them to be better spouses and better parents as a result.

What Mom and Dad Meant

Most of the unhappiness and disputes I have seen in families in and around succession has to do with arguments about what "Mom and Dad meant." Dissatisfied with who among the children gets what, the disgruntled child says that Dad actually meant to leave that asset to me, or to have had a business run by the children in a certain way. I am a great believer in ensuring that Mom and Dad make it clear what they mean long before Mom and Dad are not around. Family retreats and discussions in and around the succession process can go a long way to achieving this, and in wills, trusts, and other succession instruments, accompanying these with clear expressions of wishes can also be a good and important thing to avoid future disputes. Assuming that your children and other heirs know what you mean is not safe. Putting things in writing and explaining your thinking while you are around, and inviting discussion, is a better way of avoiding disputes.

I have seen many wealth owners who sign wills and trust documents that are put in front of them by their legal and tax advisors but which contain little more than the basics on who gets what. Standard form documents are not the way to ensure that intentions will be met. Accompanying this with explanation can go a long way to avoiding disputes, and I sometimes suggest that wealth owners also consider recording themselves to outline how they would like to see things go. With easy technology to do this today, why not have a video recording of what the wealth owner would like to see happen with their assets, including their businesses, and how they would like to see the next generation carry things forward?

The Reality of Emotions, Psychology, Aging, and Communicating with Money

I acknowledge that I am idealistic in my thinking that communication within families, early on, can go far to address many potential circumstances of unhappiness and disputes. But I am convinced that communication is critical to avoiding problems. I also believe that in today's world of wealth owners living longer and longer, the ideal is to consider making at least some transfers of wealth to the younger generation earlier to avoid children waiting to inherit until the death of a parent. Is it really right that a child should only inherit at the age of 80, when their Mom or Dad dies at 100?

I am also idealistic in suggesting that children be treated equally, to the extent possible, and that money not be used as a means of communicating within families. I acknowledge that there are many realities that come into it, including specific family issues, such as children who are unable to deal with wealth safely. Is it good to give money to my children early if they are too young to deal with what they get and may squander my hard-earned resources? Is it right to treat my children equally when one of my children has really not turned out well and has significant problems with substance abuse or otherwise? Will my children take care of me in my old age if I take advantage of opportunities to save on taxes by making early distributions?

But some of the limitations on wealth owners doing the right thing are more psychological than real. Am I afraid that my children will not visit if I don't use my money as a way to keep them interested in me? Am I thinking about treating my children unequally in my succession plan as a way of communicating my disappointment with one of my children? There is a role, in many families, for psychologists and other health professionals to be part of the succession process and to help navigate the complexities that wealth-owning families face. As part of the "stress tests" of the succession process should be questions about the psychology of money, and its effect on every generation.

Is it easier to just give it all away to charity? Frankly, no... this still causes many issues for families. Nothing is easy, and the work that families need to do is ongoing.

Can Private Banks, Trustees, and Other Advisors Get it Right?

The key to success in the relationship between wealth owners and the service providers they use is for the interests of the two to be aligned, and for there to be real openness on fees, conflicts of interest, and more.

I have not been impressed with the wealth-management industry and the leadership of many private banks, trust companies, and other players. I have also been very unimpressed with the regulators in many financial centers seeking to maintain and build the wealth-management sector of their economy. Wealth management is a big business, but a changing and chaotic one, where the players of today may well not be the players of tomorrow. We are already seeing disruption in the industry, and clearly Silicon Valley with Google, Apple, Amazon, Alibaba, etc. are going to be part of the future of banking and wealth management.

Getting it right, and aligning with the interests of wealth owners, means that there needs to be an understanding that families are about the long term and about relationships. I am critical of investment bankers running private banks, but am open to the possibility that an investment banker can learn that long-term relationships can have value, and that it is not only a large transactional fee in this quarter that brings value to a bank.

A few thoughts on strategy for private banks follow, but for all involved in the process of helping wealth owners, there is enormous opportunity given the needs that wealth-owning families have. It is surprising how misunderstood these needs are by law and accounting firms, with only relatively few having organized themselves to meet the holistic needs of wealth-owning families. Some law and accounting firms have actively stayed away from working with other than companies, thinking that serving wealth owners means routine will and trust work, not understanding that working for the owners of businesses means exposure to comprehensive tax, legal, and other issues that only the most sophisticated of advisors can handle at the higher end of wealth. For the wealth-owning family, finding the right advisors can be tricky, but the first step is to understand what you really need.

The typical private bank today focuses on asset management, which is where they think they make their money. In developing strategy, there are a few things to consider.

Asset Management is a Commodity, and Pricing Will be Increasingly Under Challenge

Markets are what they are, and it is difficult to outperform a competitor, given that everyone is dealing with the same markets. With technology, it is possible to obtain information increasingly easily, and with a variety of index and other products it is easy for a client of a private bank to replicate performance at a substantially cheaper price.

Does your client really need pages and pages of "market thinking" from you, expensively produced, when similar information is coming to them from the many private banks chasing them for business? Do they need this information when they can get it on their own from elsewhere, and where the information may be more trustworthy? Do you actually need to manage money for your clients, or would they benefit more from an honest, low-cost approach to your helping them review their total asset and investment portfolio, helping them in consolidated reporting, understanding their asset class and geographical asset allocation, and helping to guide them to lower-cost, lower-risk ways of managing and investing their assets?

Understanding What Your Clients Really Need

The needs of wealth-owning families are considerable, and vary depending on where they live, where they invest, and on issues particular to the family. Can you really provide services that address a family's real needs without specializing in families from particular countries or who invest in particular assets in particular places? How do you go about really understanding and getting to know the families you work with, particularly if your relationship managers are not trained to do much more than sell the asset-management services you think you make your money from?

Continuity and Encouraging Your People to Institutionalize Clients

If it is true that wealth owners are looking for trusted advisors who will be there for the long term, is your bank equipped to bring people onboard who will remain with the bank for their entire career? Or are compensation approaches designed to reward short-term profits, encouraging those working with clients to "sell" rather than to develop relationships? And if rewards are short term, will your people have an incentive to institutionalize clients by introducing them to specialists in other areas than their own, such as wealth planning, trust services, and otherwise? Are those working with clients incentivized to move to other banks to get promotions, or are compensation systems designed to retain staff for their entire career?

Private Banking is a Knowledge Business – Is Your Bank Being Run Accordingly?

The needs of wealth owners are increasingly complex, and the regulatory burden on banks, trustees, and others in the wealth-management industry is constantly increasing. Is your bank equipped to operate as a knowledge business, where there is a focus on capturing and sharing knowledge at all levels?

In my work with private banks, I rarely ran across any that focused on knowledge as being their main asset. In the consulting world, firms like McKinsey and others make knowledge the core of what they offer, and put huge effort into developing approaches to knowledge management and sharing that allow them to be learning organizations – companies that learn from every client engagement, and that ensure knowledge is shared internally and used externally to improve the output provided to clients and to help educate both clients and potential clients, attracting more business. If a private banker works with a client from a particular country, and in the course of setting up a succession and asset plan for that client is exposed to legal and tax advisors from that country who help put something of value in place, how is that knowledge and experience captured and shared with others in the bank who may serve similarly placed clients? Are the advisors involved invited to help in the training of bank personnel, and to help the bank develop products and services that are relevant to clients from the same country? Or does the next banker working on a similar project start from scratch, with no base of knowledge to draw on?

Complexity and Compliance are Your Friends

For many private banks, increased complexity and compliance has encouraged exits from some markets. The USA is a good example, with a number of private banks no longer providing services to Americans because of the aggressive enforcement of US tax, securities, and other laws by the authorities, in part as a reaction to the historical abuses of banking secrecy by the private banking sector. The perception that working with US clients is too complex, and that compliance with reporting and other requirements too burdensome, does not factor in that dealing with complexity is what clients need help with. The USA is the largest wealth-management market in the world – for a private bank to exit a market of that size because of complexity shows a lack of strategy and foresight, given that complexity will inevitably grow in dealing with other markets, whether involving clients from emerging economies such as China or clients from developed countries such as the UK or elsewhere.

The more complex things are, the more wealth-owning families need help. The simple reality is that the private banking of the past, where bankers would say *we don't care about the tax or other laws of your country, because we have bank secrecy – let's go out for a nice lunch* can no longer exist. In fact, such an approach to client needs was never appropriate or helpful, but too many in the industry long for the days of easy answers.

Should a Private Bank Own a Trust Company?

In the USA, it is very common for trustees to be individuals – often lawyers in law firms offering estate planning and related services. While corporate trust companies exist, they are less ubiquitous than in the international arena, where the vast majority of trusts are administered by companies. A few years ago, virtually every bank offering private banking services had their own trust companies, but with increased tax and reporting requirements affecting trustees, and more of an understanding of risk, a number of banks have been selling or closing down their trust operations.

There are really no right or wrong answers to the question of whether a private bank should own a trust company, and there are strategies banks can take to stay close to clients despite not being in the trust business. I do generally like the idea of a private bank owning a trust company, but this assumes that the bank involved is aware of the critical point that trusteeships require serious expertise and commitment, and a real focus on understanding, managing, and pricing risk. The upside for banks and clients is that a bank-owned trust company can offer a holistic and long-term solution for families, and for the private bank, is a "sticky" service that automatically connects multiple generations of the family to the bank.

A good indicator of the value of a trust or other fiduciary operation is research conducted by the Boston Consulting Group, which shows that the average private-banking client keeps an account with a private bank for six or seven years, while where a trust is in place, the relationship will remain for an average of 20 years.

Understanding the Value of Relationships and Aligning Interests

Owning the client relationship is where the value lies in private banking. High relationship manager turnover, loss of confidence arising from over-selling of products, and a focus on short-term revenue and many other missteps have forced wealth owners into the arms of independent asset managers, multi-family offices, and other providers better able to cherish and build on long-term relationships. Private banks often become nothing more than asset custodians, a low-margin and commoditized business that cannot compete given the dominance of the large players who have made massive investments in technology and otherwise, permitting them to offer solid, global custody.

There are many ways to understand the value of relationships and to align interests. One is to reflect on the statistic mentioned earlier regarding the length of time the average client of a private bank remains with the bank when they have a bank account only as opposed to maintaining a fiduciary relationship, such as a trust. If a private bank earns \$75,000 a year from a family that maintains a bank account with the private bank, the value of the client can be calculated by developing a present value of the client – projecting the expected revenue from the client for the six or seven years the client is likely to stay. Say this figure is \$400,000 – if the client, instead of just having a bank account with the bank, were converted into a client that also maintains a trust with the bank, on average, the client is likely to stay with the bank for 20 years. This will pretty much triple the value of the client to the bank in present terms, a value that is too seldom measured in typical private banks.

In fact, I believe that the Boston Consulting Group's suggestion of the enhanced value of a client where a fiduciary structure is in place underestimates the value. The reason for this belief is that where there is a trust in place, the trustee gets to know not only the wealth owner settling the trust, but also the beneficiaries, usually the children and spouse, and other family members, all of which not only helps create a stickier client relationship, but also leads to new clients, and more funds under management. And most importantly, the client family is getting what they really need – a long-term trusted advisor that really knows the family, and provides services that are holistic – focused on much more than just asset management.

Keeping the Relationship Manager (and Others) There for Their Entire Career

A key driver of success is aligning the interests of the wealth manager, employees, and clients. There are many ways of doing this, and among them is to recognize that wealth management is a business of long-term relationships, and one that requires an approach to clients that reflects that working with a wealth owner requires an understanding that the wealth owner is part of a family, and that client needs will include, by necessity, issues in and around succession and asset protection. There will be wealth managers who do nothing but manage money, but if this is the case they had better have something to offer that stands out if I am right that asset management is a commodity, and one that will, with technology and greater access to information, face severe pricing challenges.

If long-term relationships and families is what it is all about, then having client-facing staff who are with the private bank for their entire career becomes a key success factor. How can this be achieved? There was a time when a traditional private bank truly offered long-term relationship management. But this has become, in all too many cases, a thing of the past. Private banks are constantly restructuring and chopping and changing their strategy, rewarding "hunters" bringing in new clients rather than "farmers" developing existing clients. Relationship managers and others are encouraged to think short term and to move from one bank to the next in order to progress their careers. Private banks are increasingly publicly listed or otherwise faced with having to produce short-term financial results.

I know of families who years ago met their relationship managers when they were at the start of their career. The relationship manager would get to know the family when they were in their late 20s or 30s, and would visit the children at boarding school (the orphanages of the wealthy), attend weddings and funerals, and work closely with experts within and outside the bank in areas from tax and trust planning, to personal security, and otherwise. When the relationship manager approached retirement age, the relationship would be seamlessly passed on to a more junior colleague.

In my ideal world, a private bank today would create incentives that are long term, and ensure that successful relationship managers build their careers with one bank, aligning interests, and having every incentive to institutionalize clients. An example might involve reducing upfront salaries, and increasing compensation that is long term, and one element of this could be to reward the relationship manager for the added value to a bank of the client establishing a fiduciary relationship within the bank, possibly through a trust or otherwise. If the relationship manager has been with a bank for two or three years, and it is clear that they are honest, hardworking, and otherwise make the grade, the view should be that they will stay with the bank for the long term. If this is not the view, they should be exited from the bank. Once they make it past this initial threshold, they should, from many perspectives, be provided with job security, and an assurance that if they continue to perform well, aligning with the interests of the bank and of the families the bank serves, they will be with the bank for their entire career, and beyond.

If the banker, for example, has a client with a bank account and a certain amount of money under management, the client has, as mentioned earlier, a value to the bank given the fees the bank earns, and the expected number of years those fees will be paid given how long the client is likely to stay with the bank. If the relationship manager introduces the client to the trust company owned by the bank, and now the client family has a fiduciary relationship, the expected number of years the client family will be with the bank triples. This enhanced value of the client to the bank is a measurable figure, and part of this value can be shared by the bank with the relationship manager.

But rather than a one-off bonus to the banker, as many banks currently provide, the relationship manager, in my model, would receive compensation over the full period during which the client family is expected to maintain the relationship. Twenty years is the estimate of the Boston Consulting Group where there is a trust in place. The compensation to the relationship manager may not be immediate, but is being paid to encourage the relationship manager to "farm" the client family – to keep them close to the bank and to develop relationships with the younger generation and others.

The idea is to provide the relationship manager with a financial incentive to stay close to their clients, with the commission for having increased the value of the client family to the bank only continuing to be paid so long as the family remains with the bank. And if the relationship manager retires before the full 20 years pass, the commission would continue providing the relationship manager keeps links, in their retirement, with both the family and the bank, and is focused on ensuring the success of the succession process within the bank, helping in the handover of day-to-day activities to the next generation of relationship managers. In retirement, the relationship manager will continue to earn income from the hopefully many families he or she has managed to help connect to the bank, and stay close to the family and the bank beyond retirement, helping to align the interests of all involved.

This approach is not limited to trusts and other fiduciary structures, but reflects a different way of working and thinking, and one where building and maintaining relationships, rather than short-term transactional profits, are rewarded.

How Wealth Planning and Trust Services Fit With Asset Management

Many banks struggle with how and whether to offer wealth planning and trust services. Misguided CEOs look at where the bank earns its money, and think that asset management is the key. Given the need to invest in knowledge and compliance in order to safely provide wealth-planning and trust services, a number of banks are exiting those businesses, ceasing to provide clients with services beyond asset management. To me, this is a mistake, and while it is not at all necessary to have these functions internal to a bank, I am a great believer in the need to provide holistic services in order to "own" the client relationship and provide clients with value that goes far beyond the fees the client pays to the private bank.

Banks that do have trust and wealth-planning services struggle with whether these functions should be cost centers or profit centers. For me, it does not matter whether a trust company or wealth-planning service is a cost or profit center – what does matter is whether the client, as a whole, is paying a fee that ensures the bank overall is earning a reasonable profit. What this means is that having a trust company owned by a bank that ignores the value of the client to the bank in other areas is simply not a good way to operate. And on the fees a client pays, looking at this in terms of what the bank earns in total is a better way to go than having internal units competing with each other. This, of course, is primarily in the client's interest, but I am a strict believer that it is only those who put the client's interest first who will succeed for the long term.

Leveraging Networks – Share Your Ability as an Educated Consumer of Legal, Tax, and Other Services Wealth Owners Need

While very large, global private banks are able to internally provide trust, wealth-planning, and other services to complement the various areas of asset management they cover, smaller organizations may not be able to maintain the expertise necessary to cover in any comprehensive way the needs of the families they seek to work with. This does not mean that smaller organizations cannot compete. Even the largest of banks cannot provide all the services that families need, and wealth planners and trustees within banks themselves need to rely on outside experts, such as lawyers and accountants and others specialized in the many areas that wealth-owning families may need expertise in.

Managing and maintaining external networks of experts is a valuable thing for effective private banks and others in the wealth-management space. As a knowledge business, ensuring that there is an effective flow of information from those with expertise to the bank is key, as is sharing that knowledge internally. Developments on the tax and legal front affecting wealth owners, issues in and around security and kidnapping, dealing with special assets such as artwork and otherwise, and many other topics are routine areas of need for wealth-owning families.

An effective private bank leverages its networks of experts, helping to bring them together with families, and helping families manage how they consume legal or other services. When I, as a tax lawyer, was asked questions directly by a wealth-owning family, often the family, not being experienced consumers of legal services, would ask the wrong questions, or ask questions that were much wider than they really needed to ask. This would have an impact on the cost of providing a response, and also on the usefulness of the response. In the case of a private bank, there is every opportunity to help clients in their use of specialists in every area, helping to identify the right advisors for the right questions, helping to narrow the questions asked, and to manage costs and the process.

High Net Worth, Ultra-High Net Worth, Rich, …

As soon as a private banker hands me a business card that reads "Head, Ultra High Net Worth Unit," or something along those lines, I know I am dealing with a private bank that does not understand its business.

Terms like "high net worth" or "rich" are subjective terms, and have no room in communication between a private bank and its clients. It is insulting to a wealth owner to not be in the group of clients who are most valued by the private bank, and for those who are in the group that is ostensibly most valued (maybe these are the ultra, ultra, ultra, ultra-high-net-worth clients), do they really want brochures that advertise this? Perhaps there is a bit of a *nouveau riche* angle here, but to me a smart private bank simply makes *every* client feel that they are getting top service because they are getting top service – for what they pay. And it is this latter point that is the key.

Frankly, I think that segmentation of clients is important, but that the approach should simply be a matter of discipline – banks and other service providers need to match the service provided to the wealth-owning family to what the family pays. The approach should be designed to ensure that the family is receiving value for money and real assistance, but in a way that makes economic sense for the bank.

In fact, the large volume of affluent families makes it sensible for a private bank or other wealth manager to orient certain products and services to such families, delivering input efficiently, allowing for pricing to be competitive while profitable. For the wealthier families with more in the way of complex needs, services may need to be more bespoke, but again, discipline in how services are delivered is key.

What I often see are expensive resources within private banks, such as wealth planners, spending too much time reinventing the wheel with clients who are not paying enough for the time being spent, and this largely through poor knowledge management and the reality of staff spending more time with the clients they find more fun rather than the ones who might be in a position to pay for more in the way of service. And with all the private banks chasing the much smaller pool of "billionaires," is enough attention being paid to the reality that this community is over-banked and generally can often negotiate their way to much lower fees than may be economically viable for the service provider?

Putting Together Strategy, Marketing, Compliance, and Training

I spent a number of years establishing and then running a company that was involved in knowledge management and training. Among the services we provided were training services for private banks and trust companies. I had long been involved in helping private banks and others in the area of strategy, and have always been a believer in the need to link strategy with training, and also marketing and compliance functions.

I am bemused by the lack of focus by the leaders of private banks on training, CEOs more often than not relegating training to relatively low-level personnel to handle, and treating training as a "check-the-box" item on the agenda, very quickly reduced when the budget is reviewed for areas that can be cut. As a knowledge business, a private bank or other provider of input to wealth owners needs to understand the ongoing need for training, and also what exactly it is that people need to be trained in.

An over-focus on selling skills, and pushing bank products, is far from the key to success. A best-of-class approach, to me, would be for the training function to be closely tied to the strategy of the bank, meaning that the first step in the process is to develop and adopt a clear strategy. This might, among others, result in a focus on particular markets and particular segments of wealth owners, and on particular approaches to asset management.

A decision on strategy then leads to the need for the involvement of the compliance function – understanding how to legally work with clients from the markets of interest that have been identified, and how to ensure that the products and services that are adapted or developed for such clients can be marketed and serviced in a compliant way. Business issues will come up at this stage, including in relation to pricing, an important thing being for banks to understand and price risk – charging the right price for the services that are provided, and holding back from providing services that are just too risky for the bank to engage in.

The training function should be part of the strategy and compliance process, the objective being to train the staff of the private bank to implement the strategy of the bank, and to do so in a compliant way. Marketing clearly comes into the picture as well, since key to delivering on strategy is for marketing personnel to design their marketing approach to help achieve strategic objectives.

Clients often have latent needs – needs that they do not know they have. The most effective marketing is often oriented toward education, and raising the awareness of the family of their needs, and how the private bank is able to meet those needs through provision of its products and services.

Joining up strategy, compliance, marketing, and training is critical to success and efficiency, but few in the industry really get this.

Recruiting and Training Rather Than Poaching, and Focusing on Skills, Not Perceived "Ability" to Work with the Wealthy

It was perversely amusing to observe the actions of private banks a few years ago in Singapore and elsewhere, during a time of difficulty in finding good relationship managers. A perceived shortage of talent in private banking led private banks to look for client relationship managers from outside the private banking industry – and often they turned to the luxury retail business for their new recruits. While private banking is a luxury business in many ways, and perhaps has, as a business, much to learn from how luxury brands are managed and developed, the reality is that a pretty young thing, male or female, working for a luxury jeweler or car retailer does not generally have the skills needed to be the trusted family advisor in the context of true wealth management.

Where a private bank is simply looking for someone to sell its products, maybe the approach makes sense, but to me how private banks recruit, and from where, tells me much about their lack of strategy and long-term focus on aligning the needs of clients with those of the bank. I believe that private banks should try harder to develop their own talent, recruiting from business schools and elsewhere, looking for recruits from different countries, with the language skills needed to navigate a global client base. A focus on training and retention should be part of the process, creating long-term careers that encourage bankers to think of what is best for the bank and its clients, rather than on their own short-term objectives. With a good chunk of current recruiting focusing on poaching bankers with a book of business from an existing bank, the current merry-go-round of relationship managers moving from one bank to another is simply not in anyone's interests – not in the interests of clients, not in the interests of the private banks, and not in the interests of the individual bankers involved.

Do Wealth Owners Need a Bank, a Family Office, an Independent Asset Manager, or a Lawyer or Accountant to Handle Things?

From the perspective of the wealth-owning family, what they need is help in many areas, and what help they need will depend on where they live, invest, and do business. What they need will also very much depend on the individual family circumstances and dynamics. For the wealth manager, the question is whether to seek to address the needs of clients holistically or to just focus on what the wealth manager may be best at – this could be asset allocation and discretionary asset management, or knowledge about the succession process, or some other area of specialty.

Of importance to every family is to find trusted advisors – people who can help with expertise in one or more areas of relevance, but ideally people with their own networks of specialists able to help wealth owners, and who can be brought in as needed to address particular areas of need. This trusted advisor role can be played by any of a lawyer, accountant, asset manager, or other intermediary, and from a business perspective, it makes sense for private banks and others in the industry to consider the need to train staff to not only sell products, but also move toward "owning" the client relationship – something of enormous long-term value to the bank, and which aligns with what is best for wealth-owning clients – forming trusting relationships that can transition from one generation to the next.

Education is Key

For the wealth-owning family, it is critically important to think about the family's asset-protection and succession strategies and to periodically review whether what is in place really meets the changing circumstances of the family. But to do this well, and to properly keep an eye on advisors, all members of wealth-owning families, at the right age, need to be brought into an ongoing program of learning, leading to responsibility as wealth owners. Whether or not a son or daughter will be involved in managing a family business, they need to be prepared for the role they will ultimately have, even if this role is limited to being an owner of the business together with other siblings who may be involved in the management of the business. And where there is no business, just having the ownership of a portfolio of assets requires preparation.

Learning is an ongoing process, and opportunities to learn from other families and their successes and failures can also be instructive. Many private banks run training programs for wealth owners, sometimes orienting things toward the younger generation and sometimes toward the family more generally. These courses can be useful, if only to allow interaction with other families, but it is good to prepare those in the family attending for the reality that part of the objective of the bank in organizing these programs is to sell their bank. It is unlikely that the training will say much about how to review pricing and how charges are imposed and might best be negotiated, and quite likely that the training will be oriented toward the products and services of the bank rather than the specific needs of the family.

Banks that understand the principle of selling by not selling – telling the truth, and really helping families navigate the complexities of wealth ownership – generally do a better job of generating business from the education programs they run, but all too often those in charge do not really get it.

There are many education options for families outside the world of private banks and the programs they run for their clients. A number of top business schools worldwide offer education to wealth and business-owning families, and these programs can often be customized to address specific issues within individual families, something that can be particularly useful.

Your children need to be prepared... to resist the thousands of investment scams out there, to understand how to navigate difficult divorces and the ever-changing regulatory world, and to work well (and safely) with the advisors they will need to help guide them.

*   *   *

When I work with families, I often insist on meeting and discussing matters not only with the older generation, the wealth-owning matriarch and/or patriarch, but also with each member of the younger generation – individually and in private. It is here that I learn about the concerns and mistrust among siblings, and of various unspoken issues in the family. It is with this feedback that I am better able to get a sense of the needs of the family, all of which must be taken into account holistically in the succession and asset-protection plan to be adopted.

Too often the matriarch or patriarch over-emphasizes one issue or another – perhaps focusing on tax minimization or the risks of divorce in the younger generation, the complexity of which makes it all the easier for advisors to keep the family in a mysterious fog about how the family's assets are owned, administered, and, most importantly, will be passed on to subsequent generations.

Is there an adequate asset-protection and succession plan in place? Have all the right "what-ifs" been addressed? Does the next generation know what they should be doing to ensure the safety and security of the family's assets going forward?

It is possible for families to get it right. And it is very important that they do.

Addendum: The Need for Dialogue on Tax Transparency

I believe that the rough road to tax transparency can be smoothed out through dialogue and proactivity. While it is late in the day, it remains possible for much to be achieved, and the steps to be taken are urgent.

As governments grapple with reporting and taxpaying requirements associated with trusts, for example, an important role for the trust industry is to help governments understand how their tax-collection and enforcement objectives can be met while respecting the legitimate privacy and other reasons families may choose to use trusts. There are many countries, including Canada, the USA, and others, that have relatively clear tax laws regarding the taxpaying and reporting responsibilities of trustees, beneficiaries, settlors, and others interested in trust structures. Over the years, the relevant tax rules have developed in a way that reflects the ongoing need of governments to close loopholes, and to ensure that taxes are effectively collected. But in the case of the USA and other regimes, this has been done in a way that supports the legitimate and appropriate use of trusts. Broad tax neutrality in the use of trusts is a positive, as is clarity in the tax results of using trusts.

There are other countries, such as France, that have taken a heavy-handed and destructive approach to trusts, demonstrating the consequences of a government failing to understand how trusts work, and how their legitimate use to address the needs of families can be entirely consistent with full tax compliance and transparency. But it is the financial services industry that should be showing leadership in helping onshore governments address their legitimate taxing needs – proactive dialogue designed to address the needs of all stakeholders. Given that the industry has largely failed to take this leadership, wealth owners, the clients of banks and trust companies, should communicate more clearly with those they work with – and encourage a proactive dialogue with governments, and not a reactive, panic-stricken approach to the consequences of inaction in relation to past abuses.

The failure of offshore governments and the wealth-management industry to proactively address issues in and around taxation has fueled the relative success enjoyed by the USA in its efforts to crack down on offshore tax evasion. The provocative practices of the off-shore world and the wealth-management industry triggered a series of steps taken by the USA that have opened the door to global changes in exchange of information and tax enforcement. But the lack of cooperative strategies has come at a significant cost for not only the industry and the families it serves, but also for the USA itself, which despite much in the way of effort and noise, is still at an early stage of truly addressing the issue of offshore tax evasion by its residents and, importantly, citizens (with the latter being subject to global taxation whether or not resident in the USA, meaning that there remain large numbers of American taxpayers globally whose tax affairs remain to be sorted out).

The USA and Switzerland: Failed Strategies by Switzerland, but has the USA Achieved All That It Could?

For wealth owners and their advisors, it is instructive to understand that tax transparency is not a recent development, despite how many view the major recent steps to information exchange on an automatic basis.

The USA took its first major step toward addressing offshore tax evasion when it introduced a regime known as the Qualified Intermediary (QI) system in 2001. America, through the QI system, successfully encouraged banks around the world to become their partners in tax enforcement, with virtually every meaningful bank involved in wealth management having become a "qualified intermediary," required to identify and document US interests in bank accounts, whether directly owned or through, in certain cases, structures.

To avoid punitive withholding taxes on investments in American securities, even the most die-hard secrecy-based private banks signed on for a complex system that required banks globally to learn the nuances of US international tax rules. Backed up by independent audits, qualified intermediaries made many promises to the USA under the QI system, and all under agreements that were written by the USA, could not be negotiated, and could even be changed by the Americans without the consent of the other contracting party, the bank involved.

Interestingly, rather than entering into negotiation and dialogue over the request of the USA to introduce the QI system, virtually every offshore center and private bank took the defensive approach of simply agreeing to move forward with the QI system.

For many banks, the view was that the USA was a fairly small market for them, and they did not want to rock the boat when it came to the broader issues in and around misuse of bank secrecy for wealth owners from other countries. Had, however, a clear and reasonable request been made by Switzerland, or other countries, that whatever system the USA would seek to implement would have to be reciprocal, this would have delayed the QI system by years. The reality is that the USA would have been unable to deliver reciprocity given the operation of its own bank-secrecy rules and accompanying tax laws, which severely restrict any exchange of information on non-US owners of bank accounts and structures in the USA. Interestingly, this lack of reciprocity continues today, with the USA being virtually the only serious country not participating in the OECD's common reporting standard and system of automatic information exchange.

Sadly for many, the QI system was not recognized for what it was – a *first* step in tax transparency… not a *last* step. As can now be seen from the growing number of attacks on private banks by the USA, so far particularly in Switzerland, the reaction of some banks to the QI rules was to circumvent the efforts of the USA to stamp out foreign tax evasion by passively or actively working with American taxpayers to find ways to avoid reporting under the QI system. This was not a huge challenge, given the clear limits under the QI reporting system in and around the question of "beneficial ownership," which was determined under American tax principles rather than under local know-your-client or other rules. Under US tax principles, among others, the beneficial owner of a bank account, where the account was owned by a properly established and managed offshore company, was the company itself rather than its shareholders, even if those shareholders were Americans. While this did not change any other US tax principles associated with the tax and reporting requirements of Americans owning offshore companies, or rules in and around aiding and abetting tax evasion or otherwise, the limits of what the QI rules required banks to technically document were misinterpreted (or taken advantage of) by what appears to be many banks that used the QI system as a roadmap for how to perpetuate offshore tax evasion by Americans.

The abuse of the QI system became clear in and around the USA's attack on UBS, facilitated by the information the Americans were able to obtain from whistleblowers and others. After US$780 million in fines, and the turning over of thousands of US depositors, the USA scored further tax-collection successes with its various voluntary-disclosure programs. But were these voluntary-disclosure programs real wins for all stakeholders, including banks, families, and interested governments? Could dialogue amongst stakeholders have led to more effective results, and perhaps results that were less destructive of lives and businesses?

Information obtained by the USA through the UBS case played a big part in the next steps taken by America, including its successful rollout of the next step in global tax enforcement, the heavy-handed FATCA – broadly, a reaction to the abuses discovered in relation to the QI rules, and from a timing perspective, well placed to become the new global standard in automatic exchange of information between countries.

As with the QI system, the USA is still unable to deliver real reciprocity, despite reciprocity having now been documented as at least an objective in bilateral agreements that the USA has entered into. And because of its early move with FATCA, the USA has so far managed to stay out of the new system of automatic exchange of information, which involves even broader reporting requirements under the common reporting standard. In simple terms, perversely, the USA has managed to navigate itself into a position where the world's banks have become their policemen, ensuring that those with connections to the USA are tax compliant, while the USA enhances its position as the best place to maintain privacy for international families given the limited information it collects and provides to other countries.

The USA has strong bank secrecy, and there are very limited requirements regarding the information banks have to obtain from their clients and, particularly, what of that information actually goes to the US tax authorities. In the case of complex structures, where beneficial owners are not direct account holders, but rather use companies, trusts, and other intermediate investment vehicles, virtually no information finds its way to the US tax authorities – meaning that there is no information for the US tax authorities to exchange with other countries. Attempts to change these rules have largely failed, with the Republicans particularly resisting change, in part encouraged by lobbyists representing the Florida and Texas banking associations and others involved in providing wealth-management and related services to families from Latin America and elsewhere seeking to hide their money.

Information obtained by the USA also led to further attacks on private banks, again, at least so far, primarily in Switzerland, leading to the destruction of Switzerland's oldest private bank, Bank Wegelin, and significant financial and other challenges for a long list of Swiss banks, including the Swiss operations of many well-known international banks.

Along the way the US Department of Justice introduced, in effect, a voluntary disclosure program for banks in Switzerland, and itself was surprised at the significant sign-on to this, with over 100 banks (about one-third of the Swiss banking community) applying for non-prosecution agreements in exchange for disclosures of activities and data in and around undeclared accounts and the payment of significant penalties based on the value of accounts not disclosed to the USA on certain key dates linked to the UBS case. Penalties were reduced where clients of the relevant bank applied for voluntary disclosure, meaning that the arrangement had the effect of banks encouraging their undeclared US clients to come clean with the tax authorities.

But with penalties of between 20% and 50% of account *balances*, was the Department of Justice "agreement" with Switzerland a fair one for the private banks involved? Will some private banks fail as a result of the costs of the arrangement? And what of the precedent the arrangement sets in terms of penalty levels when countries like Germany, France, and many others see the figures and begin to ask themselves what their fair share should be given the volume of undeclared German, French, and other assets and income in Switzerland and other offshore centers? And what of US moves against banks outside of Switzerland, and what is still to come? And when will a well-advised government in Latin America or elsewhere turn the tables and go after the USA and its banking community for their role in hiding the assets and income of their taxpayers?

Dialogue and negotiation, with a view to coming to approaches that benefit all stakeholders, may have brought about a different result, and maybe there remains room for approaches that recognize that undeclared money is a *global* problem. There is still significant undeclared money around the world, and the financial centers involved extend geographically from Europe to the Caribbean, Singapore, Hong Kong, and the USA itself, where Miami, New York, and other centers provide international private-banking services to clients from Latin America and around the world, often without meaningful checks on whether the relevant earnings are declared in the home countries of beneficial owners.

Lack of strategy and cooperation has resulted in other lost opportunities for Switzerland and the wealth-management industry as a whole. Switzerland sought to address some of its difficulties in view of growing attention on the levels of undeclared funds within the wealth-management industry by introducing its "Rubik" strategy. A failure from the outset, even the name of the strategy apparently came under challenge from the owners of the rights to "Rubik's Cube."

What Switzerland attempted to do was introduce a very complex (and costly) withholding system designed to allow it to provide confidentiality to account holders while accommodating the tax demands of the countries of residence of the account holders involved. Among the weaknesses of this strategy was Switzerland's approach to Germany and the UK as first-takers (with Austria, a bank-secrecy center itself, an easier bet to negotiate with). At this period in history, with governments focusing on their legitimate rights to tax residents and address income inequality, it is hugely provocative to propose a solution to undeclared money that keeps secret the names of taxpayers – particularly in the case of countries, like Germany and the UK, whose tax laws are well developed, and reflect a First-World system of protection of taxpayer interests. In simple terms, while some may not like the UK and German tax systems, the reality is that both are generally free from corruption, are fair, and provide significant taxpayer protection.

The deal with Germany eventually never came to pass, because of resistance within the German political system. In relation to the UK, which had gone forward with the agreement with Switzerland with a view to enjoying short-term tax revenues, Switzerland guaranteed CHF500 million in taxes to the UK. Ultimately, the ambitious tax-collection estimates of the UK were not met, and even the guarantee figure was not covered by tax withholdings, meaning that the

Swiss banking community, which had shared in the responsibility for meeting the guarantee, had to bear part of the cost.

A complex, costly, and failed system, the "Rubik" approach evidences yet another lost opportunity for Switzerland to have shown global leadership on a global issue – undeclared funds. Switzerland's provocation of the UK, through its insistence on maintaining confidentiality for UK taxpayers, led to an expensive deal for taxpayers and, ultimately, for Swiss banks.

Switzerland has caused great harm to the world's wealth owners by misleading them for too long regarding the misuse of bank secrecy. Instead of leading the way to change, Switzerland focused on short-term profits. The emergence in a very public way of the misuse of bank secrecy by Swiss-based banks is now resulting in overreaction by onshore governments and a focus on even the very legitimate tax-planning approaches wealth owners have adopted.

Open, strategic dialogue between stakeholders may be a more effective way of addressing the changing world. This dialogue is urgent, but despite what some may think given the rapid move to transparency, there remain many, many issues to resolve, meaning that the opportunity for the industry to take leadership remains.

The Liechtenstein–UK Example: The Possibilities of Strategy and Dialogue

An example of the positive effects of open dialogue is the Liechtenstein Disclosure Facility (LDF) and the accompanying Taxpayer Assistance and Compliance Program (TACP) put in place between the UK and Liechtenstein governments.

Acting for the Liechtenstein government, I was able to initiate the LDF and TACP, with the help of the OECD, and eventually a team of advisors to Liechtenstein and the UK. While a meaningful success, and a system the UK agreed to extend beyond its original period of coverage, the huge outcry over the practices of HSBC in Switzerland led to the UK prematurely ending the LDF on December 31, 2015. This was only one of many political reactions that the abuse of bank secrecy by Switzerland and its banking community has encouraged. The political responses to abuses of bank secrecy, and Switzerland's failed strategies, are just beginning, and will have tremendous effects on wealth owners in the years to come.

As was stated in the Liechtenstein Declaration of 2009, Liechtenstein committed itself to acting as a responsible member of the global community, contributing to the global effort to help foster long-term economic prosperity and the social well-being of everybody. As a member state of the European Economic Area and part of the European single market for financial services, Liechtenstein, with its solid and modern bank-secrecy laws, was well placed to go beyond current standards of exchange of information and approaches designed to address tax fraud, tax evasion, and double taxation without compromising its commitment to privacy.

Liechtenstein's ground-breaking arrangements with the UK, which came into effect in September 2009, proved to be a success for clients of Liechtenstein's financial center, for the UK, and for Liechtenstein. These arrangements, which did not in any way compromise Liechtenstein's focus on the legitimate privacy rights of clients of its financial center, recognized that countries whose tax and legal systems respect the human right to privacy are entitled to ensure that the integrity of their tax systems remains intact.

While total tax collections remain to be seen, the UK revised upwards its initial estimates regarding the tax recoveries the LDF was predicted to achieve from an initial figure of £1 billion. The relationship between Liechtenstein and the UK has gone from strength to strength on the basis of their cooperation and foresight, including the entering into of a full tax treaty between the two countries. Most importantly, thousands of UK taxpayers have resolved their tax affairs favorably using the unique approach of the LDF.

The Main Elements of the LDF and Related Arrangements

The arrangements negotiated with the UK were based on Liechtenstein's evaluation of the UK's approach to respecting taxpayer privacy and its commitment to putting the interests of its taxpayers at the forefront. Based on these factors, Liechtenstein agreed to full transparency in relation to UK taxpayers, and to an approach designed to respect the UK's legitimate right to have access to the names of those UK taxpayers using the Liechtenstein financial center – but with those names provided to the UK by the taxpayers themselves, through their tax filings. As Liechtenstein committed to the UK the objective of ensuring that no UK-connected taxpayer would be able to use the Liechtenstein financial center without being fully tax compliant, the arrangements ensured that any taxpayers not wishing to avail themselves of the many benefits of the arrangement would exit Liechtenstein.

Among others, the relevant arrangements provided for the TACP, a tax-compliance program providing, among others, a comprehensive commitment from Liechtenstein to ensure that UK taxpayers using the Liechtenstein financial center were compliant with their UK tax and reporting obligations. Critically, this commitment, backed by agreed review, notice, and audit procedures, covered not only banks, but also a wide range of service providers in Liechtenstein, including trust companies. Specifically covered by the TACP were all forms of trust, foundation, company, and certain other vehicles, the objective of the arrangements being that "gray areas" be addressed upfront and pragmatically.

Documentation of the arrangements with the UK included a Memorandum of Understanding, a Joint Declaration (which was followed by supplementary Joint Declarations clarifying a number of issues), and a Tax Information Exchange Agreement designed to facilitate the terms of the arrangement between the two countries and to encourage the use of the Liechtenstein financial center by those considering the benefits of voluntary disclosure.

The LDF provided UK taxpayers needing to regularize their tax affairs with an attractive, simplified approach to voluntary disclosure. Among others, the LDF provided for assurance against criminal prosecution, very favorable penalty and time limitations, simplified calculations of tax payable where complex structures were in place, a "bespoke" service from HMRC (the UK tax authority) for those considering use of the LDF and their advisors, and a number of other benefits.

Recognizing that the success of the TACP and LDF would require the full cooperation of Liechtenstein's banks, trust companies, and other intermediaries, the arrangements with the UK included assurances against prosecution for past practices, as well as training and other support designed to assist Liechtenstein's financial intermediaries to adapt and thrive in a tax-transparent world while preserving and enhancing the privacy rights of the clients of its financial center.

Recognition and clarity on the treatment of Liechtenstein vehicles, such as insurance structures, foundations, *Anstalts*, trusts, and others, and a commitment by the UK to assist Liechtenstein in the development of new products designed to address the needs of the clients of its financial center in a manner that provides *tax-transparent privacy* (the full protection of privacy rights with tax compliance in the home country) is assured.

In recognition of Liechtenstein's objective of becoming the financial center of choice for tax-compliant clients, the UK agreed to extend the benefits of the LDF to wealth owners with no previous connection to Liechtenstein, thereby allowing Liechtenstein's financial center to expand its client base, and the UK to ensure that the maximum number of taxpayers could regularize their tax affairs. Most importantly, the interests of UK taxpayers being at the forefront, the arrangements were designed to be inclusive of all seeking to regularize their tax affairs on the most attractive terms possible.

It is interesting to contrast the approach of the LDF/TACP and its results for all stakeholders to the failed Rubik effort of Switzerland and to the approach of the USA in its attacks on offshore tax evasion. For the UK, the LDF/TACP provided full assurance against the misuse of Liechtenstein bank secrecy, with a guarantee that the Liechtenstein financial center would not be used to shelter undeclared UK taxpayers. For the families involved, a sympathetic approach to voluntary disclosure and the choice of leaving the jurisdiction encouraged many to do the right thing and come clean. For Liechtenstein and its banks and trust companies, liabilities for past practices were dramatically reduced, and the system introduced encouragement of new relationships with UK-connected families to be developed, as well as clarity on the treatment of Liechtenstein trusts, foundations, and other wealth-planning tools.

Despite its "win–win–win" approach, the LDF/TACP was *not* pursued by Liechtenstein or other offshore centers early on as a model... more recently it was used by the UK and its dependent territories, but Liechtenstein and others may have missed the chance to take leadership. When it had the chance to pursue similar strategies with other countries, the Liechtenstein financial services community was, sadly, more focused on the profits of past practices than what was in everyone's best interests. Strong resistance to the approach taken with the UK was expressed by a large part of Liechtenstein's financial services and legal community, putting a brake on Liechtenstein's chance to make a real difference beyond the UK.

The Practicalities of Anti-Money-Laundering Rules and the Addition of Tax Offences as Predicate Offences

Through the efforts of the Financial Action Task Force (FATF) and other bodies, global anti-money-laundering rules are increasingly designed to include tax crimes as predicate offences. In other words, for money laundering to be occurring, there must be a crime involved, and increasingly tax offences are included among the crimes that can result in money laundering. Using untaxed funds to establish a company, buy an asset, or open a bank account triggers, more and more, requirements that suspicious activity reports be filed *without* any notice being given to the wealth owner involved.

While this is an unstoppable move given strongly held (and valid) views that tax evasion must be stopped, there is a reality that how such rules are implemented will, for years to come, remain an issue for individual countries to address. While weak economies, the "anti-Wall Street" movement, and a general focus on the risks of increasing income disparities in a variety of countries make any defenses against all-crimes anti-money-laundering rules virtually impossible to sustain, the *practicalities* of all-crimes anti-money-laundering rules will mean that there will be major differences in how countries and regions address their obligations.

At the moment, the inclusion of tax offences in the anti-money-laundering rules of various countries is at a relatively early stage of implementation. Even where anti-money-laundering rules include tax offences in their coverage, individual countries develop their own approaches to implementation and enforcement. In some cases broad exemptions apply, and the standard of what constitutes a tax crime can also be different from country to country.

Enforcement of anti-money-laundering rules varies dramatically. In Hong Kong, tax crimes have been part of the anti-money-laundering rules for some time, yet enforcement is minimal, with the wealth-management industry, at least at present, broadly ignoring the rules save for countries viewed as being particularly aggressive in enforcing their tax laws. Needless to say, the next steps globally will involve increasing enforcement. For wealth owners, it is dangerous to believe that lax enforcement will remain for the long or even medium term.

Recent announcements by the FATF have received global press coverage, and virtually all secrecy countries are acknowledging that they will need to introduce tax crimes as predicate offences in their anti-money-laundering regimes. In Singapore, tax offences are now part of the anti-money-laundering regime.

These developments are all at a relatively early stage, and it will likely be a number of years before the world moves to full transparency. Countries, in consultation with the financial services industry, will try to develop practical approaches to implementing anti-money-laundering rules that include tax offences, and will naturally seek to limit reportable circumstances, and to narrow the scope of the type of tax crimes that are included. Over time, international pressure will broaden the scope, and as we have seen in relation to bank secrecy and tax crimes, it is inevitable that transparency will win out.

What the world needs, though, is a *proactive* rather than a *defensive* approach, designed to provide significant long-term benefits to affected families, offshore centers, the wealth management industry, *and* countries seeking to enforce their legitimate right to tax revenues.

There are critical practical issues associated with the inclusion of tax crimes as a predicate offence in anti-money-laundering rules.

What happens when a bank or trust company files a suspicious activity report relating to undeclared funds that are linked to the tax system of a country that misuses tax information, or where corruption and instability otherwise puts the taxpayer at risk? Is it right that anti-money-laundering rules should put individuals and their families at personal risk in terms of kidnapping, political oppression, and corruption?

And should it not be the case that anti-money-laundering suspicious-activity reports should not have to be filed if the discussion with a client is clearly to encourage voluntary disclosure? On the latter, if an intermediary is aware of tax offences, there may be a reporting requirement. If intermediaries are to encourage tax compliance, should not the anti-money-laundering rules fit in with the concept of providing a window of time during which a client can consider coming clean without fearing that he will be turned in to the authorities? Are the rules in place actually *discouraging* intermediaries from having discussions about tax compliance?

Perhaps the right way forward is for open dialogue on these issues and for countries deserving of full tax transparency to be given *more* than they ask for in relation to exchange of information in exchange for a number of benefits, such as was the case under the Liechtenstein–UK deal I was involved with. But for countries not yet ready for full transparency, full automatic exchange and other promises should really only be offered if and when legal and tax systems protect privacy and the legitimate rights and interests of taxpayers. For these countries, a simple and confidential withholding-tax approach, as described earlier in this book, could be the offer. As countries implement anti-money-laundering rules that include tax offences, the demand for a confidential and safe way to be compliant will increase – simply put, taxpayers from countries with corrupt legal and/or tax systems will fear having their assets and structures in countries where suspicious activity reports may find their way to their home country. A simple withholding system (including the voluntary elements of this) could provide an ideal solution for many.

But are offshore centers and the wealth-management industry ready to take proactive leadership? Or will we see more in the way of defensive and backward-looking approaches to the global issue of undeclared funds? What will moves designed to create fairly public registers of the beneficial owners of companies and other investment and business vehicles result in for wealth owners wanting to maintain their legitimate and important rights to privacy?

Sadly, wealth owners need to prepare for the worst.

Glossary

Annuity   There are many kinds of annuities, but the term usually refers to an insurance product designed to provide annual payments. These can be associated with retirement products, but can also be customized annuity arrangements.

Anti-Deferral Rules   Anti-deferral rules are tax rules that seek to stop taxpayers from being able to delay when they pay tax on particular income items. A common example would be where a country taxes residents of the country on a worldwide basis, and the taxpayer uses a company or other structure to earn income outside the country. Anti-deferral rules might cause the income of the company to be taxed to the resident as if that income was earned directly by the resident, without the interposition of the company.

Anti-Money-Laundering Rules   There are a variety of laws that seek to uncover funds associated with illegal activity. Increasingly, these laws, which deal with money laundering, require the filing of *suspicious-activity reports* with the relevant authorities where a financial intermediary, such as a bank, real-estate broker, or other party, handles funds that they suspect have an illegal origin. The owner of the assets is usually not notified that the reports are being filed, and the "crimes" that can trigger such reports often include tax crimes, meaning that undeclared funds can be identified by tax authorities through these reports.

Asset Protection   Asset protection is a very broad term that can cover all elements of planning undertaken by wealth-owning families. More specifically, asset-protection structures focus on the protection of assets from the claims of creditors and are used by those in high-risk activities, such as medical practitioners and others who may become subject to legal claims.

Assets Under Management (AUM)   Asset managers generally earn fees based on the quantum of assets held under management, or AUM. Where assets are held in trusts and other structures, and the assets may not be managed directly by the trustee or other legal owner, the reference can be to *assets under administration.*

Automatic Exchange of Information   Led by the OECD, the common reporting standard is the basis on which countries will be *automatically* sharing a wide range of information regarding the income and assets of wealth owners. Automatic exchange of information contrasts dramatically with previous forms of exchange of information between countries, which was, largely, information exchange on request. Countries will now receive information on the assets and income of their taxpayers outside the home country without making any request for such information.

Bank Secrecy   The laws of many countries provide varying degrees of confidentiality associated with banking relationships, including bank deposits. Bank secrecy has come under considerable attack given the misuse of bank-secrecy rules.

Beneficiary   The beneficiaries of a will, trust, foundation, insurance policy, or other structures and succession strategies are the individuals or entities that benefit on a particular event happening. In the case of a trust, the beneficiaries can be named and have fixed interests, or may simply be members of a class of potential beneficiaries who may or may not actually benefit, depending on the exercise of discretion by the trustee or other fiduciary.

Bequest   When a gift is to be made on death, such as under a will, the gift is often referred to as a bequest.

Bilateral Treaties and Other Agreements   Bilateral treaties are agreements between two countries. In relation to the interests of wealth-owning families, such agreements include tax treaties, covering a number of issues that can help address the tax exposures of families living and investing on a cross-border basis, as well as investment-protection agreements, which address, among others, expropriation of assets and political risk.

Blended-Value Investments   This broadly refers to *impact investing*, where investments are made with a view to providing blended value – returns to the investor, but also benefits to multiple stakeholders, including employees, communities, and others. Rather than giving money away through philanthropy, a number of wealth owners seek to make investments that can provide returns on capital and also have a positive impact.

Capital Gain   A capital gain is the profit on selling an asset, such as arises where real estate or shares are sold at a profit. Capital gains may be tax free or taxed more favorably than ordinary income, depending on the tax regime. Where a wealth owner is actively trading assets, the gains may be characterized as trading income rather than as capital gains, and may therefore be subject to a higher level of taxation, depending on the country whose laws have application.

Captive Insurance   A captive insurance company is an insurance company that is owned, in whole or in part, by the person who is insured. Sometimes captive insurance arrangements are designed to provide tax benefits by creating tax deductions for premiums paid on what would otherwise be self-insured risks.

Civil Law   The civil law derives from Roman law, and is largely based on statutes rather than on case law. This contrasts with the common law, which while featuring laws provided in statutes, focuses more on laws developed through judicial decisions. The common law derives from England and applies in countries such as the USA, Canada, and others, the laws of which are generally based on English law.

Common Law   See definition of civil law and the contrasts between civil and common law.

Common Reporting Standard   The common reporting standard, or CRS, was developed largely by the OECD in relation to the implementation of automatic information exchange between countries, and is designed to assist in the enforcement of tax laws. Considerable information on the CRS and the implementation of automatic information exchange is available on the website of the OECD. The CRS is designed to set out rules for determining information that needs to be reported and how determinations on beneficial ownership are made.

Controlled Foreign Corporations (CFCs)   Many countries that impose taxation on a worldwide basis have anti-deferral rules in their tax legislation. Among these are rules that focus on foreign corporations controlled by residents, and provide for current taxation of the earnings of such companies despite the fact that no dividends are distributed. These rules prevent taxpayers from being able to delay payment of tax in their home countries by accumulating income in offshore companies.

Direct Taxation   Direct taxes are taxes imposed directly on an individual or company, and would include income, wealth, and capital gains taxes, among others.

Discretionary Trust or Foundation   Where a fiduciary structure such as a trust or foundation is discretionary, the trustee or others have a discretion regarding the exercise of their powers, such as a power to make distributions. If the trust is discretionary, the trustee, for example, does not have to distribute to a beneficiary a certain amount at a certain time, but may have a discretion to decide whether or not to do so. This can allow the trustee to consider whether it is appropriate to make the distribution, and also means that the beneficiary does not have a legal right to the assets involved, something which may provide tax and asset-protection benefits.

Dividends   A dividend is a payment made by a company to shareholders out of the profits of the company.

Domicile   Some countries have tax and other laws that focus on the "domicile" of an individual. This concept is different from the question of residence and citizenship, and often includes elements of intention regarding where a person plans to remain indefinitely, making it possible for a person to be resident in a place other than their "domicile" which is, in effect, their permanent home. In the UK, individuals have "domiciles of origin" (usually their father's domicile, or intended permanent home), which can be affected by a subsequent "domicile of choice."

Donation   A donation is a gratuitous transfer, and can be a gift to a family member or to a charity or other recipient meant to benefit. Donation taxes apply in some countries, often imposed on the donor rather than the recipient of the donation. In some countries, the recipient is taxable on the donation in certain circumstances. Charitable donations are often tax free.

Estate   The estate often refers to the assets of an individual at the time of death, and in some countries the estate itself may become a taxable person during the time of administration of the estate.

Executor   The executor is an individual or entity charged with putting into effect the intentions of the deceased, and most often refers to a person appointed to the function under the will of the deceased.

Exit Tax   In a number of countries, where an individual (and sometimes a company) moves out of the country, ceasing to be taxable there, an exit tax applies. Often, the exit tax is calculated by deeming the individual to have sold their assets at fair market value, exposing any gains to taxation despite the fact that the assets are not actually sold.

Expropriation   Under international law, countries have the sovereign right to expropriate, or take away, assets under their jurisdiction. While compensation may have to be paid in relation to the expropriated assets of foreigners, in political risk planning, dealing with the risk of expropriation is a key issue.

Family Constitution   A family constitution is generally a non-binding document that sets out a variety of things relating to how the family operates, its values, how disputes will be resolved, and how succession and other arrangements will be made. Many of the provisions of a family constitution become binding by being included in related documents, such as trust deeds, shareholder agreements, and other governance arrangements.

Family Office   A family office refers to the functions undertaken for wealth-owning families in relation to investments, maintenance of assets – including holiday homes and otherwise, supervision of advisors and succession arrangements, and many other possible functions. Single-family offices look after single families; multi-family offices resemble private banks and independent asset managers in providing services to multiple families.

Family Retreat Communication within families about succession, family values, safety and security, and more is a valuable means of helping in the succession process. Family retreats are gatherings of families, annually or otherwise, providing an opportunity for review of succession and other arrangements, the review or creation of family constitutions, and otherwise. These can be formal or informal and can be organized by the family alone or with the help of outside advisors.

FATCA Foreign Account Tax Compliance Act, US legislation designed to close loopholes that existed under the US Qualified Intermediary rules and requiring financial institutions and others to automatically exchange information with the USA regarding the interests of US taxpayers, including residents and citizens, where US persons are considered to beneficially own the assets and income involved. The relevant rules pierce corporate, trust, and other structures, and provide strong disincentives to banks and others who fail to cooperate with the USA.

Forced Heirship A number of countries have laws requiring that those who die transfer at least a portion of their assets to specified family members in specific shares. These rules, which can also affect lifetime gifts, generally apply in civil-law countries as opposed to common-law countries, but are not applicable in all civil-law countries, and apply in very different ways. Forced heirship also appears in the *Shari'a* law, which is the Islamic law applying to Muslims and which is part of the laws of many Muslim countries.

Foundations Foundations are generally the civil-law equivalent of trusts, albeit with a number of important differences, such as the fact that foundations are separate legal entities, while trusts are not. In general, foundations can often be used interchangeably with trusts, and operate in many similar ways.

Freezing of Assets In political risk planning, expropriation of assets is a key risk. Also, part of the risk is the freezing of assets that can arise in a number of circumstances. This relates to assets not actually being "vested" or taken away, but "frozen," such that the owner is unable to make use of the assets or deal with them.

Gift   A gift is a gratuitous transfer, such as where a parent makes a gift to a child or a spouse makes a gift to their partner. A sale of an asset at an undervalue may carry with it elements of a gift, and where gift or donation taxes apply, can also attract such taxation.

Global Custodian   A custodian of assets usually refers to a bank that holds equities and other investments, often in the name of the custodian (which is referred to as "street name"). A variety of banks provide global custody services to family offices and other wealth owners.

Governance   Governance refers to the approaches in place to deal with how assets and structures are administered. As assets move from one generation to the next, it is very important to consider how decisions will be made when there are several in the younger generation who will become owners of assets, whether or not including family businesses. Decision making, dispute resolution, buy–sell arrangements, and many other issues are part of governance, and can be provided for in shareholder agreements, trust arrangements, partnership agreements, and otherwise.

Green Card   A "green card" is an informal reference to US permanent resident status under US immigration rules. Green card status carries with it a number of US tax exposures and while not exactly the same as citizenship, given exceptions under tax treaties, can also cause the holder to be taxable on a worldwide basis regardless of actual time spent in the USA.

Guardian   The term "guardian" is used in many different ways, and can include the individual charged with supervising the affairs of a minor or of someone who is under a disability. The term can also apply to a "protector" under a trust and to many other functions that are part of governance structures adopted by wealth-owning families.

Headline Tax Rates   The top tax rates in countries are sometimes referred to as "headline tax rates," as these are the tax rates that are focused on – say a top rate of 50%. The reality, however, is that the actual tax that wealth owners pay may be far, far lower given legitimate planning approaches adopted, tax deductions, and otherwise.

Income Tax   An income tax is a direct tax imposed on individuals or entities relating to the taxable income of that individual or entity. Salaries, dividends, revenues from sales of goods, and many other such items may be subject to income tax.

Independent Asset Manager   An independent asset manager, or IAM, is usually an asset manager who does not retain custody of the investment portfolio involved. Quite commonly, the assets themselves will be with a custodian bank, and a limited power of attorney will be provided to the investment manager, who is independent of the bank, to provide input on how the assets are to be managed.

Independent Trustee   Trustees can be individuals or companies, and many banks own trust companies that offer trust services to both bank and non-bank clients. An independent trust company is a trust company that is independent of a bank, meaning that it is not bank owned.

Indirect Tax   An indirect tax includes value-added taxes, sales taxes, customs duties, stamp duties, and other taxes that are not directly imposed on the income of an individual, but rather on other items, such as consumption.

Information Exchange   There are a variety of ways information is exchanged between countries, including information exchange on request, which is contained in Tax Information Exchange Agreements (TIEAs) and in comprehensive tax treaties. Through FATCA, and the Common Reporting Standard and related steps encouraged by the OECD, information exchange is moving toward being *automatic*, meaning that information will be exchanged even where *no request* for the information is made by the receiving country. Other forms of information exchange include *spontaneous* information exchange, which a country can perform on its own initiative, providing information to treaty partners on their taxpayers.

Information exchange also takes place where there are no tax treaties in place, as might arise through anti-money-laundering reports and otherwise.

Inheritance   Inheritance refers to the succession of assets and otherwise on death. In relation to taxation, the term is widely used in a loose way, whereas more technically, taxes are more often applied to the estate of the deceased (estate taxes) as opposed to being applied to the recipient of the assets. There are, however, countries where the recipient of an inheritance is the person to be taxed, particularly where the deceased was not taxed.

Intestacy   Intestacy refers to an individual dying without having left a valid will or other instrument that sets out how the assets will pass. Where an individual dies intestate, his assets pass under the laws relevant to his estate, which may be a combination of the laws of his place of nationality, residence, or domicile at death, and the laws applying where assets are located at death. Most countries have intestacy laws that have the assets of an intestate pass to family members of specified degrees in specified shares, and if there are no such family members, to the state. In some jurisdictions, however, such as India, Lebanon, and Singapore, the applicable laws governing the devolution of a person's estate may also depend on the religion of the deceased.

Letter of Wishes   Where a trustee, executor, or other person is provided with discretion, such as the power to determine at what age a beneficiary should benefit, or who among a class of beneficiaries can benefit, a letter of wishes may be provided to guide the trustee or executor on the wishes of the person whose assets are the subject of the arrangement. Letters of wishes and similar documents are usually not binding, and are in place only to provide guidance and suggestions.

Life Insurance   Life insurance is insurance that is designed to provide payment to surviving family members on the death of the life assured. There are many kinds of life insurance, and some policies can have investment features that allow the owner of the policy to access the investment monies in a variety of ways. A number of tax and asset-protection benefits can be obtained through the use of certain life-insurance arrangements, depending on the countries involved and the circumstances.

Limited Liability Companies (LLCs)   Most countries have corporate laws that allow for the formation of companies that offer limited liability in the sense that shareholders are not personally liable for the debts of the company – the liability of the company is limited to the assets that are owned by the company itself, and such liability does not extend to the assets of shareholders. As separate entities, tax laws usually tax companies separately from their shareholders, but in the USA, LLCs (as opposed to corporations) are treated as "flow-through" entities, meaning that taxation is at the level of the shareholder, avoiding a second level of corporate tax. While an election for treatment to the contrary can be made, LLCs can offer tax and reporting advantages given the mix of limited liability and flow-through treatment.

Living Will   A living will refers to the documenting of one's wishes regarding medical and other care in the event of being unable to make one's own decisions. In a number of countries, there are formal procedures for living wills that need to be followed.

Midshore   Midshore is not a formal term, but with increasing attacks on the use of "offshore" tax-haven companies, there is a move to the use of corporate and other vehicles that are either located in "onshore" home countries or in "midshore" countries, the latter being countries with meaningful infrastructure in terms of legal, accounting, and other support, access to a wide employment pool, and, importantly, access to tax and other bilateral and multilateral treaties.

Multilateral Agreements and Treaties   In contrast to bilateral treaties, which are agreements between two countries, there are a growing number of tax and other agreements that are entered into by multiple countries. These are multilateral agreements. Cross-border activity requires a good understanding of the bilateral and multilateral treaties that may have application.

OECD   The Organisation for Economic Co-operation and Development has both member and non-member countries that contribute to the development of economic and social policies. Critically important to wealth owners is the involvement of the OECD in encouraging tax compliance and the adoption of automatic information exchange to facilitate this, as well as other initiatives relating to helping address tax enforcement, inequality, and other economic needs.

Offshore   "Offshore" is most commonly a reference to the world of tax havens. Usually, these include zero-tax countries where companies, trusts, and other vehicles can operate with no taxation and little in the way of interference. Moves toward tax transparency and enforcement of tax laws are reducing the role of offshore havens substantially.

Onshore   "Onshore" generally refers to activities and structures that take place and are located in the country of residence of the investor and in the countries in which the investor is investing. If an investor lives in country X, a company in country X is an onshore company, whereas if the investor uses a company in a different country, say a tax haven, to hold assets, the company would be located in an "offshore" location. If the investor invests in country Y and uses a country Y company to hold the investment, that would generally also be considered to be the use of an "onshore" vehicle. If, instead, the investment is held by a company in an offshore tax haven, albeit the investment were made in country Y, the investment vehicle would be considered "offshore."

Partnerships   Partnerships are business organizations that have more than one owner or interest holder, and are generally taxed not as separate entities, but as "flow-through" vehicles. This means that the profits and losses of the partnership are taxed not at the level of the partnership, but at the level of the individual partners. Partners are generally liable for the debts of the partnership, but limited-liability partnerships also exist, which allow limited partners to participate without becoming liable for the debts of the partnership.

Post-Nuptial Agreement   A post-nuptial agreement is an agreement entered into between spouses *after* the marriage takes place, and generally covers economic and other agreements regarding what happens in the event of a break-up of the marriage. A post-nuptial agreement may be entered into where no pre-nuptial agreement was made, but may also supplement a pre-nuptial agreement, particularly where the circumstances of the marriage change, such as through a change of domicile, a change in assets and income, or a number of other circumstances.

Predicate Offence   A predicate offence refers to an offence which must first occur to trigger a reporting or other requirement. In the case of anti-money-laundering rules, these generally require that suspicious activities be reported to the authorities. What constitutes a suspicious activity relates to "predicate" offences. Where tax is a predicate offence, funds that may not have been taxed properly, when handled by an intermediary, may thereby give rise to the obligation for a suspicious-activity report to be filed, which may then lead to the tax obligation being enforced.

Pre-Nuptial Agreement   A pre-nuptial agreement is an agreement entered into between individuals *prior* to a marriage taking place. In some countries, such an agreement is binding in relation to economic and other areas of the marriage; in others, the pre-nuptial agreement may only be persuasive in the event of dissolution of the marriage. In some countries, pre-nuptial agreements are not respected by the courts.

Private Trust Company   A private trust company or PTC is generally a trust company that has been established for use by only one family in relation to one or more trusts that the family may put in place. PTCs can take many forms, and are often administered by professional trustees or by directors who are appointed for the purpose.

Probate   Where a will is in place, it is not automatic that the assets of a deceased person go to those specified as beneficiaries under the will. Probate is the legal procedure for proving the will is the valid last will of the deceased.

Retrocession   The term retrocession is a nice word for "kickback." Increasingly prohibited under laws protecting the interests of clients of banks and other asset managers unless specifically approved by the client, retrocessions refer to payments asset managers receive from third parties, such as managers of investment funds the asset manager orients investments toward. It has not been uncommon for banks and other asset managers to receive retrocessions and to keep these amounts without informing their clients of them. In other words, the investment manager makes investments on behalf of their client and receives compensation as an encouragement to make the investment over and above the fees the client pays to the investment manager. Clearly a conflict of interest, many jurisdictions now prohibit retrocessions that the client has not specifically approved. Sadly, the approvals from clients often appear in small print that the clients do not focus on.

Rule Against Perpetuities   Under common law, it is possible for assets to be legally owned by someone, but for someone else to have the beneficial ownership of the assets. In a trust, the trustee is the legal owner and the beneficiaries have the beneficial ownership. The rule against perpetuities is a legal concept that requires there to be a time limit within which the legal ownership of assets passes to the beneficiaries, meaning that, at least traditionally, a trust cannot last forever. This rule, however, has now been replaced by legislation in many countries that allows trusts to last indefinitely, without a time limit. The traditional rule against perpetuities required that assets be vested within "a life in being plus 21 years."

Shareholder Agreements   Where there are shareholders of a company, a shareholders' agreement is an important governance document that provides for many eventualities, including procedures on decisions being made, how shares are bought and sold, financing of the company, dispute resolution, and more.

Shari'a Law   *Shari'a* law, otherwise known as Islamic law, derives from the *Quran* which may form the basis of the legal system in many Muslim countries and includes, among others, forced heirship principles that affect how assets pass on death and otherwise within families.

Tax Avoidance   Unlike tax evasion, which refers to the illegal activity of not paying a tax that is legally due, tax avoidance generally refers to finding a "loophole" that allows for the tax to be avoided.

Countries can attack such avoidance using anti-avoidance rules, such as a general anti-avoidance rule (GAAR) and in other ways. Tax avoidance is also increasingly coming under attack on moral grounds, both in the corporate and individual tax areas.

Tax Evasion   Tax evasion is the crime of not paying a tax that is legally required to be paid.

Tax Planning   Tax planning means understanding the tax laws that have application, and undertaking a course of action designed to legally allow for tax exposures to be mitigated.

Tax Residence   Most countries have rules that determine when a taxpayer, whether an individual, a company, a trust, or other vehicle, is a resident for tax purposes. In the case of individuals, these rules are usually either or both of objective and subjective. Objective residence rules would include residence rules that focus on days of presence. Subjective residence rules would include references to the intentions of the individual regarding where the individual lives. Residence rules are also affected by the possible application of tax treaties which commonly contain residence "tie-breaker" rules designed to address the double taxation that could arise where an individual or entity is considered to be resident in more than one country at the same time.

Tax Treaty   Tax treaties include comprehensive bilateral agreements between countries that deal with a number of areas of taxation, including information exchange, the avoidance of double taxation, reductions in withholding taxes on dividends, interest, royalties, and other amounts, residence "tie-breaker" rules, and protections from taxation on business profits in the absence of the maintenance of a permanent establishment in other than one's country of residence.

Territorial Tax System   In a territorial tax system, it is generally only locally sourced income that is taxed. A territorial tax system can be contrasted to a worldwide tax system, where a resident is taxed on worldwide income, including both locally sourced and foreign-sourced income.

Tie-Breaker Rules Tax treaties commonly contain "tie-breaker" rules designed to determine which of two countries has the right to tax a taxpayer, whether an individual or entity, as a resident. These rules can be very important in tax planning, particularly where there is a physical presence in more than one country and/or other cross-border activity.

Transfer Pricing Transfer pricing refers to the allocation of revenues and costs between related entities. If a taxpayer conducts business activities in several countries, and has companies in each country involved in the conduct of business, how prices are set between related entities will affect the tax exposures. There is currently considerable focus by tax authorities and international bodies on the abuse of transfer-pricing rules as a means of improperly reducing tax exposures.

Transfer Taxes Transfer tax is a general term covering gifts and bequests. Where there is a tax on gifts and bequests, these can generally be referred to as transfer taxes.

Trusts and Parties to a Trust A trust is a very flexible arrangement that involves a "settlor" transferring assets to a "trustee" who becomes the legal owner of the assets, holding the assets for "beneficiaries" who are the beneficial owners. An optional party to a trust may be a "protector," who has certain oversight over the trustee. There are many, many forms of trusts, making them flexible wealth-planning tools.

Wills A will is a document that sets out the intentions of an individual regarding what should happen to assets owned by the individual on his death. Whether or not a will is valid depends on the laws having application to the assets of the individual, and it is not uncommon for individuals to have more than one will where they own assets in various countries.

Withholding Taxes Withholding taxes are taxes that are imposed at the source of income, and are designed to ensure that tax laws are complied with. One form of withholding tax applies when certain types of payment are made to foreigners, such as dividends, interest, and royalties. In some circumstances, the taxpayer may be able to obtain a refund of all or part of the withholding tax given the application of a tax treaty, or the filing of a tax return or otherwise.

Worldwide Taxation   A majority of countries tax individuals and companies resident in those countries on their worldwide income. Residence rules determine who is a taxable resident, and the tax system usually provides for relief, in the form of tax credits or exemptions, for foreign taxes paid, so as to reduce the possible impact of double taxation. In the case of the USA, worldwide taxation is not only based on residence, but also on citizenship and the holding of a right to permanent residence ("green card" status).

Index